Daddy Danced the Charleston

Daddy Danced the Charleston

Ruth Corbett

South Brunswick and New York: A. S. Barnes and Company
London: Thomas Yoseloff Ltd

© 1970 by A. S. Barnes and Co., Inc.
Library of Congress Catalogue Card Number: 69-15768

A. S. Barnes and Co., Inc.
Cranbury, New Jersey 08512

Thomas Yoseloff Ltd
108 New Bond Street
London W1Y OQX, England

SBN: 498-07393-9
Printed in the United States of America

Contents

1

We Weren't That Funny

Do you remember when there were no frozen TV dinners—in fact, no TV? You could dance down the primrose path to the Charleston instead of shaking to a frenzy in a discothèque. You weren't square if you listened to Wayne King waltzes or did a little cheek-to-cheeking in a semi-darkened ballroom. "Wanna buy a duck" wasn't chanted by a poultry salesman and "I do not choose to run" didn't mean a baseball player refused to leave home plate.

A few fashions of the thirties. (Courtesy Detroit *News*, Meyer Both Co.)

If the foregoing puts a light in your eye, you're of the era in the twentieth century before psychiatrists had a therapy for healthy anxiety. We didn't wake up with pep pills, go to bed with sleeping pills and use other pills to kill the pain in between. A third of our income didn't go in the tax pot, our thinking wasn't done by mechanical brains and we didn't have a haunting fear of "the bomb."

Young people hero-worshipped the good guys, boys got haircuts and speed wasn't an end in itself. Automobiles were transportation instead of lethal weapons; we didn't cringe at Communism or debate whether God is dead. Maybe we *had* something in the "good old days," or maybe it's the rosy aura of nostalgia along with forgetfulness.

How much have we forgotten? Occasionally we like to reminisce, either with a contemporary who remembers, or to a youngster who will listen. One day I waxed nostalgic with my daughter about a balloon ascension. It was in a small Michigan town and all of the townspeople packed lunches and gathered in a field on the outskirts to watch the liftoff. She seemed to be listening intently, but when I finished she looked at me tolerantly with chin cupped in her hands and only asked, "Is *that* what you call the good old days, Mom?"

I was disappointed and showed it. "What's so bad about the good old days? After all, it wasn't ancient Rome!" Then I pondered about the period that we hold so dear; what was so good about it? What was remembered and how much forgotten of just yesterday? I was guilty of laughing at old-fashioned clothes. Were we that funny? Certainly the Depression wasn't amusing, nor World War II. It's true we didn't travel as fast or crash as hard—except in the stock market. Besides, it wasn't very long ago, so how could everything be archaic as my daughter called it?

I looked at her ridiculously ratted hair with bangs covering her eyebrows, black eye makeup and colorless

These newspaper clippings stressed temperance and war: a more confident era. (Courtesy Detroit *News*)

lips. My eye traveled to her above-the-knees shift and I started to laugh uncontrollably. Who was funny? Maybe she'll laugh at *her* getup in 1990!

If you're not ashamed to admit you like to reminisce, we can have fun in these pages. You're no more living in the past than a student reading a history book. You are merely not forgetting that there was a day before yesterday.

My husband triggered the creation of this book when he threatened to throw away long-collected old pictures and clippings from the three decades, 1920 to 1950. No pretense or claim is made that all of the names and events are included. Your "five foot shelf" would expand to ten to hold them. It will be better if you can indignantly say, "She's left out the most important part!" Then your memory will be spiced into exercise and you can enjoy the good old days still so near, yet one day further away every midnight.

From these advertisements you can see that dentists still advertised themselves as painless and movies were only thirty-five cents. (Courtesy Detroit *News*)

This montage proves art was much discussed, then as now. (Courtesy Detroit News)

2

According to the Papers...

We read in the papers such events as Roosevelt's Bank Holiday, March 5, 1932.

"What's new?"—"All I know is what I see in the papers." This was a typical street corner exchange between acquaintances in the twenties. Perhaps they repeated it after Will Rogers who made the remark famous in 1928 and thereafter. We cannot accuse the beloved Mr. Rogers of being unoriginal even though John Bright said as early as 1861, "I know nothing but what is in the papers." It was a natural reply to the profound query, "What's new?"

We've been saturated with instant news in the last forty years—via radio, so we could do other things while listening, and television; we can see live battleground scenes and the real shooting war while sitting in our easy chairs. We can see the facial expressions of the candidates when they make elaborate campaign promises. But what of the newspaper, that ancient form of news dissemination? It's had some tough sledding with the noisy competition all around, but it endures and still gives something the other mediums lack. Mark Twain, in his customarily penetrating manner, summed it up in 1906: "There are only two forces that can carry light to all corners of the globe—the sun in the heavens and the Associated Press."

The papers are excellent barometers of the times and the printed word stands still while we read it, whereas the spoken word may be half-heard, then gone. With broadcast news we're cheated out of crossword puzzles, interesting little fillers in back corners and the classified ads. What are some of the events we've read and talked about in the three decades?

The year 1920 got off to a headline beginning when the fourteenth census was taken. It showed there were 105,700,000 souls in the Continental United States. Almost everything west of the Mississippi was still called "the wild and wooly west."

We now have servicemen in many foreign quarters, but in 1920 the last forces came home from France, leaving 17,000 officers and men on the Rhine.

The event that would bear disastrous results was the voting in of the eighteenth amendment while our men were fighting overseas. The decade of the "speakeasy," "blind pig" and "rum-runner" was about to begin. There were those who maintained it was a great law—the innocent people like my grandmother, tucked away from the mainstream—the nondrinkers who judged the law good because they saw no open saloons on Main Street, U.S.A. Gangsters liked the law too because of the rum-soaked empires they built by breaking this law.

In the 1920 Presidential election Warren G. Harding with running mate, Calvin Coolidge, won easily over the Democratic ticket of James Cox and Franklin Roosevelt. Many still blamed the Democrats for getting us into World War I. There were other candidates; Eugene V. Debs tried for the Presidency under the Socialist banner and William Jennings Bryan was "always trying" with the Prohibition Party.

An interesting sidenote to the political campaign when Calvin Coolidge ran for the Vice-Presidency: the convention wanted candidates to lead the country back to "normalcy" after the great war. A determined delegation

Warren G. Harding, who won easily over Cox in 1920.

from Massachusetts thought their Governor Coolidge should be one of those men. But he was so quiet that no majority knew of his virtues. Hard, Yankee common sense was a quality his supporters esteemed, but how could this be promoted? To inform the 984 convention delegates of the vital facts, a leather-bound book was published in an unheard-of rush so they could at least read about Calvin Coolidge. Speeches, based on this book, easily won the nomination for him.

Toward the end of 1920, the net cost to the United States for its part in the first World War proves that no war is cheap, no matter when it occurs. Not counting the suffering and loss of life, the dollar cost was $24,010,-000,000.

In 1921 there were some high spots that may recall a memory. It became apparent from several high-up sources that the United States would not join the League of Nations, thus blasting Woodrow Wilson's idealistic dream. The Immigration Bill passed, so the influx of aliens would be limited. More than half of the foreign-born population became naturalized or had filed first papers. This year also saw Ex-President Taft installed as Chief Justice of the United States and the Tomb of the Unknown Soldier was placed in Arlington Cemetery with highest honors.

COOLIDGE FOR VICE-PRESIDENT

A drawing of the era depicts the nomination of Calvin Coolidge, Harding's running-mate, and later President. (Courtesy R. R. Donnelley and Sons Company, The Lakeside Press)

11

The New York skyline from Midtown New York. (Courtesy National Bellas Hess, Inc.)

A 1922 article about the super city of the future might have been written yesterday about our present metropolitan conditions. The writers felt there were deep-seated structural defects that left masses of population in environments unfit for welfare and happiness. Traffic in the streets was congested so that it placed intolerable burdens on commerce and endangered human life.

Squeezed between arms of the sea, bound to an 1811 street plan, the city built into the air; it bridged and tunneled the rivers; it burrowed underground and thrust transportation tentacles out until people traveled fifty miles to work in the heart of the city; it crowded thousands into breathless slums. They should see it now!

If complaints were made about city crowding, there

The New York skyline from downtown (left) and from
Bedloe's Island (right). (Photos by Chester Janczarek)

were other disapprovals in 1922 concerning the trend in music. It was as though the last original melodic thought had been uttered. There emerged a jangling of chord progressions without harmony, violent and unrestrained. Bedlam came to the realm of music. A thousand demons were loose in a quiet world where echoes of the plaintive pastoral had died away. The conservatives and the radicals of music were at war. Those who tolerated Debussy, Ravel and their Russian rivals couldn't listen to Stravinsky and Schoenberg. Even the least offensive such as Rimski-Korsakov and Strauss, were classed with ultra-modernists by those who by creed defended the classics from the musical cubists and impressionists.

If the events of 1922 have grown hazy, these are news reminders: the Child Labor law was declared unconstitutional, since in those days any infringement of States Rights was an important impediment; Alexander Graham Bell died and the national debt was reduced! In case you'd forgotten early labor problems, unrest and strikes

Ailing Woodrow Wilson (left) rides to inauguration with President-Elect Harding. (Courtesy Detroit News)

were disrupting businesses then. John Wanamaker, of the store that bears his name, who'd also been Postmaster General, died at a seasoned eighty-four.

Few of our citizens saw Presidential inaugurations as they happened. Camera angles changed slightly, but there was a similarity in the settings for incoming Presidents Coolidge, Hoover and Roosevelt. By Herbert Hoover's time, microphones were added for the ears of America. Now it's taken for granted that if we wish to see the ceremony, we turn the television knob. Here President-Elect Franklin Roosevelt rides to his first inaugural with Mrs. Roosevelt, E.R. and Joseph T. Robinson on March 4, 1933.

By 1923 the American troops that had kept the "Watch on the Rhine" were called home. It was usual to hear of new laws and the sharpening of teeth in old ones, to attempt Prohibition enforcement. As an example; President Harding didn't agree that enforcement agents should be under Civil Service. The War Department ruled Puerto Rico and decided that it should come under United States' Prohibition laws. The Attorney General upheld this decision. Prohibition was extended to Puerto Rico. The Supreme Court held that intoxicating beverages on either American or foreign ships could not enter United States waters.

President Harding died in August of 1923, and the following day the oath of office was administered to Vice-President Coolidge in Vermont by his magistrate father.

Here's the fairy tale of 1923; the Secretary of the Treasury announced that the total debt was reduced again and by the middle of 1924 he anticipated a surplus over expenses of $200,000,000! This *must* be a story, in the face of present-day debts. But it must be remembered that Harding and Coolidge were against bonuses for soldiers and financial aid for farmers. Coolidge was fanatically economical.

Woodrow Wilson died in 1924 after a lingering illness that had incapacitated him completely. Many said he died

The swearing-in of Theodore Roosevelt, Calvin Coolidge and Herbert Hoover. (Courtesy Detroit News)

Franklin D. Roosevelt riding with his wife to his inauguration (Franklin D. Roosevelt Library)

of a broken heart over the outcome of his work in the League of Nations cause.

George Eastman, of Kodak fame, gave twelve and one-half million dollars, divided between several schools. James Duke said he'd give a third of his forty-six million dollar gift to Trinity College providing it was thereafter known as Duke. It was!

There were sharp Ku Klux Klan clashes with the forces of law in Herrin, Illinois, and several were killed. This brought the state militia out when trouble flared again.

If Robert M. LaFollette had gotten enough votes in the election the year before, he would have served only from March 4 to June 18, 1925, before dying at the age of seventy-nine. Other notable names that left us this year were Amy Lowell, the poetess, and William Jennings Bryan, who had also contended for the presidency three times. It emphasizes the importance of carefully choosing the Vice-President.

We were reading in 1926 about the successful flight of Lt. Commander Richard E. Byrd over the North Pole . . . the passing of Luther Burbank, much labor upheaval in the coal mines and more Ku Klux Klan uprisings. Eugene V. Debs was finally done with his earthly problems, including the Industrial Workers of the World, better known as the I.W.W. Top hostesses fluttered over a visit from Queen Marie of Rumania.

Radio became a force in 1927 and the Radio Control Bill was new law. All broadcasting had to be licensed, and that year radiophone service was established between New York and London.

Sacco and Vanzetti were still in the news, fighting for their lives and freedom, but all appeals had been exhausted. They were sentenced to die on or about July 10, 1927. Their agonizing suspense lengthened when the Massachusetts Governor stayed execution until August 1. By the third of August, Governor Fuller stated he'd thoroughly investigated the evidence and would interfere no further with the execution of Sacco and Vanzetti. The edict of the law wasn't carried out until August 23—for murdering two men in 1920, a crime which they were convicted of in 1924. They paid for the crime in life as well as in death. It was a famous case that proved what the ultimate in appeals can do.

This period couldn't be passed without the name Teapot Dome cropping up. Much attention was focused upon Secretary of the Interior Albert B. Fall, who "fell" when President Coolidge investigated the Naval oil releases with representatives of both political parties as counsel. Secretary Fall refused to testify on the grounds that it might tend to incriminate him. Does this sound familiar? The whole Teapot Dome affair received national scandal proportions and forever reflected on Harding's administration.

At this time workers were struggling for something we forget hasn't always existed; the eight-hour day. The newspaper said that a bonus bill was passed over the President's veto, that several indictments were handed down in the Teapot Dome scandal and the most famous

two in the courts were still Sacco and Vanzetti. The entire radical political world was stirred over them.

Women began to climb politically with the election of two to governorships; Nellie Tayloe Ross as the Governor of Wyoming, followed by Miriam (Ma) Furguson in Texas. President Coolidge got a term on his own, with Charles Dawes as his running-mate.

There was aviation news when two out of four planes from the Army completed round-the-world trips, taken in hops of less than five hundred miles each. If some were doing new things, others were partaking in the oldest event—dying. Names in the obituaries included Henry Cabot Lodge and Samuel Gompers, President of the Federation of Labor. This was when William Green became the longtime head of the organization.

There were many who thought President Coolidge was a dour-faced do-nothing executive, but a chorus readily echoed, "Why rock the boat when it's sailing in smooth waters?" Yes, why—but those glassy waters of prosperity, wild stock speculation and wild violation of the prohibition laws were covering the treacherous rocks that lay shallowly under the surface . . . Depression! Luckily for him, Coolidge "did not choose to run again."

There was color in the Presidential campaign of 1928 when Herbert Hoover came against Alfred E. Smith. Governor Smith of New York was the first Roman Catholic to make the run for the highest office, and although his personality and policies were liked by many, heads shook against the possibility or desirability of having a Catholic head this country. There were Protestants who believed that the Pope would have a direct line from the Vatican to Washington in order to dictate American affairs. Al Smith sang "The Sidewalks of New York," and called for reforms in the Prohibition Amendment and Volstead Act, but this popular wish of many people wasn't enough to override the built-in prejudices. Mr. Hoover won and reforms concerning liquor had to wait until his defeat in 1932.

The public liked to see portraits of men they were coaxed to elect, and their families. Al Smith posed with his wife, daughter and granddaughters, including the family dolls.

You who were too young or yet unborn undoubtedly know, as we who suffered through it, that 1929 will forever be known as the year of the stock market crash. If Ralph Waldo Emerson had been writing in this year, he could have said "The crash heard 'round the world," instead of "shot." There was a foreboding slump in the stock market earlier in 1929; it was like a dress rehearsal for the real show which opened in Wall Street the week of October 24 to 30. Paper fortunes burned from the friction of wild, frenzied selling—men frantically scurried, payed, borrowed, maybe stole with the hope of shoring-up tottering "house-of-cards" marginally-bought holdings. Let's pray that such a scene never plays again! Every day's newspapers told of suicides . . . men going to their desired deaths because of being wiped out.

If the mass of people were befuddled about what was

Al Smith poses with his wife, daughter and granddaughters. (Courtesy Detroit *News*)

happening on Wall Street (the average man didn't buy stocks then), the alleged financial wizards were no more knowledgable about it or of what to do. Every day platitudes were uttered by informed men, in vain attempts to explain. Instead of screaming and running through the streets, others tried to be lullabyers, the sedative to calm the nation's tattered nerves. They intoned, "This can't last, it's just a passing phase that will soon be forgotten with our rapid return to normalcy." But what was normalcy? It couldn't have been the days after the war when rents suddenly shot from $20 to $90 per month: it couldn't have been the Florida real estate boom when people bought swamp lots, unseen, for fantastic prices; or the newly made millionaires whose only claim to the title were sheaves of worthless paper—shares that weren't paid for.

A sketch of Herbert Hoover, c. 1929. (Courtesy Detroit *News*)

Into this cauldron walked the new President Hoover. His ready-made job was staggering and Coolidge was a wise man in "choosing not to run." Hoover reaped most of the blame a distressed public had to pin on someone. It was only odd that so much fell to him when actually the Depression was nearly worldwide and the trend started in Coolidge's administration.

A newspaper didn't land on the streets without its quota of Prohibition news . . . shootings among the underworld gangs to whom this law was a plum in their liquor- and blood-stained hands. The worst aspect was not among those who would be criminally bent in any generation, but the thousands of ordinarily law-abiding citizens who found themselves in speakeasies in order to have a drink. How odd this law must have seemed to other civilized countries where such an idea could not have been conceived!

Advertising of old line European alcoholic beverages had to be tailored especially to our market. One advertisement said in 1926 that it was always delightfully old, and yet refreshingly new, non-alcoholic Vermouth, the choice of the *beau monde*. French was freely interspersed in our language then.

Now a girl would ask her boyfriend in for a nightcap drink, but here was a suggestion offered in 1926; "When Prince Charming escorts you home and broadly hints that he'd like to linger awhile, ask him in. Tea for two is at its best after a long ride in the outdoors."

Another ad stated that Vermouth was especially prepared for the United States in the same way as always with the single necessary alteration of the original formula. They were subtle about the absence of alcohol.

Headlines screamed of raids on even the plushiest drinking parlors, with "paddy-wagons" hauling surly men and screeching women off to account for their illciit activities. Detroit gained notoriety from the rum-running across the Detroit River from Canada, and the Purple Gang grew lusty. A favorite recommendation for liquor was that it was "just off the boat." To which someone would ask, "Scraped off?" This inference came from the awful fact that people were so drink-hungry that they'd imbibe poisoned brews, drink bathtub gin, go blind and insane as an aftermath of wood alcohol, canned heat, perfume, flavoring extracts or anything that promised a kick. Making a batch of home brew was a common occurrence in many American homes—otherwise respectable homes. It was a spreading violation that enforcement agents couldn't cope with. With crackdowns and arrests, there was a legion that didn't feel contrite . . . not over breaking a law they didn't think sensible. It could have been the first mass disrespect for law and its enforcers.

Although prohibition was a festering sore on the American scene, Hoover tried to uphold the law, but government machinery and personnel was most concerned with the top priority problems—unemployment and the Depression. It could have been called the "relief regime," so many bills were passed to aid various groups; unemployment relief, drought and farm relief. This was one time when states didn't have to fight for their rights because the Federal Government wished to dump much of the problem at local levels. Voluntary relief measures were called for along with work programs.

Wages were falling as corporations made cuts. It was contagious once a big company started the trend. Runs on banks were regular occurrences. The little people were terrified at the loss of life's savings and they began to hoard what they could recoup. Some hapless souls were too late and found no more money when they got to banks. By October 30, 1931, there had been 2,342 bank failures. How forlorn these imposing buildings looked with their ornate ceilings and marble columns

After long and futile attempts to get mobster Al Capone, the law finally clamped onto him for income tax evasion. Americans could read all about it in such publications as *Liberty Magazine.*

that whispered of a wealth and solidarity that no longer existed. It was bitterly incongruous that as time passed, the highly decorated banks became houses for a miscellany of businesses from florists to being rented for shoe and clothing sales.

This was the face of a President beset with heavy problems in an ailing country and he couldn't have found it easy to feign a smile.

The face of President Hoover in a tragic time—he couldn't have found it easy to feign a smile. (Courtesy Detroit News)

One of the biggest stories in the annals of crime came on October 24, 1931, when the law finally clamped onto Al Capone for income tax evasion. After long, futile attempts to get the all-time big racket boss, this tax mechanism was the only card to turn the trick. He was sentenced to eleven years, fined a mere $50,000, but the court costs were double this amount. It was enough to break his Chicago reign, even though his top lieutenants contacted him many times . . . while dividing the ill-gotten empire among themselves.

If the twenties were called "roaring," the next decade earned the title, "terrible thirties." There was gang rule, accompanied by the collectors of protection money. Any illegal or immoral thing was obtainable in the teeming cities, if you knew enough to say through a peephole in a door, "Joe sent me."

A happier aspect of the time was the opening of the

Boulder Dam a-building. (Photo by Chester Janczarek)

great George Washington Bridge across the Hudson River between New York and Fort Lee, New Jersey. The immense Boulder Dam was underway, later to be named after Hoover.

In 1932 came the suicide death of George Eastman who had given much money to the betterment and education of mankind. He left a brief note saying, "My work is done, why wait?" He'd been generous in life, and it continued after death when he left the bulk of his fortune to schools and charities.

One dark, frustrating note of this year was the dogged, unsuccessful bonus march on Washington, D.C. There was news in the forming of the Reconstruction Finance Corporation which made big drains on the United States Treasury as it granted astronomical sums to ease various depression areas. The House of Representatives had enough Democrats to be able to have one of their group, John Nance Garner, as Speaker of the House. There was difference of opinion between Congress and the President on relief measures. Signs were more and more evident that the pendulum was on the swing away from the Republicans after all of the years they'd ruled. Long queues in soup and bread lines, the penniless, jobless people plodding the streets, hordes milling around the country on railroad "bum" trips, hundreds of applicants where one opening existed—these people were ripe for a change. It's doubtful if some cared what they changed to, so long as something showed promise. Twelve million jobless people was a force to be reckoned with. They made their wishes apparent when the time came to make X's in the voting booths. Franklin Roosevelt received the biggest popular vote anyone had enjoyed to that time. In every hamlet the swing was toward the Democrats. Hoover could no longer control the reins that were

President Hoover takes time out to pose with oysters and fish. (Courtesy Detroit News)

Vice President John Nance Garner, with Mrs. Garner, returning to Washington for the 1938 Congressional session. (Photo by Acme)

loosely whipping around the runaway economic Depression.

It's an American peculiarity that in the midst of President Hoover's greatest travail, there was a retinue of gift bestowers, usually bringing something representative of their part of the nation. He took time from pressing matters to be photographed with oysters, oxen, fish, keys to cities and their donors.

When we flipped to the entertainment pages of our papers, what fare was at the local theaters and concert halls in 1932? We could listen to a noted baritone, Lawrence Tibbett, of opera, concerts, films and radio.

Joan Crawford had newly arrived in "Rain," Clark Gable and Jean Harlow were sizzling the celluloid in "Red Dust." Gilda Gray was shimmying in person with eight great acts. If you craved movie music and an all-star cast, there was "The Big Broadcast" with Bing Crosby, Kate Smith, the Boswell Sisters, Donald Novis,

In the thirties, baritone Lawrence Tibbett was a star in opera, concerts, films, and radio. (Courtesy Detroit News)

19

Stars of the day were Joan Crawford, Clark Gable, and Jean Harlow. (Courtesy Detroit *News*)

the Mills Brothers, Vincent Lopez, Cab Calloway and the "Street Singer," Arthur Tracy. If all of these entertainers left you wanting, you could still see Laurel and Hardy on the same bill.

A fact not generally remembered is that the proposal for repeal of the Prohibition Amendment was first brought forth in Herbert Hoover's administration. Most people lump it in with the credits given the following President. The major debit event of the dying regime was the many bank closures, starting in Detroit, as ordered by Michigan's Governor to halt further drains on the reserves. It was called a "bank holiday," but when people read the gaunt headline, they muttered in a dazed, uncomprehending manner—numb and unbelieving. It spread to other states like panic.

It was the dawn of the New Deal and an administration that lasted into an unprecedented stretch of twelve years. Scarcely had the inaugural voices died away when the new President Franklin D. Roosevelt declared the bank holiday for the entire nation, to give the distressed institutions a breathing and retrenching period. In short order he gained discretionary powers unknown before, so he could act promptly and decisively on the major

In 1930 the man who'd later be known as "F.D.R." sat in the New York Governors chair in Albany. (Franklin D. Roosevelt Library)

issues. In rapid succession he proposed bills that were quickly passed concerning Federal economies, the return of light 3.2 beer, unemployment relief and curbs on the manner of stock buying. He started development of the Tennessee River Valley and industrial measures for recovery. In spite of all this unparalled authority, the public in general had confidence in him and backed up his New Deal program. Dissenters and critics were drowned in the onward rush.

People felt more hopeful and were told "the only thing to fear is fear itself." We may not have been better off, but we felt better about it. There were the new beer gardens to inspect while sampling their wares. The Sunday paper featured an article for hostesses to whom beer was an unknown item—not of their time. The "beer buffet" was suggested so that an erring lady wouldn't serve layer cake with the new beverage.

It said, "Now that beer is again legal, many a hostess is desirous to know how to serve it, what to serve with it, and the new technique and etiquette of beer, which is far removed from the swinging door of the gas-jet age and a bucket of suds. Beer has at least brought back the almost vanished taste for foods which are sour, sharp, spicy and bitter. We have perhaps gone whipped cream and ice cream-sodaish for just too long!"

If newspapers printed beer snack menus and recipes, they also gave space to artist's ideas for beer garden décor. An article stated; "The return of beer is opening a new field to interior decorators and mural painters. The new beer dispensary must vie with the ritzy speakeasy in its artistic appeal. We must expect that women, many of whom have acquired the habit of going to speakeasies, will be generous patrons of the popular places in the new beer era." A young designer recommended green as a restful color for peacefully emptying your tankards, but said definitely that yellow doesn't go with drinking.

A Detroit group of artists got publicity when they said; "With the return of the stein-on-the-table, restaurants should take on a genial, old-fashioned, homey air conducive to long, quiet evenings and good conversation. This spirit flourishes best in a setting that is gay, humorous, whimsical and colorful." It further said, "The successful restaurant where the long-awaited 3.2 beer is to be served (New Deal restaurants), should have a touch of Bohemia." Would you say that the beer bars have succeeded with these suggestions?

The editorial page gave the "Culture Budget" for busy persons. You had to, "Make one visit to a museum each month, visit six art exhibitions at a half hour each, hear two concerts or recitals, listen to four classical radio programs, see two plays per month, read one outstanding non-fiction work—biography, memoirs or history—every two months, reread one classic every two months and read one volume of poetry every two months. This won't hurt you, no matter how much you know—and it's better than thinking about the depression."

Roosevelt brought a New Deal to Washington. (Courtesy Detroit News)

In the *Detroit News* feature section for June 25, 1933, Cyril Arthur Player wrote; "This is the story of today. President Franklin D. Roosevelt has declared war on poverty, on inefficiency, on neglect of natural riches, on unemployment, on human misery. It can be styled the NEW DEAL, if you wish, but essentially, the narrative is continuous." Indeed it is, because some of these phrases sound amazingly familiar in the Lyndon Johnson Great Society programs.

The National Recovery Administration was to curb elements thought to have contributed to the Depression. But by 1935 the Supreme Court had declared it illegal.

As the New Deal shifted into high gear, we entered what some called the "alphabet soup" era. The bureaucratic mechanism had too many agencies to name, so initials were used for simplification; NRA, AAA (not the Automobile Club), FERA, CCC, HOLC, TVA, PWA and WPA. If you misquoted a set of letters it might send you far afield. The National Recovery Administration (NRA) was to curb, regulate or eliminate elements thought to have contributed to the Depression. But by 1935 the Supreme Court had declared it unconstitutional. This was also when farmers were first told what to grow, and were paid NOT to grow.

The Home Owners' Loan Corporation assumed home mortgages to try to keep purchasers from foreclosures. These hard-hit people were given new mortgages for fifteen years at five per cent interest.

Now the cry arose that with the vast controls the government had over many vital things, it was actually in business. But despite these drastic changes in former ways and means, people generally followed along cooperatively.

Labor troubles were constantly broiling as laws and recommendations for workers, unions, wages and hours were brought on. We had a deficit of four billion dollars, but it was considered justifiable with the improved public morale.

If it seemed that what John Public read in his papers was much rosier, the New Deal was not without bitter opponents. Many began to call the Roosevelt moves Socialistic, as revolutionary as Russia's "five year plans." Some among the wealthy used their powers to pull backward on the recovery reins, hoping to discredit the governmental scheme. Above all of the cry, the President's voice confidently spoke to us with assurance that the American system and philosophy was being preserved.

One of the most significant changes that received President Roosevelt's signature was the Social Security Act on August 14, 1935. We started paying one per cent from our incomes, to be matched by employers, in 1937. No one could anticipate then how high the percentage could go while they envisioned themselves comfortably provided for in their declining years.

In January, 1934 we learned that Billy Burke would continue the *Follies* begun by her late husband, Florenz Ziegfeld. (Courtesy Detroit *News*)

In 1934 we could get a lot of entertainment for our money, providing we could acquire a quarter or half dollar. A January Sunday paper told us we had exciting doings on the New York stage where Billie Burke, true to her promise, put on the Ziegfeld Follies even though husband, Florenz Ziegfeld, had passed on. Opening night really sparkled when the furs-and-jewels crowd thronged the theater to see the rollicking Fanny Brice.

Laurel and Hardy delighted audiences of the thirties in such films as "Sons of the Desert." (Courtesy Detroit *News*)

Laurel and Hardy were still going strong in a piece, "Sons of the Desert." Many familiar star names cropped up. Most are no longer with us because of death, retirement or the fluctuation of public taste; Ruby Keeler, Dick Powell, and Adolphe Menjou for example. James Cagney and Ginger Rogers are still occasionally seen.

The big coming attraction announced that the picture you'd been waiting for was nearly here, "Dinner at Eight," and it promised to have more stars than "Grand Hotel." Singer Ruth Etting was in an Eddie Cantor picture—and many Midway entertainers from the Chicago World's Fair were in a stage revue.

With 1936 another election was upcoming, bringing all of the usual predictions, editorials and surveys. The Republican nominee was Kansas Governor Alfred Landon, who ran with Frank Knox. Their campaigning plan was to make capital of criticisms of the Roosevelt policies, and in a surprising switch, "Alf" Landon was supported by Al Smith, who'd deserted the Democratic Party.

Out of the stress, flamboyance and change in this decade, a September 1936 article talked about moderation. It's problematic whether the writer was indirectly slapping at the New Deal when he said that moderation must always be characteristic of true leadership. The program of a great leader is a compromise between what is beneficial in the long run and the expediencies of the present.

Governor Landon fought hard, but he might as well have stayed home, because Franklin Roosevelt came up an even stronger winner than he had against Mr. Hoover —an additional four million votes were added to his margin of safety. The people voiced their approval but the going wasn't as easy with the Supreme Court where his measures were dealt heavy blows. The best procedure was to do something about the troublesome court and its unconstitutionality decisions. The President did this immediately by a move that caused a furor in the Senate—over the so-called Supreme Court-packing attempt. He tried to make the advanced age of the major-

ity of Justices the issue. "Old age begets inability to meet changing conditions." Now senators of his own party were sharply critical.

If there seemed to be an emergence from the Depression, there was another slump in 1937, (slight recession) when strikes riddled the automotive and steel industries' recovery.

Every copy of our papers told about bill-passings, naming huge sums of money to make them operative . . . astronomical amounts that were incomprehensible figures to the average citizen. The national deficit was growing like cancer cells from forty billion dollars in 1938 to an additional five billion by the year's end. If this was alarming, there was also an imminent war brewed for serving in Europe—and come it did in 1939. The Nazis were more than "on the march."

We had to be fed something besides the grimness of a world exploding and the staggering national debt. Bathing suit styles were surveyed with a narrowing eye as they disappeared thread-by-thread. By an old ordinance, it was unlawful for a woman to bathe in waters within a city unless wearing suitable clothing that covered the body from neck to knees. There was also controversy about men's bathing trunks: whether they should be with or without tops. So suits had tops that could be zippered on and off, depending on where you swam.

When election time came in 1940, we were busy with war goods manufacture for ourselves and the fighting allies—the Depression was nearly forgotten. However, the war conditions in Europe were ominous. What could a new, unseasoned man do if he stepped into the Presidency at this time? Another hard-bound American tradition was scrapped when Roosevelt ran for a third

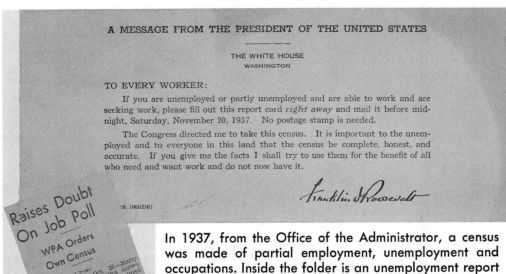

In 1937, from the Office of the Administrator, a census was made of partial employment, unemployment and occupations. Inside the folder is an unemployment report card on which everything pertaining to a worker's status was asked.

term. Wendell Willkie was no competition against not only a firmly entrenched President, but a difficult world situation. We were warned of the doom that could follow any change of course. December 7, 1941, was on its way as we worked again, built houses, bought automobiles and generally felt prosperous. The Japanese bombed our ships out of recognition in Pearl Harbor that quiet Sunday of the 7th as we were about the peaceful business of reading the Sunday papers.

From a journalistic standpoint, this was a busy time. Newsmen were scattered around the globe, sending back constant, vivid reports of the fighting, but what were we reading and doing at home besides running the defense plants?

People were talking about the War, the resultant erosive emotions, reports of Raymond Gram Swing, the "Beer Barrel Polka" annexed by British troops. Newspaper headlines of this day were contrasted with those of twenty-five years previously when huge black letters said simply, "WAR." We could see the effect of war on the theater, clothes—even to the new corset. We felt an uncertainty as though squeezed into a tightening world by a big nutcracker.

There were many who stayed glued to their radios, listening to all newscasts and analyses, until a form of nervous jitters developed. George White put on his "Scandals," and we read Ludwig Bemelmans.

A much-publicized man was Martin Dies, whose Committee for Investigation of Un-American Activities not only fired into any suspected Red hanky-panky, but was in turn set upon by his critics. Mr. Dies was accused of publicity seeking, being unfair, slipshod and a one-sided revealer of evidence from witnesses who were not first investigated.

As if our national scene wasn't giving the journalists enough to write about, a man who held no higher office than mayor was making news columns crackle. Frank Hague, variously called Boss Hague or "I am the law," raised hackles in New Jersey. He may have been a relic of the old political bossism, but he made his presence felt, particularly in matters of free speech and assembly, as when Socialist Norman Thomas attempted to speak in Newark, New Jersey. Hague swore great Americanism while he wielded dictatorial power. Writers warned that if the 1938 depression grew worse, Hague's doctrine and practice could spread—even to considering New Dealers radicals who should be egg-pelted.

Other thoughts in these days: what Martin Dies would say to Earl Browder, the Communist; wonderment about Grover Whalen's World of Tomorrow Fair in New York, also the good sound of "Somewhere over the Rainbow." We saw a movie version of "The Women," and talked about the new comedy, "The Man Who Came to Dinner." We read Dorothy Thompson's writing on the War and discussions of Chamberlain, Daladier and Hitler. We tired of stories of those just in from the war zone, and read a book, *The Hundredth Year*, that told of roots

planted in 1936 for the war. The German Embassy was displeased with Clare Boothe's play, "Margin for Error," Lindbergh made alarming speeches about Germany's strength, and we listened to Prokofieff's "Peter and the Wolf." Meantime, Charlie Chaplin still worked on his satire of Europe's strong men, "The Great Dictator." It would be interesting to know how soon names of those who surrounded Roosevelt will be lost to the ages. Do you remember Paul McNutt, Jimmie Roosevelt, John L. Lewis, Harry Hopkins and Madame Perkins?

Thomas E. Dewey never had a chance in the 1944 election—especially with the War still going on.

Although we were embroiled with wars on two fronts, a 1944 election had to occur. No matter who the Republicans might have pulled from their hats, he wouldn't have a fighting chance. "Don't change horses in midstream," was the common slogan. Roosevelt must see the War through, no matter how many terms were involved! This election was an interruption to the business of the day. While Thomas E. Dewey went heatedly around the country trying to drum up votes, Roosevelt gave fireside talks on radio. Dewey had the popularity or recognition of being a successful special prosecutor, but this didn't weigh heavily enough for the voters to give up the President we were used to. Even if Roosevelt warned us about fear, we were never more fearful as a nation. We were now accustomed to leaning toward the central government and many dubbed the President "The Great White Father."

Roosevelt was only slightly into his fourth term when, after the Yalta Conference, pictures came to us that showed a man who looked ill and rapidly aged. Suddenly on April 12 at Warm Springs, Georgia, he suffered a cerebral hemorrhage and was gone. People by the millions around the world were stunned and our nation mourned the loss of its leader and Commander-in-Chief of the Armed Forces.

Only slightly into his fourth term, the ailing F.D.R. suddenly died on April 12, 1945.

Vice-President Harry Truman immediately took the reins and soon was sitting in the World Security Conference with Churchill and Stalin. President Truman's quick ending of Japanese hostilities are found in the story of World War II.

Before we were completely in the War's grips, what entertained us? "Dr. Cyclops" was scarey and beautiful Linda Darnell starred in a story about Hollywood. For advanced prices you could see "Gone With the Wind," but you'd have a considerable wait to see it at popular price. In New York, Kate Smith celebrated her ten years as first lady of the airlanes. Lana Turner dashed away from Metro-Goldwyn-Mayer, saying she was retiring from pictures to be a good wife and mother. Elsa Maxwell wrote a movie script on the subject she knew best—debutantes.

If you wanted to be modish, you wore a redingote dress, and Emily Post could advise you how to behave correctly under all conditions. Prudence Penny wrote about ways to serve eggs because they were cheap and full of protein.

Taxation came up for a lot of discussion and editorializing in 1942 and 1943. There was talk about "forgiveness" and "redistribution of wealth," and one group of defense workers declared that they had no intention of

President Truman waving, J. Howard McGrath, Vice-President Elect Barkley, Mrs. Truman, Margaret Truman, and Mrs. Barkley returned to Washington after the elections. (Zweig-WHNP Photograph, Harry S. Truman Library)

Paramount, Graumann's Chinese, Loew's State, Carthay Circle and United Artists Theaters showed the screen epics of this era.

If you wanted to be modish, you wore a redingote dress.

paying income tax. The quick reply was that there was plenty of jail room. The squeeze was on as many cashed War Bonds and patronized loan companies at an alarming rate, to scrape up a cash lump big enough to pay their taxes. Thousands of people were paying income tax for the first time, and a plan had to be devised whereby the tax dollars would not be spent before the date to pay them. It wasn't human nature to see that sum just laying there. The time was ripe for withholding from salary checks—the only conceivable way to assure the government of its money demands.

In 1945, as today, we were prisoners of the cigarette habit.

Russians closed transportation routes, we flew supplies in by Allied airlift.

Life at home was generally on the upswing as salaries, employment and prices soared. Television began to invade homes and planes flew at supersonic speeds. We were learning about sonic booms.

In 1949 new aerial records were made when Air Force bombers flew non-stop around the world. Trials of Communists were held and Alger Hiss got star billing in news stories that unfolded facts about Communist workings, propaganda and entrenchment within the vitals of our country. America survived one of the most trying tests in its history, and could not be quite the same as before. We read it all in our newspapers.

What was happening at home as average citizens plodded through their duties while yearning for the War's end? We dreamed of the day that rationing would end and we wouldn't feel like beggars in long lines to get a little piece of butter or a package of cigarettes. Hoarders, the despicable people, would be eliminated, and black marketeers could not reap pots of gold from basic human needs. We could dream of going more than a few miles in our cars without running out of a minimum gas ration. We might even buy a new car!

Stars and tears were in our eyes when we heard that our men were coming home, especially if they'd gotten through the conflict sound in mind and body. Great adjustments and understanding was necessary for many who hadn't been this fortunate. Any war has a reconstruction period, but we had to recover from the greatest illness the world had yet known!

Price ceilings, frozen salaries and fixed rents could become history, but we worried about the possibility of prices leaping out of sight. There was a race of veterans to start small businesses they'd dreamed about while crouching in foxholes. For every ten who tried enterprises in which they were inexperienced, nine failed outright or gave up. Many were dissatisfied with going back to their old jobs and milled around seeking something new.

While U.S. individuals were working out their salvations, headlines told of mass unrest in industries and large-scale strikes in mines, steel companies and railroads. These crippling stoppages caused government seizures to put the wheels into motion.

In 1948 the United States assumed a worldwide role for the first time. We put the Marshall Plan for European aid to the test. Labor at home still ground its jaws about passage of the Taft-Hartley bill the year before, and the "Cold War" had already begun in Berlin. When the

The newsboy hawking his extras has largely vanished from the scene.

Whether tracking down dark alleys to get a story, walking the halls of capitals, balancing a teacup at a fashionable affair, or getting sparks in their hair from a holocaust, our newsmen and women have fearlessly risked their necks and comforts to bring us tomorrow's story today. For every newshawk portrayed as a glib, fast-talking, hard-as-nails character, there's an army of hard-working, earnest people performing the job they've chosen—to let us know what's going on in this wide world.

3

What Happened to Money?

Did you pay income tax in 1920? If so, you were a member of the exclusive upper class. Of course, you may not have yet been born to the worries of taxpaying. Although my father worked steadily all of his life, he never knew the "joys" of paying as much as one cent of income tax. We spoke enviously of people who made enough money to be singled out for the tax—as if it were a status symbol. Does this seem incredible? What then has happened since?

Then, as now, inflation was a matter of concern. (Courtesy *The New York Times*)

This subject could sink into the intricacies of economics, but we're considering the average, ordinary person who was called the "working man." It's sufficient that we—who were weaned before the market crash of 1929, managed to live through the Depression, escaped enemy bullets in World War II and are still climbing the spiral staircase of inflation—still like to speak of the days when hamburgers were a nickel.

Of course we can't mention many merchandise prices, but you might cry dollar signs with a glance at a *Detroit News* ad for a leading department store. Hurry with the figures fresh in mind, to a merchant who carries comparable goods. Or can you find comparable quality in what would have been the same price range?

"I'll Show You a REAL Bargain"

"And you will agree with me, too, when you see this cherry colored dinette suite at this smashed price. I said I'd go the limit and here's how I back it up. Draw top table and four chairs **$29** *Use Your Account*

"Bed Prices Take a Drop"

This "real bargain" would be an even bigger one today. (Courtesy Detroit *News*)

Do you remember the last time you saw a bona fide *drop* in advertised prices? Not sales where they claim you'll save money—but a complete drop. It would be sweet to a shopper's ears if it didn't herald a drop in the whole economy. There's the rub!

The next time on a trip when the motel keeper says "Twenty dollars for the night" without apology while you're wincing, look at this ad for the new Lincoln Hotel. No one was charging bed tax either. The wrecker's ball has since eliminated the Lincoln to make way for bigger things.

When you were staying in New York at the new Lincoln Hotel, you might have nourished the inner person with these foods from the menu at Dempsey's, and still have had enough change left for an evening on the town.

Those were the days! Curtains for a dollar! (Courtesy the Pontiac, Michigan, *Daily Press*)

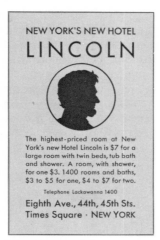

NEW YORK'S NEW HOTEL

LINCOLN

The highest-priced room at New York's new Hotel Lincoln is $7 for a large room with twin beds, tub bath and shower. A room, with shower, for one $3. 1400 rooms and baths, $3 to $5 for one, $4 to $7 for two.

Telephone Lackawanna 1400

Eighth Ave., 44th, 45th Sts.
Times Square · NEW YORK

Both the Lincoln Hotel, and the room rates, are a thing of the past. (Courtesy Davis Publications, Inc. *School Arts* Magazine)

SUPPER SUGGESTIONS	
STEAK MINUTE with O'Brien Potatoes	1.75
FILET MIGNON with Fresh Mushrooms and French Fried Potatoes	2.00
BROILED PRIME HAMBURGER STEAK with Smothered Onions	1.50
BROILED DOUBLE LAMB CHOP (1), French Fried Potatoes	1.25
HALF BROILED SPRING CHICKEN, French Fried Potatoes	1.50
Scrambled Eggs with Beech-Nut Bacon	.95
Ham and Eggs, Country Style	.95
Scrambled Eggs with Deerfoot Sausages	.95
WELSH RAREBIT	1.00

A menu from Jack Dempsey's restaurant. Where can you get filet mignon for two dollars today—or even for twice that amount?

Someone usually argues, "When things didn't cost as much, we didn't make as much, so where's the difference?" Logical as this sounds, it still doesn't cure the anemia of the de-valued dollar or the difficulty of adjusting to now-against-then.

In 1934 all standard brands of cigarettes were one thin dime; ground beef ranged below fifteen cents per pound and other foods were scaled accordingly. If you could grasp a ten dollar bill, it would buy more groceries than you could carry. The problem was to get it—or better yet, to get a job that paid enough to live on.

Maybe you were among the thousands looking for work and were fortunate to be *the* one hired for twenty dollars per week. If that didn't satisfy you, there were plenty who were glad to change places with you. The average wage for a topnotch secretary was twenty-five dollars. The first job I got after nearly a year of looking, made me very happy at eighty dollars per month. For this colossal figure we sometimes worked seventy hours a week, not daring to complain. Instead of overtime pay we were given fifty cents for dinner money. It would buy a meal because a moderately good neighborhood restaurant had a top price of sixty-five cents for a full-course dinner. This paid for sizzling steak with all the trimmings.

For amusement, two could see a double feature at the neighborhood theater for twenty cents. If you were extremely flicker-hungry you could go on change night to see four features which might include dishes, glassware and bingo as added inducements.

When you looked at your salary check, the figure was the same amount you were hired for—no deductions, withholding or other shrinkage. If you were thrifty enough to have a bank account, these institutions gave you 1 per cent for the use of your money. There was no boom yet of saving and loan associations offering attractively higher interest.

The beautician still performs these same services; but he'll charge you $16.00.

While mentioning attractiveness, if you wished to be beautified at the neighborhood salon, a glance at these prices on the card for my old beauty parlor gives a hint of the bargain grooming. When I left Detroit the price

for such a visit had climbed to $7.95. On the west coast the same ministration was $16.

Did you wish to buy a new automobile? It could be done for a trim $700. The car wasn't heavy with accessories, but it got you where you were going and usually brought you home.

This is just a sampling of prices where I lived. Each of you can tell an economic story with localized variations. Only pity was written in the eyes of those fortunate individuals who had steady, established jobs through the Depression. They undoubtedly saw breadlines, but never tasted their bitter fare. "Panhandlers" were everywhere and no one escaped the pleas for a dime for a cup of coffee. Actually, coffee was only five cents but the second cup wasn't free. When coffee jumped to 7 cents, then a dime, it caused a furor.

If some items were much lower than today, others remained nearly the same or became less. Radios, for example, were cheaper after the novelty wore off. They'd been $200 or more from about 1925–1930, and that was a lot of money to scrape into a pile all at once. Credit didn't flow as freely as now—"Nothing down and 39 years to pay." A typewriter in 1929 continued at about the same price for many years.

In 1939 we built a brick, five-room house that would be considered modern yet today. This delightful home cost a total of $5800. After three months of occupancy, building costs began to rise and would have added $1000. We couldn't have guessed how far this could climb. By 1950 there weren't comparable dwellings for less than $10,000. When the house was sold in 1956, it brought $19,000 and would have gotten more if speed of disposal hadn't been an issue.

What was happening in the tax department? Taxmen sharpened their pencils gradually to a vicious point for the laboring citizen. If we deplore income taxes, we may blame the lawmakers of 1913 who first ratified the Six-

A DODGE BROTHERS
TOURING CAR AT
$795!
F. O. B. DETROIT

Roadster - - - - $795
Coupe - - - - $845
Sedan - - - - $895
F. O. B. DETROIT

DODGE BROTHERS, INC. DETROIT
DODGE BROTHERS (CANADA) LIMITED
TORONTO, ONTARIO

DODGE BROTHERS
MOTOR CARS

They don't make Dodges like they used to—and they don't charge the same either. (Courtesy Dodge Division, Chrysler Motors Corp.)

teenth Amendment empowering Congress to lay and collect taxes on income—then appended the tariff law of that year to include an income tax that has remained a permanent source of revenue.

It was 1924 when Congress first attempted to differentiate between earned income and unearned income. Since then tax forms have continually grown more complex and incomprehensible to some of us, including Philadelphia lawyers. There's no status symbol value left in the tax picture as the collector bends to the level of youngsters with summer vacation jobs that help pay for their next year's schooling and clothes.

It was natural to wonder why an automobile could no longer retail for under one thousand dollars—taxes. Unless the manufacturer could produce a car for $200–$300, the price including tax would have to exceed $1000. Wipe away a tear as you scan this 1926 Dodge Brothers advertisement.

Probably the majority of average citizens understand the explanations of economics to the approximate degree that Einstein's calculations can be comprehended. It usually sounds like doubletalk written in turkey tracks. It's simple to say that inflation and deflation refers to the fluctuation in the quality of money as shown by its purchasing power, but there are many ramifications that complicate the subject thereafter.

Consider the "gymnastics" that some long-established companies were forced to perform when the Depression-into-War times of the thirties and forties came. Few were unaffected so it matters little what the product was in the changing picture. In the thirties, International Silver saw the character of its business change more in five years than it had in the previous century. This wasn't gradual, but a sudden revolution that had to be adjusted to by a company whose entire tradition was to manufacture expensive, quality goods. It couldn't sell quality lines and was forced into production of cheap silverware to compete in chain store promotions and department stores' basement sales. A major depression was a stern master as wages were slashed twenty-two percent and salaries cut as much as fifty percent. High-pressured promotional drives were used for the first time in International's history in order to survive.

Some of you weren't around then and may be asking how it climbed to today's level. After World War II we were bent double under a public debt so large that it was hard to read a figure and translate it into dollar terms. We used to hear about millions and now everything was equated in billions. Inflation was becoming worldwide, but we had the enlarged aggravation of colossal spending for foreign aid, plus huge defense spending and domestic social improvement programs. So-called "limited" inflation was started when the New Deal wanted to remedy the Depression sickness. During the War we were deliberately deprived of some of our plentiful spending money by "emergency" high taxes. We were busy producing war machines—not civilian goods. However, what we assumed were temporary tax measures have not only remained, but have been upped and upped to cover vast governmental spending for full employment, unemployment insurance, public housing and such.

Meantime, the working man cried for more money in the face of high taxation, prosperity or what is called the "soaring economy." The labor unions were the instrument for getting the worker his dues, and in turn, the manufacturer reflected this wage rise in the cost of products. Anyone for a balloon ride?

This illustration reminds us of the days when we could get something for five cents at a Woolworth's.

Today the nickel won't buy much; in fact we either lump it with other small change to make an exact amount or save it for a parking meter. What did it formerly buy? You could get a cup of coffee, any of numerous candy bars, a *Saturday Evening Post* or *Collier's* magazine to read while sipping the coffee or eating the sweet. The dime store had countless nickel items when the store name meant that nothing was over a dime. George Marshall made the famous remark, "What this country needs is a good five cent cigar." We had them.

"The good five-cent cigar" is a thing of the past, too. (Courtesy Detroit News)

A multimillionaire built one of Chicago's biggest skyscrapers, bought Catalina Island off California's shores, owns the Chicago Cubs baseball team, plus other costly possessions; but he did all of this with the sale of nickel packages of gum—Wrigley's! And, isn't it strange that a package of his gum is still a nickel?

Are there any bargains left? Yes. Consider your utility bills and you'll realize that, as companies claim, they offer one of the last real bargains. Many rates have been lowered in recent times by government edict. Although it's hard to believe as you look in your skinny wallet, statisticians say that the percentage of your earnings spent for food is less than five years ago. If the taxes were removed from a gallon of gasoline, it would roll back to the good old levels. Of course the item bearing the classic tax story is the ordinary loaf of bread.

We no longer have penny cafeterias where a meal could be bought for a few cents, we can't send letters for two cents, penny postal cards are a memory. We can't read the dailies for two cents or clutter the living room with Sunday papers for a dime, but I'm sure that some form of money is here to stay even though it may closely resemble credit cards. And they'll have to arrange it so that people can acquire goods with whatever medium—otherwise, back to wampum and shells. The trick is to keep the article of exchange close to you—very close.

4

The Wheel Started Something

Were you brash enough to be an automobile pioneer who scared or squashed cows, horses and chickens out of normal growth while you jolted on alleged roads in a coughing gas machine? How could we have foreseen they would someday swarm like locusts everywhere, glutting superhighways, freeways and other elaborate roadway systems that man has devised to handle the traffic load? There are few places in the world where natives haven't seen some form of motor-driven vehicles. When this inestimable mass of metal stops, then the problem begins! Parking automobiles is a major business, major problem and major headache as we've finally realized.

If from each need new sciences, professions and jobs are born, motor cars have whelped traffic engineers, road planners, architects who design inside parking buildings or facilities underground—and these are but a few connected directly or indirectly with the car. "The automotive industry has never stood still . . . each year has brought marked mechanical improvements, better values and more artistic offerings," so said a booklet from General Motors in the thirties.

When the horseless carriage began hesitantly to appear, it was truly named. It was so likely to break down en route to the next block that it's a question why detachable hitching equipment wasn't included so a horse could come to the rescue. It's understandable why the first cars looked like buggies, for who had seen what an automobile should look like? Evolution takes time, and through the years we've seen drastic changes in the auto image.

An ad for Henry Ford's Model F, 1905. Other makers were charging $2000 and up. (Courtesy Ford Motor Company)

This chart traces the evolution of the automobile from the "horseless carriage" days through 1947.

Ford showed a car in 1905 that looked like a more logical contraption with hood, steering wheel and a place for the back seat driver. It was his Model F, phenomenally low-priced at $1200, considering that other makers were charging $2000 and up.

This 1910 Studebaker "40" had such advanced features as the windshield. (Courtesy Studebaker Corporation)

In 1910 Studebaker had a desirable model incorporating many improvements such as the windshield, convertible top, gas lights and nice bright brasswork. Studebaker was not a Johnny-come-lately in the business.

Ladies loved the noiseless, clean, easy-to-operate electric. A 1912 Anderson is shown here.

No account of automobiles could exclude the electric car—boon to the ladies with its noiseless, clean, easy lever operation. Of the many electric cars seen, I can't recall ever seeing a man in one. Because of the limitations of power, it was recommended for running around town on shopping or social calls. It would have been useless on a rough dirt road in the country on a moonless night—with a dead battery!

This Saxon was a forerunner of today's compacts.

The natty little Saxon roadster was a forerunner to our sports cars and compacts. Later Crosley built a small car but it had a limited life. We craved the authority of size.

A montage of trademarks from the days when America had many more than four automobile manufacturers.

Although the automobile business has congealed into a limited field of major car companies, this wasn't always so. Everyone was hopping into the swim and some managed nicely before sinking in the big pond. For these names that you may remember, many others are not shown. Some died a-borning while others were here so long and satisfactorily, their demises were almost mysteries. Did you own a:

Stutz	Winton	Graham Paige	Grey
Chalmers	Grant	Wills St. Clair	Cord
Scripps Booth	Roamer	Whippet	Dort
Peerless	Rickenbacker	Maxwell	Crosley
Auburn	Willys-Overland	Marmon	Jewett
Star	Willys-Knight	Haroon	Dusenberg
Jordan			

With so many kinds, how confusing it would have been if they'd offered as many models for each make as we have today!

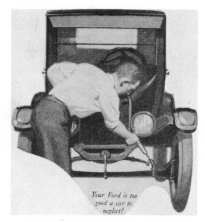

Proper maintenance of your Ford is urged in this old ad. (Courtesy Alemite Division, Stewart-Warner Corporation)

A happy owner behind the wheel of the "Tin Lizzie." (Janco Fotos)

Of all automobiles ever manufactured, none could have been the brunt of more jokes and derisive remarks, yet sold better and traveled farther, than the modest "Tin Lizzie." The Model T was the most famous that Ford ever made. My father owned nine in a row, which should be a good testimonial. Dad did the tinkering we now call "car care." He taught me the fine points and except for the weight of major parts, I could take the Ford apart and reassemble it at the age of ten.

About forty-five years ago my father taught me this verse that summed up the sentiments of a Model T owner:

Of my old Ford everybody makes fun,
They say it was born in 1901.
Well, maybe it was, but this I'll bet—
She's good for many a long mile yet.
The fanbelt slips and the horsepower squeaks
A piston grips and the radiator leaks,
She shakes the screws and the nuts all loose,
But I get 40 miles on a gallon of juice.
If I can't get gas, I burn kerosene—
And I've driven home on Paris green.
With the high-priced cars they give you some tools,
Some extra parts and a book of rules.
A wire-stretcher and a pair of shears
Are all I've carried for fifteen years . . .

It was a nostalgic day when the last Model T was sold and the revolutionized Model A's appeared. They were nicer in styling and appointments, but it was the end of a great era in automotive history, so sentimentality was unavoidable. We'd driven between Michigan and the Pacific Coast in both directions in Model T's and tire or engine trouble was negligible.

There are still Model A Fords in perfect condition. One coupe takes its owner, Arthur Grube, to work every day. Mr. Grube is a member of the Model A Ford Club of America, San Fernando Valley chapter, in California.

The streamlined age had begun by 1940, as a Ford of that year clearly demonstrates.

Model-A Ford coupe . . . still in good working condition.
(Courtesy Arthur Grube)

By 1940 the Ford had grown into a modestly stream-lined, smooth-skinned car. The gear shift was on the steering column and the car boasted of two windshield wipers, two sun visors and two air horns, all included in the price! It boasted of a V-8 engine.

A company that diligently romanced some of Mr. Ford's customers was Chevrolet. It advertised its tidy little squarish coupe in 1925, with one of the earliest suggestions of a second car for the family. It was fortunate for a long time if a family had one.

The Chevrolet touring cars of the early thirties sported a feature that was not repeated for many years —the absence of side brace obstruction such as comes with the hardtop of today.

The Chevrolet tried to woo away some of Henry Ford's customers. This is a 1925 coupe. (Courtesy Chevrolet Motor Division, General Motors Corp.)

A Chevrolet sport roadster. Note low, low price. (Courtesy Chevrolet Division, General Motors Corp.)

A Chevrolet touring car, c. 1932. Note the absence of
side brace construction. (Courtesy Janco Fotos)

Economy was always Chevrolet's key word. For example the sport roadster of the twenties sold for a mere $555. Can you imagine going into a dealer today and driving out with a new car for *that* price? It would only be a down payment!

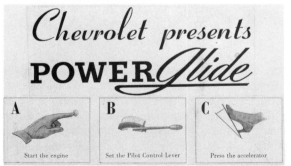

Chevrolet stressed feminine appeal when it introduced Power Glide automatic transmission in 1950. (Courtesy Chevrolet Division, General Motors Corp.)

Chevrolet introduced the automatic shift, Power Glide, in 1950. "Driving is as simple as ABC! . . . and that's all there is to it! No clutch, no gearshift, only three driving operations." (This sold me.)

Like an earthquake, the car industry had rumblings under its ground. It was reasonable to expect that with so many manufacturers, not all could succeed. Some failed from plunging beyond finances, or entered their products in overcrowded fields. Others had cars with inferior engineering. There were good, usable cars that the public wasn't attracted to in sufficient numbers. "You can lead a horse to water but you can't make him drink." Likewise, a prospect at a dealer's can't always be led to buy. One year's output could ruin a company if the mechanical flaws cropped up too regularly. It's true that a "lemon" can come in any make, but if they're all lemons—BEWARE.

There were cars too advanced for their time and the public wasn't ready to accept them. The Scarab looks like a forerunner to the Volkswagen Bus, but who was ready for it in 1935?

The Graham Paige was impressive in its early stages of streamlining. It appeared to be in motion when standing still due to the front end design.

We are so accustomed to automatic transmissions, it's hard to remember when we had the first one. Was it near 1950, give or take a year? It needn't have been, although few may remember that Reo came out with the "Biggest engineering advance of 1934, made by Reo

This 1935 car, which might have been a forerunner of the Volkswagen bus, was called, appropriately enough, the Scarab. The public didn't take to it kindly. (Courtesy E. L. Johnston)

It was commonplace in my childhood to see 1923 Hudsons—the Phaeton and the Speedster. Young people today mostly see the large, open cars carrying gangsters with machine guns in television shows.

In 1937 the Hudson Motorcar Company made the Terraplane to compete in the "low price field." Hudson probably had its biggest boost with the "step-down" model after the second World War. It was low to the ground, compared to others, and hugged the road well at high speeds.

Studebaker, the pioneer, was the first to produce a new car after the automobile starvation during World War II. Its 1947 name tag was appended by, "Studebaker, first by far with a postwar car." Besides being snapped up by eager customers, this model revolutionized our prewar concept of design. Perhaps the timing was more than perfect, because it might not have succeeded if it appeared in normal times. One comedian quipped about this Studebaker, "You couldn't tell at a distance which direction it was going." It had an unheard-of expanse of glass wrapped around the back.

Streamlining was a Graham-Paige feature.

in 1933." It was called the "Self-Shifter, leverless automatic." In their booklet about this "brilliant achievement" they explain the workings and advantages over old, conventional manual shifts. They say, "The Reo Self-Shifter has not only come to stay, but it leads the way toward greater safety, convenience and real pleasure in driving." What happened to it?

Some companies added quite different models to their regular line to rekindle a waning market. Sometimes it worked for awhile. In the twenties and early thirties the Hudson and Essex were familiar sights on the road. The sharply squared 1922 Essex Coach sold extremely well. "Until Essex brought out the coach there was no closed car at a moderate price on a first-rate chassis," Hudson told its dealers.

Soon there were new postwar running mates—Kaiser and Frazer. Henry J. Kaiser was a super industrialist, road builder, cement specialist and famous for his "Liberty Ships" during the war. Ford built the immensely sprawling Willow Run plant to make wartime bombers. After that need was over, the Kaiser-Frazer Corporation made the new cars there. The "bustle-back" body became popular and everyone followed suit. Many companies left an optional choice for the customer: the bustle-back or teardrop design. The latter looked longer—a bigger car. Competition was stiff, once all of the giants snapped into postwar production.

Later the Henry J. was born to add a smaller, cheaper car to the Kaiser-Frazer line. Although this automotive enterprise became a memory, they were good cars as

The 1933 Reo boasted an automatic transmission. (Courtesy Diamond Reo Truck Division)

The 1922 Essex Coach featured elegance. (Courtesy American Motors Corp.)

In 1923, Hudson featured the Phaeton (left) and the
Speedster. (Courtesy American Motors Corp.)

*It
Almost Drives
Itself*

It's so easy to have a
TERRAPLANE
Sent out on Approval

Ease of handling was the theme this ad for the 1937
Hudson Terraplane tried to get across. (Courtesy American Motors Corporation)

Jokesters accused the 1947 Studebaker of not being certain in which direction it wanted to go. Customers snapped them up, though. (Courtesy Studebaker Corp.)

The Kaiser was another postwar development, shown here in a Western setting. (Courtesy Kaiser-Frazer Owner's Club)

The Frazer was Henry Kaiser's attempt to get into the luxury market. Note the heraldic emblem. (Courtesy Kaiser-Frazer Owner's Club)

attested to by loyal owners who have a national club today. In fact, a Henry J. parks in the carport next to mine!

The rumble seat brings back thirties memories. (Courtesy Chevrolet Division, General Motors Corp.)

This 1924 advertisement details the features of the Chrysler Six. (Courtesy Chrysler Corp.)

No account of the thirties' automobiles could be countenanced without mention of the rumble seat as you of that generation will remember. It was dear to the hearts of young people, but grandmother would have had a struggle to maneuver in and out of one considering the feat of stepping from the little toe-tread atop the back fender.

Walter P. Chrysler was another motor car old-timer, even though he was considered a latecomer by other manufacturers. The company innovated spring suspension and balloon tires. Chrysler, of course, has survived, becoming one of the "Big Three."

Nothing could have been more sporty than the 1930 Chrysler Pursuit convertible with the front and back windshields. The wind could still tangle a girl's hair if she rode bareheaded.

To prove the difficulty of selling the public something too different, there's the case of the Chrysler Airflow model. Its engineering improvement, economy on gas and smooth ride could not offset the reaction, "We just don't like the looks of it!"

After the venture into advanced styling, the entire Chrysler line espoused an extremely conservative look.

The 1936 Airflow showed a modification of the waterfall grille. The company promised that "Yesterday's tiresome journey is just a refreshing jaunt."

When DeSoto entered the Chrysler family in 1928, it adhered to the roadster style of the day but was smaller, less costly than the "big brother." The corporation

The 1930 Chrysler Pursuit featured front and back windshields.

After the Airflow failure, the Chrysler line took on a more conservative look. (Courtesy Chrysler Corp.)

The Chrysler Airflow of the thirties had many advanced features, but the public didn't care for its looks. (Courtesy Chrysler Corp.)

The 1936 Airflow showed a modification of the waterfall grille. (Courtesy Chrysler Corp.)

started the present-day usage of several trade names under the parent head, such as General Motors.

The 1934 DeSoto looked like an identical twin to the Chrysler Airflow. One feature that supposedly lessened wind resistance was a cover over the rear wheels—detachable for tire changing.

By 1940 DeSoto was not only more powerful and larger—way up to 100 horsepower—but it gave you a "floating ride," cradled *between* the axles. It advertised warning signals to let you know when gas, oil or water was low, and greater visibility through a one-piece rear window. The greatest delight was a headline we see seldom anymore . . . "Lower-priced."

The 1934 DeSoto sported Airflow styling. Note the detachable rear wheel cover. (Courtesy Chrysler Corp.)

The original DeSoto, in 1928, featured roadster styling.
(Courtesy Chrysler Corp.)

The 1940 DeSoto had grown larger and more powerful. (Courtesy Chrysler Corp.)

Chrysler was the only "Big Three" Company that did not have a car competitive to the Chevrolet and Ford. That was a good reason for the advent of Plymouth and it gave the rivals a good run for their sales. They were used extensively in Detroit for taxicabs.

The Plymouth was Chrysler's answer to the Chevy and the Ford. (Courtesy Chrysler Corp.)

Dodge could say it's been around long enough to know the country. The Dodge has always been distinguished by "Dependability," and originally individual with a different gear-shifting pattern than the standard. All things change and also the Dodge Bros. product. When aviation became increasingly popular, planes and pilots were often used for backgrounds.

Chrysler bought the Dodge Bros. Company in 1927 and has let it continue with its own name ever since. During the mid-thirties its style varied little from the other Chrysler cars.

Two names confusable by their similarity were Hupmobile and Oldsmobile. In 1930 these two-passenger-with-rumble-seat cars were contenders in Hupmobile's stable. They had only six cylinders but an imposingly long hood and long price for that year, $1075. Custom equipment was available at extra cost.

An airport was the setting for this Dodge advertisement of the twenties. (Courtesy Dodge Division, Chrysler Corp.)

The 1930 Hupmobile was stylish . . . and expensive.

The 1934 Hupmobile sported a three-piece windshield. (Courtesy Detroit *News*)

The Pierce Arrow was noted for the headlamps that rose out of the fenders. The chic sportswomen were indicative of its social status.

Three views of the classic 1933 Silver Arrow. Pierce Arrow built just five of them. (Courtesy *Automotive Industries Magazine*, a Chilton publication.)

Hupp produced a very sleek design in 1934, with divided front bumper, vertically oval headlights and divisions in the windshield. One day we looked and Hupmobile was gone.

Names that breathed class, prestige and status have sadly passed. One of the first that comes to mind among defunct cars is Pierce-Arrow. In 1933 Pierce-Arrow produced an eye-popper, the ultra-streamlined Silver Arrow. It had 12 cylinders, 175 horsepower and it could go the phenomenal speed of 115 m.p.h. It was priced at $10,-000, f.o.b. Buffalo. To magnify how exclusive this Arrow

was—only five were to be built that year.

Even though classic with the look of European cars, it was not generous with the rear windows or tail lights. The running board disappeared, too.

Whenever a man of taste and means went shopping for an automobile befitting his station, he might choose a Packard instead of a Cadillac or Lincoln. If you're of my generation, you thrilled to have the neighbors see your beau pull up at your house in a Packard Roadster.

In 1934 Packard made a 12 cylinder custom sport coupe that bore some resemblance to the rear design

A classic Packard Roadster of the thirties. (Courtesy Studebaker Corp.)

46

This 1934 Packard 12-cylinder custom sport coupe resembled the Silver Arrow of the year before. (Courtesy Detroit *News*)

My favorite Packard was a ritzy, rakish convertible phaeton. An advertising man I knew declared that by a certain year he'd have his first Packard—his yardstick of success. He got it on schedule and it was this model.

The radiator piece above the grille was Packard's identifying mark. You can see it sitting proudly atop this four-door convertible. (Courtesy Studebaker Corp.)

and streamline concept of the Silver Arrow of the previous year.

The *Detroit News* Automotive section in 1934 said that "The automobile industry has taken leadership in the recovery movement by the development of 1934 cars so unmistakeably better in comfort and utility that they create a practically new automobile market. It has blazed the way to better times by a fearless but well-calculated capital expenditure for comprehensive motoring improvement, and by greatly intensified sales and advertising efforts." Hopeful words for the dire depression years, uttered by C. W. Nash of the Nash Motors Company.

This same note of confidence in the future was exercised in 1938 when the Packard Company came out with forty-one models. It offered the Packard Eight, Supereight and Packard Twelve in six chassis models on five wheelbases. It was a try to have something for everyone.

Packard kept an identifying mark, regardless of the year, in the design of its radiator top piece above the grille.

There can be several reasons for the demise of a proud car and it's not our concern to explore these. But Packard gradually slumped. One year the styling was atrocious; it also needed a broader market. The last recouping device was the Packard Clipper, smaller and catering to the middle-price field. For a year it was like a shot of adrenaline when a backlog of orders piled up from people who appreciated a quality name. But like most stimulants, it wore off and by 1956 Studebaker had bought the Packard Company. The magic was gone and we no longer "Asked the man who owned one."

In the *General Motors Magazine* for January, 1933,

A 1938 Packard Phaeton convertible meant status. (Courtesy Studebaker Corp.)

the company announced, "the most outstanding values its motor car divisions have ever produced." One of these values was . . . "a most important advancement in comfort and safety—the new Fisher No-Draft Ventilation system, individually controlled." We've had our "wind wings" so long, young people have perhaps never seen cars without them.

The class standard which has survived and prospered is Cadillac. Other large, fine automobiles were and are made, with or without custom bodies—but there's something about a "Caddie."

first Coupe de Ville appeared. Advertised were the "low-swept lines of a convertible with the comfort and convenience of a closed car."

Fitting between Cadillac and Buick was the LaSalle, a division of Cadillac. Perhaps the comparison could be "as the Bentley is to the Rolls-Royce." In the 1934 model, the windshield fit narrowly between the top and high hood.

The 1940 model was one of the last LaSalles, mainly recognizable by its sharply curved horizontal grille. So many things were new then that we now take for

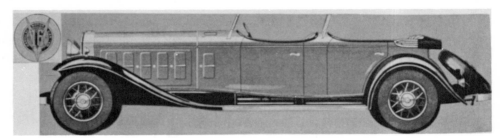

The classic 16-cylinder Cadillac was a thirties favorite. (Courtesy Cadillac Division, General Motors Corp.)

Cadillac advertised its 16-cylinder model with the headline that simply read, "Sixteen Cylinders." Can you imagine opening the long hood to gaze at 16 cylinders? The copy said, "It is impossible to arrive at an adequate conception of the Cadillac V-16 until you have experienced a demonstration—for there is no mode of transportation, whether on land or sea or in the air, more completely luxurious than travel in this distinguished car. Priced from $5,350 to $15,000 f.o.b. Detroit." It should have been luxurious because that was before prices were inflated.

The 1934 LaSalle. Note the sporty windshield crammed between the top and the high hood. (Courtesy Detroit News)

granted; Security-Plate glass, more effortless steering, adjustable front seat, chromium plate—"the new treatment that preserves indefinitely the original sheen." LaSalle announced prices of $2295 to $2875.

The Cadillac custom limousine of the thirties. (Courtesy Cadillac Division, General Motors Corp.)

In the thirties, Cadillac built a custom limousine for the elite of Cadillacdom before the fishtail fin developed on rear fenders. It's a rarity now to see a chauffeur-driven car, but could you envision the lady-of-the-house sliding under the wheel of a car like this to do the marketing?

The late forties' Cadillac built after postwar production could resume, and the new trend in styling had begun. The rear fender style was distinctly new and the

This sporty 1940 LaSalle was one of the last to be manufactured. (Courtesy Cadillac Division, General Motors Corp.)

The fishtail arrived in the late forties on the Cadillac Coupe de Ville. (Courtesy Cadillac Division, General Motors Corp.)

Do you recall the Buick Marquette of the late twenties? The tires appeared to be what hot-rodders call "slicks." There's very little that particularly stands this car out from other roadsters of that era.

The thirties' Buick marched in the parade toward streamlining. There's an amusing aspect to living in Detroit when new car models are in the designing stages. Top-drawer secrecy surrounds every company's upcom-

The Buick Marquette of the late twenties. Note the fur-coated man and the short-haired girl. (Courtesy Buick Division, General Motors Corp.)

The Buick of the thirties featured streamlining. (Courtesy Buick Division, General Motors Corp.)

Oldsmobile featured the rocket engine in 1950. (Courtesy Oldsmobile Division, General Motors Corp.)

ing designs. There are no-trespass signs in ad studios and agencies where photos of the cars must be seen for the preparation of advertising. When the unveiling day arrives, the cars are so similar, it's as if the designers had looked over each other's shoulders.

The buck-toothed, portholed Buick Roadster of 1950. (Courtesy Buick Division, General Motors Corp.)

Whirlaway Hydromatic Drive was another new 1950 feature. Again, note the appeal to the ladies. Arrows indicate shift selector lever and absence of clutch. (Courtesy Oldsmobile Division, General Motors Corp.)

The 1950 Buick Roadmaster is still seen rolling along our roads. In the late forties Buicks appeared with "hood holes." They were first round, four for the Roadmaster and three for smaller models, then changed shape somewhat yearly. Comedians can always squeeze a joke out of something different on cars, so the Buick didn't escape. But the biggest laugh "all-the-way-to-the-bank," was for the fellow who made artificial holes to bolt onto any car. He must have sold thousands of them. The most ridiculous example I saw on Detroit streets was a spanking new Lincoln with eight artificial holes bolted onto the shiny, new fenders.

Each year manufacturers stressed more length, rangier cars, higher horsepower and longer wheelbases. As parking space diminished yearly, it took more room to park each car! Is it any wonder that the public was ripe for compacts?

The 1950 Oldsmobile may bring back a memory to you. It was the year the new Whirlaway Hydra-Matic drive was introduced. The combination of automatic transmission and rocket engine was termed, "Oldsmobile's new power package."

"No gears to shift! Just sit and relax. Both hands are always free for steering—for signaling—for safety!" Oldsmobile said this in 1950, but Reo had used the same sales talk in 1934.

Once upon a time until the early thirties there was a car called Oakland, which came from Pontiac, Michigan. It was a fine automobile, bought by many people throughout the land . . . until one year it grew lemons on its fine vehicle tree. There was a tumult from the customers, and bad public opinion cut down the vehicle tree. That's the story of why there's no more Oakland.

The Pontiac was born in 1926 and eased into Oakland's spot. It fitted into the General Motors family between Chevrolet and Oldsmobile. The Pontiac might have been termed a "Depression Baby," for it was whelped shortly before the market crash. The new series, Pontiac Big Six, was pushed by large, colorful magazine ads. The tidy price of $745 was displayed prominently in each advertisement. The 2-seater coupe was popular for many years.

The now-defunct Oakland. (Pontiac Car Division, General Motors Corp.)

$745

A Pontiac six of the late twenties. (Courtesy Pontiac Division, General Motors Corp.)

Pontiac first offered GM's Hydra-Matic transmission in 1948. A booklet dealt solely with the smooth advantages of the easy-to-handle Pontiac with the automatic shift which cut the 15 motions of starting a car from parked into high gear down to three simple motions.

The series of "Silver Streak" Pontiacs ran through 1955; then the styling changed. Although I cannot speak for the familiar 1950 model nationwide, it sold well in its own back yard.

Ford had to compete with Cadillac, Imperial and Packard to hit the upper-bracket market and plump up the range of choice. Lincoln and Mercury served this pur-

1 START MOTOR
2 SET DIRECTION CONTROL (FORWARD OR REVERSE)
3 STEP ON ACCELERATOR!

A brochure described the merits of Pontiac's Hydramatic transmission in 1948. (Courtesy Pontiac Division, General Motors Corp.)

The familiar "Silver Streak" series of Pontiacs. This is the 1950 model. (Courtesy Pontiac Division, General Motors Corp.)

wealthy who had chauffeurs to sit in the uncovered portion of this custom limousine.

A later model trimmed the slowly dying running board, streamlined the fenders with generous aprons and incorporated the lights into the fenders.

Lincoln distinguished itself by designing one of the all-time great classic cars—the old Continental. When it ceased to be, it was a collector's item.

Meantime, Lincoln was enduring the same stresses many car makers faced because of the Depression and

The austere, dignified Lincoln limousine of the twenties. Note the uncovered chauffeur's seat. (Courtesy Lincoln-Mercury Division, Ford Motor Co.)

pose. In the twenties, Lincoln was a steamship-long car, with the fold-up additional seats in the seven-passenger vehicle. It was an austere and dignified car for the

War. Money had to come from a broadened, diversified market. This modest Lincoln bears little resemblance to the limousine. Packard made the Clipper, and Lincoln

The Lincoln of the thirties was somewhat streamlined. Note the incorporation of the headlights into the fenders. (Courtesy Lincoln-Mercury Division, Ford Motor Co.)

The Zephyr was a lower-priced Lincoln which never really caught on with the public.

The back seat of a limousine was good for lounging.

came out with the Zephyr, but it was not extremely popular.

There was automotive news in 1956 when Lincoln gave rebirth to the Continental which is still richly and classically designed, without a maze of brightwork to clutter the lines.

Let's look inside some of the cars you may have never entered, or have forgotten. In the twenties the ladies lounged in the back seat by peep-hole windows, compared to present glass expanses. Sedans weren't fitted with shatterproof glass until later, and some people regarded them as death traps. The interior fittings were deluxe. For years many car windows were equipped with shades, some fringed and having fancy ornaments dangling on the pull-cord ends. Real swank included a bracket to hold a bud vase!

The "white tie and tails" crowd entering the spacious back compartment of a glassed-off, chauffeur-driven limousine, equipped with extra pull-out seats. There were lights in the back corners and a hand strap that slid along a bar, plus a vertical handle to grasp by the door. This was posh in 1941.

A posh crowd entering a posh limousine, around 1940.
(Courtesy *Harper's Bazaar*)

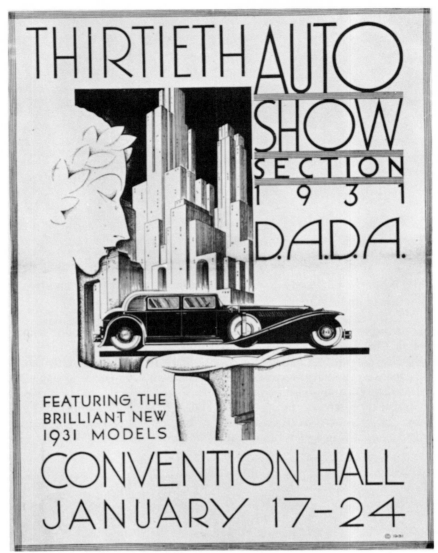

The artist had a field day drawing this design for the show announcement in the Detroit News. The hood on his dream car could have covered 32 cyclinders.

Automobile shows were not exactly big business before 1901. In Detroit, the car-show breeding ground, the display of 1931 models was called the 30th Auto Show. A news article called it a "Monster Exhibition." It further said, "Justification of the faith of this city and the state of Michigan in the ability of the automobile industry once more to set the pace for the country will be demonstrated when the Detroit Auto Dealer's Association opens its thirtieth annual automobile show in Convention Hall."

In 1931 many names appeared in the Auto Show that would merit blank stares from youngsters today—unless they are antique car buffs. Some represented were: Auburn, Austin, Buick, Cadillac, Chevrolet, Cord, Chrysler, DeSoto, Dodge, Dusenberg, Durant, Essex, Ford, Graham, Hudson, Hupmobile, LaSalle, Lincoln, Marmon, Mathis, Nash, Oakland, Oldsmobile, Packard,

Pierce-Arrow, Plymouth, Pontiac, Reo, Studebaker, Willys, Willys-Knight, Federal, Gotfredson, and Paige. Consider the competition of this size! When the 1934 Detroit Auto Show was announced, there were already nine less names so the mortality rate was high!

The evolution in passenger automobiles was followed in kind by trucks and other commercial vehicles. In 1929, many trucks were propelled by Exide Batteries. The driver and cargo didn't have the softening of air to cushion the bumps—his tires were solid rubber.

Fire may not have changed with time, but the equipment for fighting it has. Old-time hook and ladder trucks could squelch the blaze after they had sped to the scene —we hoped.

But if the heavy duty trucks had enough muscle for the hard jobs, the lighter ones could nevertheless look sleek.

In 1929, Exide battery-powered trucks ran on hard rubber tires. (Courtesy ESB, Inc.)

Fires haven't changed much, but this drawing proves that firetrucks certainly have! (Courtesy Pontiac *Daily Press*)

This Reo custom paneled truck had limousine-like elegance. (Courtesy Diamond Reo Truck Division)

As long ago as the twenties, Greyhound Busses carried passengers across the country. (Courtesy General Motors Truck and Coach Division)

Greyhound can prove that "leave the driving to us" has been a suitable slogan for more years than we've heard it. Their busses were a familiar sight across the nation's roads long before we had Interstate superhighways.

Do you remember the corner gasoline station that serviced your car in 1929? Texaco was there to do it although the mechanisms looked different—especially the gas pumps. Much change came to pump styles. It was considered a vast improvement when a glass cylinder was atop the pump. The amount of gas you ordered was forced into the glass container with gallon marks down the side. My father would only patronize stations that used this because he liked to *see* what he bought. The

Gas pump styles have changed through the years, as this painting made for Texaco by Saul Tepper clearly shows.

fuel was manually pumped, so the attendant had had a lot of exercise by the end of his day.

Have you considered the number of accessories we take for granted as standard that weren't always? It was some considerable time after the invention of the self-starter before it wasn't an optional feature. Many a man was kicked by a crank—or worse—had an arm broken. What about windshield wipers? Usually only one was added on and manually operated by a harassed driver. While fighting through a storm he had the additional problem of grabbing the little knob on the wiper to swish snow or rain away. If you wanted to signal the driver behind you about an intended stop, you could install a brake light, again, just one. There were few items pulling electricity from the battery in 1920.

We were thrilled with the first car radio. True, it was in the car; but the vehicle had to be parked with a ground wire attached to a guy wire on a utility pole or such.

A curious device was invented to discourage car thievery because car insurance wasn't common in the twenties. It was a heavy metal gadget resembling a single handcuff with a pointed fang-like prong sticking out on the side. This bracelet was locked around one of the wheels for the night, assuming that no one would try to limp down the street, rotating the point—it would have looked mighty suspicious. But what if the owner lost the key?

Driving in storms has never been fun, but Weed Tire Chains were there to help as long ago as the twenties.

Storms posed another early day problem besides windshield cleaning. Usually the rain had started to fall when the side curtains were hauled out. Then a mad dash to find the proper ones for the openings—next to pull slots over turn-buttons on the car. Some of the dingy celluloid windows were broken out or cracked and no matter how you strained, one piece didn't fit the hole it was designed for. Recall this the next time you curse a shower!

While most of us eagerly look at each new year's automobiles, not all people share this enthusiasm. These are the collectors of antique cars—an expensive hobby. Three famous collectors of our time have been James Melton, the singer; Jack Benny, of Maxwell fame; and Peter Helck, the foremost industrial illustrator who has a passion for old racing cars. Henry Ford's Greenfield Village in Dearborn, Michigan, has a fine collection that includes an exhibit of the history of transportation back to antiquity.

The difficulty and cost of collecting comes first for the search for cars, the initial price, then reconditioning and obsolete parts replacement. These may have to be handmade. If you should see the Glidden Tour with bright, shipshape old cars and appropriately costumed passengers whizzing along the highway, you'll see a magnificent array of automotive history.

Weed Tire Chains made winter driving safer as long ago as the twenties. Note that this driver has placed them on all four wheels. (Courtesy American Chain and Cable Co.)

Antique Car collectors do not share the majority's enthusiasm for the annual model change. (Courtesy CBS Radio)

Here is a glimpse of an early thirties General Motors plant in Pontiac, Michigan. (Courtesy General Motors Corp.)

Where were all of these gas machines made? Of course Detroit gained its name, "The Motor City," from the number of cars made there, although plants have been widely scattered.

The automobile has changed the complexion of living and the face of the world probably more than any other single factor. There are predictions of what may lie ahead in motordom, but as long as people are people, the best safety devices and fruits of engineering genius will not keep automobiles from being a blessing and curse—all in the same breath!

5

All Aboard!

"The time will come when people will travel in stages moved by steam engines, from one city to another, almost as fast as birds can fly—fifteen or twenty miles an hour." This was Oliver Evans's dream in 1813.

After his sage prediction, Mr. Evans couldn't have envisioned how large this "steam-engine-with-stage" could grow as a business influencing our way of life.

The historic moment of railroading was in 1869 when the Union Pacific and the Central Pacific, from the Missouri River to San Francisco, met at Salt Lake City, with ceremonies due the first transcontinental line connection. The greatest era of building track miles on railroad lines was the decade between 1880 and 1890 when easily 70,-000 miles of rails were laid. This type of growth has not

The steam engine of the nineteenth century evokes a more romantic era. (Photo by William Gordon)

occurred since, inasmuch as the logical routes drawing the country together were already made. Beyond this, change has been in multiplicity of tracks on a given line, improvement in equipment and service.

One adventuresome and fearful fact of train travel until the West was considerably tamed was the train robbery. It has made much material for writers of western television drama and movies—if not sheer joy for those who experienced the real thing.

In 1926 an advertisement for the Union Pacific Railway announced excitedly that on November 14th of that year, via the Overland Route, there would be two sixty-three hour "flyers" which would save a day's travel to California. By leaving Chicago at 8:00 o'clock in the evening, you'd be in Los Angeles the third day at 9:00 o'clock in the morning. This was fast traveling in view of the time consumed if you were adventuresome and leisurely enough to drive a 1926 car to the West Coast. The feat took us two weeks and a day in a Model T Ford, and my father boasted about it. "Not one puncture or blowout in all that distance!"

Can you remember any sound that evoked more wistfulness and haunting loneliness than the wail of a steam locomotive whistle at night? It usually brought some reaction if nothing more than . . . "There goes a train."

Children were always fascinated by trains, especially if they came within easy viewing distance. It was perhaps the old lure of travel to faraway places maybe better than where you were.

It was standard procedure when motoring on a road parallel to tracks to race the train and wave to the engineer. He was a friendly fellow who always waved back. In the vastnesses of the 1920's West, he might be the only human being seen for hours.

The Northern Pacific races through the Rockies.

Cinders in the eye were a problem in passenger trains pulled by steam locomotives like this one.

Waving to the engineer became an American tradition
in the twenties. (Courtesy Kelly-Springfield Tire Co.)

What were the old wooden coaches like? They had small windows that traditionally stuck, but an opening wasn't advisable if the cinders and smoke wafted back to you. In summer there was *no* air-conditioning. The seats were usually a plush or velour and on particularly old coaches the dust found a home in the upholstery.

A hand print could be left if you slapped your hand against the seat-back once. I can still remember the stuffy, dusty smell of coaches when first entered. A pull rod on the back could reverse the seat's direction if four wished to face each other. A table could be hooked to the wall for eating, writing or games to pass the time.

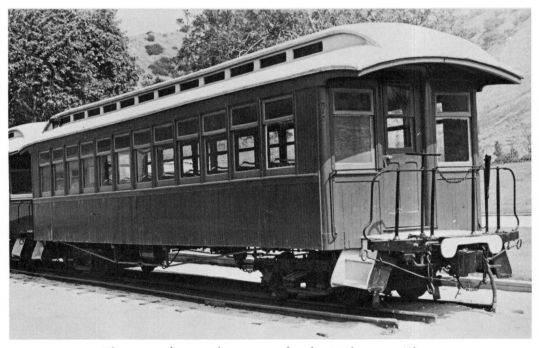

These wooden coaches were a familiar sight once. (Photo
by William Gordon)

Wooden baggage cars rode behind the tender. (Photo by William Gordon)

The old wooden baggage car rode behind the tender where fuel and water were kept for the locomotive. Do you recall the "baggage-smashers" who tended cargo from the platform?

On some smaller trains, a combination baggage and passenger car was used.

If you were lucky enough to be taking an overnight trip, then there'd be the thrill of sleeping in a Pullman berth—that is, if you didn't wish to save the money by sitting in the cheaper "chair car." George Pullman was a successful inventor and capitalist, whose first sleeping car was with the train that carried Abraham Lincoln's body for burial. Mr. Pullman had such immediate demand for his cars that he could scarcely fill the orders.

A combination baggage and passenger car. (Photo by William Gordon)

Pullman berths were fun—if you didn't have to take the upper berth.

The Perris, California, station is pleasing to the eye, and is much favored by artists. (Photo by Roy Brent)

Getting off the train and right into Grandma's arms for a Christmas visit was always a high point of the year. (Courtesy Pennsylvania Railroad Co.)

He not only headed his Pullman Palace Car Company, but was president of the New York elevated railroads. The only problem with the Pullmans was for the person elected to the upper berth if he had rheumatism or was affected by claustrophobia and sleepwalking.

Eating was a necessity on a long trip, so the dining car came into existence. On my first long journey by train, the porter's singsong fascinated me, "Last call for dinner in the diner at the rear." But I didn't get to see the magic realm at the rear because my thrifty parents brought a box lunch for the whole trip. It grew less than appetizing toward the end.

A few quaint relic stations still remain if you look for them, usually tucked by the tracks in smaller towns. The station in Perris, California is a favorite subject for artists.

If your trip took you for a holiday, it was an ecstatic moment of bursting forth to greet grandparents or other relatives seldom seen. It was great for children, while parents struggled with armloads of presents. If there was clean, fluffy snow in the country or small town, you were a part of the kind of Christmas we nostalgically recall.

In time the wooden coaches were replaced by metal ones. Do you remember slapping from wall-to-wall while trying to traverse coach corridors? I can still hear the syncopated music as the wheels ground over rail-joints and passed the ding-dinging signals.

Special coaches, quite removed from the conventional type with rows of uniform seats on either side of an aisle, were built. In them, train travel was stylish and comfortable.

Narrow coach corridors were great for losing your balance. (Photo by William Gordon)

These metal coaches were a great advance over the old wooden ones. (Photo by William Gordon)

A favorite stand for politicians was the rear platform on a train where he could "stump the country" with short speeches at the nation's grass roots. The train would hesitate a few minutes for man-to-man talk in numberless small communities where the tracks led. Many a president used this campaign tool.

My stepfather was a trainman for many years. One of his common expressions was, "They passed him like the Century passed a bum." The train he was referring to was the 20th Century Limited, a "crack" train that made it from New York to Chicago in eighteen hours. Two other well-known, fast and popular train names, especially favored by Hollywood celebrities, are Santa Fe's "Chief" and "Super Chief."

As fondly as steam locomotives are remembered, there's no escaping that they did intermittently let out belches of thick, black smoke which rolled with the wind over a wide area as they started or pulled a long grade,

Special coaches like this one made train travel comfortable and stylish. Note the deluxe lights, wallpaper, pictures, and period furniture. The upholstery is pale rose velvet and the carpeting wall-to-wall. (Photo by William Gordon)

The "20th Century Limited" is ready to pull out. (Courtesy Penn Central Railroad)

A favorite stand for politicians was a rear platform on a train. (Photo by William Gordon)

heavily loaded. In this day of smog, additional smoke isn't needed.

The evolution of engines has been violent in the last forty years. With the steam-driven vehicles, the boiler grew larger and longer as the height of the chimney shrunk until it barely protruded. Streamlining came almost as drastically to them as with Diesel engines.

Along with the modern revolution came ultra-streamlined engines and coaches. In 1934 the aluminum trains were introduced and could attain a speed of 120 miles per hour. However, for reasons of safety, speeds of trains have not increased—except for the new high-speed experiments.

Familiar Sante Fe trademarks. (Permission for use of coyrighted trade mark courtesy the Atchison, Topeka & Santa Fe Railway Co.)

Thick belches of black smoke are fortunately a thing of the past.

The brakeman manually uncoupled connections between cars. Youngsters used to be badly or fatally injured when, as a daring prank, they'd attempt to jump across between cars. It was characteristic of a heavy train to jerk and lurch suddenly, throwing or crushing the daredevil children.

The "Twin Cities Zephyr" sported vista-domed passenger cars. (Courtesy Chicago, Burlington & Quincy Railroad Co.)

There were numerous jobs for the brakeman while en route. He checked wheels, brakes and load while skillfully walking atop the speeding train. He hopped off to change signals, grabbed onto the moving caboose and waved directives to the engineer.

Some of the regular patrons of railways were a populous group of non-paying passengers known as hoboes—professional tramps or, in the Depression years, the jobless who milled around the country for want of anything else to do. Railroad "dicks" or detectives were their enemies as they policed trains. Word got around about the towns to stay clear of. The free riders would sit like

Cars were coupled manually by the brakeman. (Photo by William Gordon)

Brakemen went about their errands on walks like this one. (Photo by William Gordon)

birds on a phone wire along the top walkway. If concealment was advisable, hoboes "rode the rods"—a dangerous way to go, to not mention the discomfort while wedged in the works under the car. There were those who had less desire of fresh air who found an empty boxcar and made it home. "Going on the bum" was common even with married couples who wanted to try their luck at finding work in a new location.

As much as we're accustomed to the quaint caboose, few have had a peek inside. You might say it's an office and home-away-from-home for the crew. Paper reports are made here, meals eaten—there are sleeping bunks and a pot-bellied stove. There's everything needed except room to spread out. Heating is likely modernized by now.

Masses of freight cars of all types—tankers, boxcars, refrigerator, coal and flat cars, make a jungle of freight yards, along with the turntable. A faceful of cinders was guaranteed with a trip through here. In movie chases this locale makes an effective honeycomb for cops and robbers to run through.

If you've ever watched a passing freight train while held up at a crossing, or counted the cars, as my daughter always did, you couldn't have missed the many painted emblems or trademarks on the cars' sides. Mr. Walker Evans shares my enthusiasm for collecting bits of Americana that's on the scene one day . . . gone the next, then largely forgotten. A few of these insignias may strike a familiar chord in your memory.

Hoboes would try to hop freights during the Depression . . . and detectives did their best to keep them off. (Janco Fotos)

Then as now, freight cars of all types made a jungle of the yards. The insert depicts yards in Detroit. (Photo by Chester Janczarek)

The airlines, busses and private motor cars have robbed the railways of many passengers during the last several decades. Planes are speedier, busses cheaper and your own car goes on your schedule where you want it to. The web of transcontinental trucks and air freight have taken profitable cargo; but trains carry on, because they can still haul loads that would stymie the biggest trailer-truck. Trains certainly cemented the far reaches of this country in the past century and they still have their own brand of service and effectiveness. They go in weather that a plane couldn't pass through or land in—hold more passengers comfortably with the option of adding coaches. If you aren't racing the clock, a pleasant trip can be had with each window framing a picture of America. It's seeing our country at ground level where lots of people prefer the solidity of steel tracks under them, and let the engineer do the driving. At least some of us have tasted the joys of trains before speed was all-important and travel was exciting.

The caboose is the freight train's office. (Janco Fotos)

Just a few of the many painted emblems you could see on the sides of the freight cars. (Courtesy *Fortune* magazine, from an article by Walker Evans, "Before They Disappear")

70

6

We Left Solid Ground

Most people have dreams occasionally in which their bodies can rise and fly about at will.

> The birds can fly,
> An' why can't I?

The question writer Trowbridge gave Darius Green and his Flying Machine in 1869 expressed a logical feeling about man's dream of flying. It laces through history —even to several mentions in the Bible. Nearly all writers who mentioned flying spoke of it as a silly, irrational idea with "some new-fangled contraption."

Like many dream concepts, that contraption came as early as the sixteenth century when balloons became a fad, especially in France. The first American ascent was as early as 1793.

At one time man thought that the only way to fly would be to have wings tied to his arms.

Author's rendition of America's first balloon ascent, 1793.

In order to fly, it was believed necessary for him to have wings tied to his arms since he only had birds to emulate. Interest in balloons died considerably after frequent accidents occurred in the nineteenth century, plus the limited maneuverability.

In spite of experimentation through the 1800's, no one was successful in actually getting man "off the ground" with a machine until that historic day, December 17, 1903, when the Wright brothers flew at Kittyhawk, North Carolina. Even though Wilbur and Orville Wright established flight as a reality, public interest was lax and aviation was a livelier subject in Europe in the early twentieth century. Finally America got underway in 1915, but the greatest impetus was World War I.

It is presumed that the first American airport was Simms Station, unless Kittyhawk could be called one in a stretch of imagination. The field at Simms Station was rough and small, so a catapult device was erected for launching planes. Even though crude, it was a forerunner to future assists in plane takeoffs.

The Wrights' former bicycle business suffered as increasing attention was diverted to building more aircraft. In 1909 the bicycles were forgotten and a plane company was formed; and more people were hired. Shortly thereafter, the first American flying school was set up at Montgomery, Alabama.

An early "aeroplane."

Europeans considered the airplane (or "aeroplane"), as a possible military item early in their experiments. The War distilled aero-progress into concentrated form, but thereafter advance lagged because of little interest or foresight into the peacetime commercial value of planes.

The word *ace* had great meaning in World War I, with such magic names as Captain Eddie Rickenbacker, who brought down twenty-six enemy planes instead of the five required for an ace rating. After the War, photographed dogfights between our doughty little biplanes and the Germans made exciting fare for moviegoers in many war pictures.

A notable squadron during the first World War was the 50th. This rough and ready group couldn't boast of a star-studded roster of aces who went into direct combat with the Germans. Instead, they had the less glamorous job of infantry contact patrol in De-Havilland-4 planes, commonly called "flying coffins." Despite the flyers' lack of opportunity at acehood, the 50th squadron had two winners of the Congressional Medal of Honor.

If the average "John Citizen" of America had better sense than to step inside a danged flying machine, the postwar era found records being established by spunky

Perhaps the Red Baron was leading this German squadron of the World War I Era. (Courtesy Twentieth-Century-Fox)

Henry Ford figured in aviation when he became enough interested to financially help William Stout develop an all-metal monoplane. Out of this venture came Ford's Tri-Motor planes that were used as late as 1938.

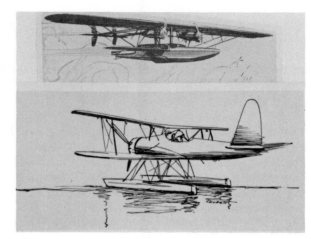

Seaplanes were coming of age at the end of World War I.

A DeHavilland 4 Plane.

pilots who were bringing public attention to what airplanes could do. The first world altitude record was set in 1920 when Major R. W. Schroeder got up to 33,113 feet. The following year Eddie Stinson stayed in the air longer than anyone had—with twenty-six hours of continuous flight. This record didn't stand long because two fellows, Kelly and Macready, bettered it by eleven hours. Then they flew non-stop across the continent in 1923.

The valiant little "Pride of Detroit" circled the globe.
(Courtesy Valvoline Oil Co.)

The most exciting air performance after the war was accomplished by Army pilots flying around the world. Two of the four starters succeeded. The "Pride of Detroit" ventured the long distance to girdle the earth.

As early as 1918, air transport of mail was established between New York and Washington by Army aid to the Post Office. Expansion and improvement of planes and service steadily progressed and in 1925 an Air Mail Act was passed to transfer such operations to private carriers. This did much to stimulate aviation all the way from experimentation for better mechanisms to public acceptance of air transport reliability, even though many people were mighty reluctant to let planes carry their mortal bodies.

We sometimes forget how early some aerial ideas were advanced to reality without fanfare. Seaplanes were coming of age. In 1918 at war's end, the Navy wanted to send its "flying boats" across the Atlantic and a record was set when one of these planes carried 61 men. Although Lindbergh got all of the world's adulation and fame, the Atlantic had already been crossed non-stop by one of the seaplanes. A month later in 1918, Alcock and Brown flew from Newfoundland to Ireland.

The helicopter is a name of more recent date after its forerunner, the autogyro, that Juan de la Cierva put together in 1920. This type might be in operation today if the superior helicopter hadn't been developed by Sikorsky. Man had long toyed with the possibility of a craft

Juan de la Cierva's autogyro was a forerunner of the helicopter.

that could rise vertically, then hover in the air without the necessity of forward flight.

The great potential of the "choppers" or "windmills" wasn't realized to the fullest until later. Igor Sikorsky didn't get into high gear with manufacture for military and commercial use until 1939.

The one touch of magic that aviation needed for a full-fledged aerial enthusiasm was provided in 1927 by a "Lone Eagle" in a tiny plane called "The Spirit of St. Louis." Charles A. Lindbergh took off from Roosevelt Field in foggy, uncertain weather at 7:25 o'clock in the morning of May 20. One brash headline called him the

"flying fool," but this could only have come from a person who thought that none but fools went up in planes. No nickname could have been more inaccurate, considering the long planning and detailed calculations before the flight. If many wondered about or prayed for Lindbergh's success and safety, they only waited about thirty-three and one half hours to know that he had landed. Paris opened her heart to this shy, earnest man. "Lindy" was the happy word on everyone's lips while a hero never had more acclaim. The only person of more recent times who even approached this type of adoration was John Glenn when he orbited the earth, but the worship was short-lived by comparison to that of "Lucky Lindy." If everyone went quite mad emotionally in Paris, a thunderous ticker tape parade in New York brought to Lindbergh the realization that he'd accomplished a monumental triumph. What he'd done with the tiny dot-

Charles A. Lindbergh.

Charles A. Lindbergh's marriage to Ann Morrow in 1929 created a stir. (Courtesy Detroit News)

in-the-sky fired imaginations, speeded the cause for aviation and gave the world's youth a star to tie to even though multiple groups had flown the Atlantic previously.

When Lindbergh married Ann Morrow in 1929, the romantic dreamings of America's girls were tossed aside, but she was certainly the perfect mate to share his interest in flying. Together they made other historic flights.

After the War the Orteig prize of $25,000 went begging from 1914 until Lindbergh's flight because no one had followed its stipulations by flying non-stop from New York to Paris. There were many unsuccessful attempts, but after Lindbergh made it, many more tried. No less than Commander Richard E. Byrd and Clarence Chamberlain succeeded—only to land in the Berlin area. Byrd tried again but he still didn't land in Paris. There was a rash of crossings tried by those who ended in disaster.

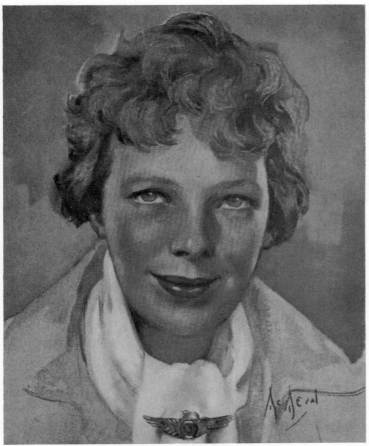

Amelia Earhart came to prominence in 1928. (Courtesy Joan B. Leech)

Amelia Earhart came into aviation prominence in 1928 as a follow-up to Lindbergh—female version. She first flew with two men from Newfoundland to Wales, establishing herself as the first woman to cross via air. By 1932 she soloed from Newfoundland to Ireland, becoming the first person to go across alone since "Lindy." There was ample reason for her acclaim as she soloed the first Pacific flight from Hawaii to California in 1935.

Her prowess at plane controls was rewarded by many decorations, including the Distinguished Flying Cross. She was the charming subject of Neysa McMein, the famous illustrator.

When it was starkly announced that Amelia Earhart was overdue on a leg of her 'round-the-world flight in 1937 near New Guinea, most Americans were sure that by a miracle she would turn up. We waited and anxiously listened for a hopeful word that never came. Some time later her husband, George Putnam, identified a scarf that was believed to have been hers. This awakened anew the steadfast belief that she was alive on a remote island and would appear when a passing ship rescued her. My mother never gave up the hope, even after she was officially declared dead in 1939.

General Italo Balbo ambitiously led a flotilla of planes from Italy to Chicago in 1933, without mishap. Atlantic flights were no longer novel or bringers of fame. The last colorful bit to this part of America's aviation history was Douglas Corrigan with his "wrong-way" crossing from New York to Dublin, Ireland. He afforded much amused admiration because of his bland explanation that he'd thought he was going the opposite direction in his ancient, single-engine monoplane. He was reprimanded for the unauthorized flight, but succeeded in the nine year old plane whereas many others failed after acquiring new and elaborately equipped planes. "Wrong-Way" Corrigan made one movie concerning the trip, during a brief flurry of publicity, but his was not an actor's personality, and he soon sank into obscurity.

A mid-air refueling, about 1930. (Courtesy Texaco Inc.)

So much was happening aerially that keeping all of the activities in chronological order was difficult. The craft was going farther, faster and more foolproofly, but one problem had to be solved for the long-distance, non-stop flights. The planes had to be dangerously overloaded with spare fuel or the best plane in the world would have to land when it ran empty. Refueling from one plane to another in mid-air was the answer.

Planes were proving what they could do in the frozen vastlands of Polar regions. The outstanding leader of Polar exploration was unquestionably Richard Byrd. More than eleven years elapsed between the idea and the action in 1925 when Lt. Commander Byrd was accompanied by Donald MacMillan in Navy amphibians to survey large sections. The following year Byrd flew with another famous pilot, Floyd Bennett, over the North Pole. By 1929 he sighted equally cold Anarctic scenes and the South Pole. Many more expeditions occurred to the top and bottom of the world, and Byrd formed Little America as an expedition settlement in Antarctica. After World War II it became common to fly over the North Pole on weather missions, but it took the Byrd "ice-breaking" and reports of his findings. The first man deservedly earns the fame.

Passengers boarding this Eastern Air Transport biplane in 1925 didn't take air transportation for granted the way we do now. (Courtesy Eastern Airlines, Inc.)

Radio telephones were a big improvement in air safety.

In the work of improving plane equipment for more safety, a big step forward was the introduction of radio telephones for plane-to-ground communications. Consider the previous problems of landing without this assist of instructions!

Flying across our own broad nation was first done in crippled stages as early as 1911 by Calbraith Rodgers. His crude plane was practically rebuilt in the process, but he was followed year after year by many who did the hop non-stop with speed records being the primary interest. Well-known names in air circles were engaged in this, such as Frank Hawks in a plane-towed glider in 1930. Roscoe Turner in 1933. Howard Hughes sliced the time to 9 hours and 27 minutes. Each junket pared the time and records were only made to be soon broken.

We marveled at the ease of dashing across our country from dawn to dusk. It was said that words written in New York today were read in California tomorrow. By airmail the pulse of business was speeded and the far-flung activities came to arm's length.

The passage of the Air Mail Act in 1925 speeded the carriage on regular transports of passengers along with the mail. The Eastern Air Transport biplanes did not

The "Graf Zeppelin" returns home after completing a globe-girdling flight in 21 days, 7 hours, 32 minutes— a new record. (Courtesy Newspaper Newsreel Syndicate)

closely resemble our huge, sleek jet liners of today, but those who were passengers probably thrilled much more than we do now.

A smart interior for air travel in the thirties was different. There was cozy proximity between the pilot, co-pilot and passengers. There was a narrow aisle and only one seat row on either side. Any serving was done by men as the stewardess hadn't yet made her bow.

Perhaps the names, Pangborn and Herndon will stir an aviation memory because they made the first non-stop Japan to United States trip in 1931. The B-29 Superfortresses even made news with a record-breaking flight from Tokyo to Washington. Two never to be forgotten names in air history are Post and Gatty. Around-the-world flights were inevitable as other pursuits paled, and the lumbering first try at the new distance endurance took 175 days. Post and Gatty really cracked the whip on time in 1931 by doing the stint in a whirlwind 8 days and nearly 14 hours. Two years later Wiley Post took the same plane and went alone. He bettered the time by approximately twenty hours.

We seldom think now of the thrill of those pioneering and record-breaking flights. After World War II the trip around the world was a commonplace that rated little attention—it was routine. There were other remarkable records and new feats to try. If pilots tired of long distance, speed dashes and new connecting trips between the United States and other countries, then they turned to testing how continuously they could stay aloft, using mid-air refueling. The fad was all but abandoned by 1949 when fliers Barras and Riddle stayed up for forty-two days!

Yet to be established were successions of speed-per-hour records, each outrunning the previous title holder. Then the jet outmoded all former speed concepts. Altitude was another aspect of flying in which records pushed up to nearly 34,600 feet. European pilots outshone us until they made the ceiling up beyond 56,000 feet in 1938. Getting off the ground is such an established fact in this space age that the loftiest figure of past machines-with-propellers seems tame. But within fifty-eight years from the day that Wilbur Wright hit the unheard of height of 361 feet, we've progressed beyond all dreams.

Air vehicles couldn't be discussed without mention of the ill-fated dirigibles. Disasters with this type of craft began before the twentieth century, and seemed to continue at a great rate. The earliest explosion resulted from benzine vapors, but fortunately many of the early accidents didn't include large loss of life. There was a real thrill in seeing a dirigible aloft—the great size and novelty of it, but always the fear for its safety.

There was a set of disaster possibilities, noticeable by frequency of occurrence. Storms destroyed amazing numbers, particularly the Zeppelins. They could be battered to pieces by stormy winds and explosion was always a danger when they were hydrogen-filled. The Goodyear dirigible, "Akron," exploded, killing the owner and his

A photographer friend journeyed to Lakehurst, New Jersey, in 1937 expecting to get a picture of the beautiful "Hindenburgh." He photographed a tragedy instead. (Loaned by Lorne Braddock)

four assistants. In 1921 a United States Naval dirigible buckled, crumpled and exploded, killing all but four of sixty-six aboard. In the next year the U.S. Army lost one with thirty-five passengers. Another year and another great loss when the "Shenandoah" gave up in a storm, killing all in the control cabin. The whole gory, flaming story of the giant rigid airships is one of exploding, crumpling, burning and crashing, punctuated in 1931 by the horrible blow-up and burning of the immense "Hindenburg." One man I knew happened to be at the scene in Lakehurst, New Jersey, when the disaster occurred. Many had gathered to watch the mooring of the huge craft when all at once their unbelieving eyes saw the great ship disintegrate in flames. My friend had enough calmness to grasp his camera and get pictures of the horror instead of the beautiful, intact ship he'd intended to photograph.

The "Graf Zeppelin" was one of many dirigibles used by Germany but at least half of them burned, due to the flammable lifting gas. Non-rigid airship construction after the rigid structures' ill-fated roles, was speeded for American Naval escort service during World War II, and had a good record. The Goodyear Company built the tremendous Zeppelin airdock at Akron—the largest structure in the world without internal support. They were under contract to build the "Akron" and "Macon." Interest died after the line of rigid ship tragedies. The smaller Good-

upward trend of more passengers, cargo and air miles each year. Instead of merely being a means of travel, planes have become luxurious, distances and times have melted, lopped in half when companies acquired fleets of jet planes. It was cause for excitement on June 28, 1939 when the inaugural flight of Pan American Airways

The "Graf Zeppelin." (Courtesy *The Christian Science Monitor*)

A Goodyear zeppelin. (Courtesy Goodyear Tire & Rubber Co.)

year blimps, "Columbia" and "Mayflower," travel hundreds of thousands of miles in their public relations jobs —beautiful by day and "skytacular" by night with blinking lights along their sides. You've likely been pleasantly surprised more than once to spot a Goodyear blimp.

The story of the airlines and their growth is one long

"Dixie Clipper" took place. It left Port Washington, New York, with twenty-two paying passengers, a crew of eleven plus a mail cargo.

Do you think that the Wright brothers envisioned the day when people would sit in luxurious quarters, eat gourmet meals and watch movies, rather than glory at man's ability to rise 361 feet from the ground?

7

There Have Always Been Dictators

"We know as a people, as a nation, that we are at the crossroads in America. Soon we must determine whether or not we are going to preserve Anglo-Saxon institutions in this country or join the other nations of the earth under a dictator." Hatton Sumners said this in a 1937 House of Representatives speech, but his reference to dictatorship was anything but new.

Even ancient Rome was called a republic, but a dictator was appointed during a crisis when it was expedient to have a strong man in control to straighten matters out fast. Our century must be the most crisis-ridden time in all of history if the dictator situation is a criterion. But they come to power now as a result of revolution, resulting in the violent overthrow of a czar, president, monarch or even a weaker dictator. Every strong man in the forefront of revolution must dream of himself as dictator—or fancy himself as the savior of his people and the world.

In modern times, particularly the decades in this century that we're recalling, dictators have grown all around us—Stalin, Hitler, Mussolini, Franco, Mao Tse-Tung and Castro . . . to name the most prominent. They are spawned in times of upheaval, unrest and dissatisfaction of peoples who thought a change was necessary, sometimes to their later grief.

The biggest and longest enduring movement started in the nineteenth century when two men co-authored a famous document, *The Communist Manifesto*. Karl Marx, of Jewish parentage, teamed up with Friederich Engels, a German Socialist, when the former became actively interested in Socialism. Together they wrote many books and papers of an informative, inflammatory and propagandistic nature. Marx operated in France until the character of

Karl Marx.

Friederich Engels.

his work earned him an expulsion. Then he became an English resident and continued writing, even to contributions to the New York *Tribune* and *Putnam's Monthly* in America. Odd as it seems, he was never in Russia.

After his death in 1883, Engels carried on further volumes of Marx's *Das Kapital,* the bible of Socialism.

Nikolai Lenin.

If the architects of the Socialistic building were dead, there were carpenters ready to continue hammering the nails of the new order, following the blueprints already made. An outstanding figure to emerge was Nikolai Lenin, a Russian leader of the Bolshevist movement. (In 1919 the Bolshevist Party was renamed the Communist Party.) With Lenin's push for violent overthrow, he ousted the minority group of the Kerensky Social Democratic Revolution in 1917 and began to build his concept of a more purely Marxist state over the bones and shambles of the Czar's society. He fancied himself the great man of destiny for the working class.

At Lenin's side, Leon Trotsky was a worker very willing to help build the proletarian order. To be in the front of a revolutionary system was to live dangerously, as he was exiled to Siberia, imprisoned for his activities, but never dampened in his spirit for spreading the gospel of Communism. He escaped and continued—even to America's shores in 1917, to try to keep us out of World War I. Peacemakers sometimes have ulterior motives.

Joseph Stalin.

After Lenin's death in 1924, Trotsky naturally felt his chances were excellent for the top position. But he hadn't

reckoned with another upcomer who gained strong support—Joseph Stalin.

They differed in their interpretations of Communism. Whereas Trotsky wanted to inflame the world with the doctrine, Stalin believed the realistic job at the time was a gargantuan fence-mending at home. Meantime, Trotsky was growing embittered as an exile again, living one place and another until he was assassinated in Mexico in 1940.

By 1924 Stalin's work was rewarded when he became the Russian dictator and outstanding figure of world Communism. He didn't remain static because after a nonaggression pact with Nazi Germany, Stalin decided to flex his muscles when Germany had all but bagged Poland. When the spoils were divided, Russia came out with three-fifths to Germany's two.

In 1941 Stalin received the title of Premier after annexing the bordering countries, Latvia, Lithuania and Estonia. Finland didn't like having Russian troops quartered there, but its resistance only netted it defeat from Russia's overpowering military might.

Being a strong realist, the Soviet leader turned his guns against an aggressor—Germany. By 1943 he was Commander-in-Chief of the army and soon Marshal of the Soviet Union. Hitler's chances of turning European tides in his favor soon changed when the overbearing weight and fierce fighting of the Russians stalled the previously victorious Germans. Their nonaggression pact was a scrap of paper.

Stalin's constantly inscrutable expression was well underlined by his surname, given him by Lenin. Stalin means "man of steel." When he gained complete power over the millions of Russians, he liquidated enemies and banished those who didn't agree with his roughshod methods. He was considered by the fastidious members of the party to be a crude man, bearing out his humble, peasant origin. Whenever a known person was seen or heard no more, it was assumed he'd met a firing squad or become a resident of Siberia.

The familiar symbol of Communism.

Do you remember how many Americans believed that the only problem was to rid the world of Stalin and Communism would magically dissolve, because they KNEW that the Russion people hated him as much as we, and would gladly help in the overthrow? This dream was disspelled in 1953 when Stalin died.

Lavrenti Pavlovich Beria had scarcely became a known

name in the United States when he was reportedly executed for high treason, the same year he'd risen through the ranks to Deputy Premier. He conducted purges of Stalin's enemies after much previous experience as head of the secret police and other "plum" party positions after the Bolshevist Revolution. It took an expert skater to skirt the thin ice in high places while playing Russian roulette for high position.

Benito Mussolini. (Janco Fotos)

Nikita Khrushchev.

An earnest worker amid the Soviet's top brass was the First Secretary of the Central Committee, Nikita Khruschev, who did not let the thought of being top man escape him. After Premiers Beria, Malenkov and Bulganin in rapid succession, Khruschev took his power-wielding and card-playing turn and had shuffled them in his favor by 1958.

Like his chief predecessor, Khruschev was a man of the peasantry, but with a different personality. While we waited for the Communist dream to fall apart, the new Premier did the Russian housekeeping as he felt it should be done. Now he was our threat as he rattled sabres, wrote his "Mein Kampf," and banged his shoe on the United Nation's table to push Russian weight around the world. He softened some of the hard core practices of Stalin, but we didn't enjoy his shouted remark, "We'll bury you!"

About 1919 and 1920 two busy movements were being shaped into solid masses from nebulous beginnings. The slightly earlier one was the Fascisti formation from the disgruntled World War I veterans who weren't happy with Italy when they came home. They found a leader in Benito Mussolini, who'd mulled around with Socialism, been in trouble for his ideas and became editor of a paper, *Il Popolo d'Italia*. The greatest awareness of Mussolini and his followers was the influx of Communism and the foothold it had gained. As the weak regime in power wasn't making conditions better, the young Fascist organization donned black shirts and went

to work, ousting Red flags and pulling out Communists and Socialists by the roots they'd grown, especially in industries.

The party was growing in numbers and enthusiasm so that by 1922 it held a great meeting in Naples. The government tried to reckon with the Fascisti by offers of cabinet positions. Benito would have none of this—he wanted to BE the government! The Fascisti staged a tumultuous march on Rome as Mussolini met with King Victor Emmanuel at the King's invitation. The monarch hardly realized that within one half hour, he would no longer be the ruler except in name. The sceptre was firmly in Fascist hands and was wielded rapidly to whisk away as many old rules as possible. If there was shock as the new order made strict laws, eliminating all but the elements of a dictatorship, the people went along with their anti-Communist leader. Not everyone was a Fascist, but it wasn't advisable to shout the fact. There was one political party and it made the rules. Mussolini became known as Il Duce in 1923.

During the following decade Italy slowly but certainly changed from a representative government to a dictatorship with actual outlawing of other political parties, a constant strife to regain territories lost in World War I settlement, and agreement with the Vatican over the separation of church and state influence on youth. The Church was given the right of religious instruction but all physical and cultural education passed to the government. The old system was unable to establish order or satisfaction amid the radical uprisings. The Italian people had little choice but to vote their confidence and hopes for a better set of conditions under the Fascisti and help eradicate the evils of the monarchy. Each new law gave new powers of absolutism, including press censorship, outlawing of strikes and lockouts. By 1929 the people were given the right to vote only "yes" or "no" to a block of four hundred candidates for Mussolini's Grand Council. Il Duce decided to boost Italy's population by rewarding producers of more children, and making it difficult for single men to get official jobs. He smiled on every mother with a new baby—the more, the better. He would have loved the Dionne family!

In 1935 border trouble between Italian Somaliland and Ethiopia foreboded action ahead. Troops rushed to the area and Haile Selassie's Ethiopia fell under Italy's superior forces, while the Emporer fled to England. It seemed to the Italians that their leader was getting things done, and his era of popularity bloomed. Previous unemployment and unrest was being alleviated, even though the way of life was no longer free.

Il Duce's personal life began to reach Italian ears in the form of common gossip. A French woman, Magda de Fontanges, was so proud of her affair with Mussolini that she went to great ends to publicize it. This didn't help his prestige.

The seizing of more territory consistently rated among Mussolini's ambitions and after the Ethiopian victory, his men grabbed Albania. The success of Franco in Spain enhanced Fascism's power and thousands of adherents developed in other countries.

The term we often heard, Rome-Berlin-Toyko Axis, originated in 1937. Mussolini lined up with the German Nazis after the latter had beaten France down, so Il Duce declared his war against France. He flexed his and the soldier's muscles when in 1940 he tried to move into Greece from the Albanian borders. More than once Nazi forces had to bolster the Italians when they'd get into a push too big to handle—even to Greece. Meantime the support and enthusiasm of the Italian people had to be whipped up as their dictator became more frantic for personal adulation and prestige with the enlargement of the country's territory.

When the Allied forces were joined by the Americans, the wide spreading of the Fascist operation was pushed back where it came from and Italy was invaded. Mussolini's stock fell fast, as well as his dreams of reestablishing a Roman Empire.

Window-dressing of alliance and love were exhibited, but the feeling was not deep when Mussolini was given a resounding welcome on a visit to Hitler in 1940. Italians wished the Rome-Berlin Axis could be broken.

The older Mussolini grew, the more disdainful he was of age. He had a bag of tricks to give the appearance of youth—such as running with his men, having statues that showed him as a Roman god and carrying on a love affair with a twenty-three year old girl when he was fifty-six. The more his empire slipped, the louder he bellowed to the throngs about their great future destinies. He posed for pictures in childish rompings, bare-chested in the snow, and played down the very existence of several grandchildren.

Patriots were still in Italy, men who loved their country more than they loved Mussolini. The dictator's non-invincible underside showed and the people were neither happy nor proud. By 1943 Mussolini had resigned his prime ministerial post and within three months the Italian soldiers surrendered gladly to the Alies. The ire of the Italians welled over in 1945 when the dictator was seized

IF GERMANY WINS
WHAT ITALY WANTS

A World War II Headline.

Adolph Hitler.

with his mistress and a few loyal Fascists and was literally murdered. Any good he'd done was buried with his bones in a pauper's grave. The end of Italy's Fascist experiment had come.

The king, who had remained as a figurehead, abdicated. His son, Prince Umberto, became King Humbert II, but his reign was distinguished by its brevity—thirty-five days; then he also abdicated.

While Fascism took stabs at problems in its realm, another potential strong man of Europe gathered steam as fast as possible, starting in Munich beer cellars. Adolph Hitler was a name beginning to be heard in 1921, after his growing interest in politics from 1912, service in the German Army during World War I, then the return to a badly beaten Germany torn by money problems, including large reparation debts. When Germany became a republic in 1918, Adolph Hitler was *not* pleased.

Some of Hitler's fanaticism was the outgrowth of an unhappy childhood in poverty, hate for his drunkard father and Austria, the place of his birth. He joined the German forces, renounced his Austrian citizenship and devoted himself to his adopted country. The only parent Hitler loved was his mother—his father's third wife. She was the source of the name Hitler, which was her maiden name.

Service in the German Army was an escape from a miserably dull frustrating life. An art school wouldn't accept him, he did menial jobs and was rejected by the Austrian Army. He learned early to hate, and to the Jew's misfortune, his hatred turned on them.

Hitler was not to be ignored once he was inflamed by Fascism. As early as 1923 he attempted a Munich "beer hall putsch" with General von Ludendorff. After the failure of this, he served one year of a five-year sentence for the try.

The word Nazi came into being as an outgrowth of the National Socialist Workmen's Party which was Fascist-inspired. Hitler was constantly active and agitating through the shuffles in the republic's elections and changes of officialdom. The firmest stander against him was President von Hindenburg. The upstart Nazi gained supporters, but by numerous power plays, he wasn't yet able to grasp the desired plum—the chancellorship. Hitler made more than one try to get a commanding majority of votes for his party. On strong advice from von Papen, von Hindenburg finally made Hitler the Chancellor in January of 1933. The President's sleep must have been troubled that night.

Strong suppression of demonstrations by all opposing parties was evident, and it was believed that acts the Nazis perpetrated were blamed on Communist agitators. Hitler soon retired the old Reichstag, and under a new group was made a dictator for four years, following the old Roman custom of appointing dictators for short periods—at least, at the start.

What the Nazis promised as their vague program was not much different than other parties desired or prom-

ised. Against the Versailles Treaty, the Germans were rearming, there was distressing depression, and things could not be administered readily by the government's parliament. Hitler's fiery oratory gave the Nazi Party the edge as the propaganda machine was ably oiled by Joseph Goebbels.

It only took a few months to show Hitler's hatred of the Jews. They were ruled out of all civil service jobs, deprived of making a living; Jewish students were excluded from schools and books written by Jews were burned.

Little time was required for the German people to realize what the new regime intended to do. Not only were strict laws made against the Jews, but the Christian churches came under fire. The Protestants banded together for a solid front, and Catholics suggested unity to insure a Christian power.

Originally President von Hindenburg had made von Papen Vice-Chancellor as a check and balance leverage against Hitler's possible ambitions, but this was utterly ineffective in the face of gathering totalitarian force being daily strengthened. The Reichsfuhrer's house was put into rigid order with brutal measures such as blood purges within his own party, sterilization of anyone with hereditary disease, Nazi "church members" to watch for any wrong words in minister's sermons. Other political beliefs were dissolved. Hitler designated how many could attend universities. including a drastic cut in the ratio of female to male students. He wanted young women to stay home and enlarge the population.

In 1933 few were brave enough to vote "no" in alleged elections, for already concentration camps were spreading —inhuman torture chambers with unbelievable conditions. Without charges, trials or sentences, political prisoners were herded into these jungles of agony, with the keys virtually thrown away. To not approve of the government was to invite this terrible disaster.

It was a sad note for Germans in 1934 when Paul von Hindenburg died at a mellow eighty-six. He was beloved as a war hero and firm patriot. Hitler lost no time in assuming the Presidential role as well as Chancellorship, almost before the funeral dirge died away.

The Versailles Treaty was all but scrapped, Hitler argued that his country could or would not stop rearming unless all of the other treaty signees would cease armament. This lip service caused other powers to renew their defenses when it was apparent that Germany was on its way to arms superiority with no regard for agreements. The restless, embittered youth were mobilized at a time when economic conditions seemed hopeless. Country-wide conscription was in force.

Italy and Germany became "pals" when mutual sympathies for Franco's revolution in Spain were exhibited and there was agreement against Russia and Communism. Hitler released a peace dove over other parts of the world to flutter down with its message of goodwill while he went merrily ahead at great speed with his war-making machinery. Italy likewise proceeded with military preparations and the people were put into near-wartime economies for saving. You couldn't be bristling with this much armament and nowhere to go. Germany was on her way when she took overly impressed Austria.

Hitler and Chamberlain.

Neville Chamberlain.

It was a sad item in history when England's Neville Chamberlain and representatives from France, Italy and Germany met at the Munich Conference in 1938. With a false sense of security, Prime Minister Chamberlain was so passionate for "peace at any price" that he appeased Hitler's appetite by trading off Czechoslovakia's Sudetenland as an offering. At least, he thought matters were settled and was assured by Hitler's word to that effect.

It was a situation that Chamberlain was no match for and his umbrella became a symbol of appeasement in all

of the free world. To Hitler the alleged settlement was like red-to-a-bull. He swept into demoralized Czechoslovakia and took it as a lion tackles the docile lamb. By 1939, *der Fuehrer's* appetite was whetted to a keen edge as he seized Memel from Lithuania. It was not the slightest deterrent when England and France threatened to fight if moves were made against Poland. It was as if they were calling Hitler's next move in advance. Germany's war machine moved with dizzying speed and met so little resistance that it took much more than it fought for.

Some believed Hitler's barrage of words scared Chamberlain into making the deal that ruined Csechoslovakia. When the Prime Minister expressed fears that war would ruin civilization, Hitler quickly answered that this might be true for countries that were struggling to preserve outmoded capitalism and democracy—but not for Germany! He predicted that England would surely have a revolution.

Berchtesgaden.

The beautiful chalet in the grandeur of the Bavarian Alps near Berchtesgaden was Hitler's idyllic retreat. It was in this building that Chamberlain sealed the fate of Czechoslovakia.

Editorial cartoon from The Detroit *Times* shows Hitler and Mussolini celebrating their victories.

Hitler was the master of Europe in 1941, but someone who didn't worship at his temple set a time bomb that missed by a mere ten minutes—otherwise the course of history could have been changed in a Munich beer garden. *Der Fuehrer* lived to hear "Heil Hitler" again. In 1944 he again narrowly escaped a bomb put in his headquarters. Obviously some of his own officers didn't care for their leader.

The men in early struggles for organization and promotion of Nazism later formed the inner circle of the Nazi government. Hermann Goering met Hitler in 1921

Hermann Goering.

when both were fired with the wish to overthrow the German republic. He later built the air force to great strength and got the army and secret police (Gestapo) into working order. He'd even been named by Hitler as his successor. Most Americans saw Goering as a fat, loathesome man sodden with all evils, including drug addiction.

Joachim von Ribbentrop was a wine merchant-turned-Nazi-organizer who climbed to foreign minister for his reward. Dr. Paul Goebbels was probably the best educated of Hitler's henchmen, since he had a Ph.D. degree. He held several posts, the ultimate being the head of the propaganda ministry. Heinrich Himmler had the sadist's job as chief of the Gestapo and death-dealer of all regime opposition.

No matter how powerful an organization or well-planned a concentrated effort, there mercifully seems to be a last ditch where an inevitable tide sweeps mankind out of the boiling cauldron unbalanced men would force it into. Hitler's Nazi Germany was no exception. When the waters of fortune did change direction, it was an awesome surge that left the power-crazy dictator unable to cope with the reversal. As the sands shifted on the sleazy shores, the allied Hitler and Mussolini were like madmen groping for the crack in the dike.

This Detroit *Free Press* headline heralded the death of the mad dictator of Germany.

In the final days, the chaos Hitler swaggeringly swore to Chamberlain would never come to Germany came. Suicide was executed with the aspects of a pact. After snuffing out millions of lives in the infamous ovens, the Nazi "brass" chose to do their own killing of themselves. Much mystery shrouded Der Fuehrer's demise because the body was never found. Speculation ran high that he had been spirited from Germany to a safe haven in South America. Even accounts of those who supposedly last saw him were doubted. After April 29, 1945, he was never again seen by the German people. Goebbels, Goering and Himmler committed suicide.

Just prior to World War II, when dictators were daily company in our newspapers-with-breakfast, another absolute ruler appeared who less directly disturbed us. He was Francisco Franco, trained to be a career militarist who graduated to revolutionist when he became dissatisfied with the republic in Spain. He headed the military school at Zaragoza in 1933 until the cabinet closed it. He rose to generalship at the slight age of thirty-two, and service followed in Morocco against the Riffs until he was recalled to Spain as the military Chief-of-Staff.

Political vagaries scrambled the direction of life in Franco's case after only one year back in the homeland. He was exiled to the Canary Islands, but didn't stagnate with this turn of fate. He returned to Morocco and prepared a force of the Spanish Foreign Legion to fight in a Fascist overthrow of the government in Spain in 1936. It was a civil war that continued until 1939. At that time the loyalist forces gave over Madrid, and Franco, as leader of the revolt, declared himself dictator. He received other Fascist aid and comfort from Hitler and Mussolini, because, like them, he was an enemy of Communism. Numbers of Americans gave money and volunteered for military service for this cause. One of my fellow-workers, a card-carrying Communist, left propaganda pamphlets weekly on our desks.

Communism for China was an almost native byproduct of its deplorable conditions of continuing warfare and mass poverty. So many were illiterate that elections as we know them could not nurture a representative government. Because of the mass plight, dictatorships and the rule of warlords was possible. A great famine from 1927 to 1929 caused such suffering in several provinces that banditry became almost a necessity to stave off starvation, especially in rural districts.

Chiang Kai-shek.

If the Chinese populace was ripe for Communism as a savior, there was help when Sun Yat-sen asked Russia's advice in 1923. Michael Borodin came and gladly advised, but with the idea of recruitment of another Communist satellite—not as an aid to unite scattered provinces under a Nationalist head. Sun Yat-sen's motives were idealistic, and for a free, democratic constitutional government. By 1927 this dream was nearly realized through the efforts of General Chang Kai-shek. Only Manchurian warlord, Marshal Chang Tso-lin, held out with several provinces he controlled, and with no love of a united plan. Communist Russia became like the "Man Who Came to Dinner" in its zealous reorganization of government forms, the army and other activities not of the guest's liking. This was tolerated until Dr. Sun's death—then anti-Communism flared. After much battling, Gen-

eralissimo Chiang Kai-shek became President of China in 1928.

The country ran far from smoothly. In 1930 bandit armies roamed at large, murdering, looting, ousting missionaries, conducting civil wars and massacres. The Reds found this good territory for their hands.

All through the thirties there was anything but peace as continual struggles upcropped, jealousies flared and Japan bombed and warred over Chinese cities. Communists gained a two hundred mile strip along the Yangtse River and agitated everywhere. Manchuria remained a sore spot between China and Japan.

Mao Tse-Tung.

There's always a strong man "waiting in the wings" for the right cue. China had this man in soldier, politician, poet and scholar, Mao Tse-Tung. He became interested in Socialism and the Marxist doctrine while in teacher's college. When Sun Yat-sen's revolutionary movement, known as the Kuomintang, was in high gear, Mao was a member of it as well as follower of the Communist ideology. There was a definite break, however, when Chiang Kai-shek massacred many Shanghai workers in 1927.

Mao Tse-Tung had a comrade in War Lord Chu Teh. These two formed the Fourth Workers and Peasants Red Army. By much work the Chinese Soviet Republic was established in 1931. Mao Tse-Tung was the logical chairman to be elected for the provisional government. During this time Chiang Kai-shek got rid of Communists wholesale and the Kuomintang forces pressed hard against Mao's Reds.

After a six thousand mile march northward in the mid-thirties, Mao's position and authority over the Communist movement was unchallenged. While he established soviet headquarters in Yenan, the Japanese made trouble with the invasion of Manchuria. In the same manner as squabbling boys in a neighborhood, they united when a rival group from another street invaded. Mao's Soviet army sought to make a united front with the Kuomintang. This arrangement was agreed upon providing Mao discontinued his agrarian revolution. By 1945, when World War II ended, the Communists had gained ground and strength even though the Japanese were as aggressive against China as they were with the United States at Pearl Harbor.

It wasn't as if attempts weren't made to unite China after the war; Mao Tse-Tung even had a conference with Chiang Kai-shek for this purpose. But the Communist was sensitive and educated and he resented the peasant-like reception given him by the other leader. Even General George Marshall's efforts for a coalition agreement met with failure. After the boys from the other street went home, the two Chinese strong men resumed their private war in 1946.

The Kuomintang was on its way out amid bitter hostilities between the factions. Chiang fled to Formosa with his Nationalist followers, and Mao was the supreme ruler of China under the Communist banner of the People's Republic of China. Another enemy to our way of life was born.

A "Johnny-come-lately" dictator who is much alive at this writing, is another cause for keeping us on tenterhooks—Fidel Castro. He was educated in law in Havana, was exiled to the United States from Cuba when only

Four dictators—Stalin, Mussolini, Hirohito, and Hitler— seen as the four horsemen in this South American publication. (Courtesy Lorne Braddock)

Fidel Castro.

twenty-two for rebellion against another dictator—Fulgencio Batista. Castro quickly organized a small rebel force and returned to Cuba the following year—1956.

Fierce guerrilla warfare continued until New Year's Day, 1959, when Batista finally gave up and fled to the Dominican Republic. Through the thirties and forties there was a veritable parade of presidents, too numerous to mention, and Cubans must have been scarcely able to say who the current executive was. In 1940 under Batista, Cuba had a new constitution, labor legislation and social security. It was on our side in World War II.

After Castro's revolt, called agrarian reform, he was hailed by most Cubans enthusiastically as a hero. It wasn't until later that his Communist associations came to light. It was another takeover and Dictator Castro ruthlessly got rid of his enemies, even of some who had fought with him in the hills. The big American tourism died, for we were suddenly "enemy Imperialists."

A speech by August Bebel in 1871 to the Reichstag, sums up our considerations of dictators we've known: "All political questions, all matters of right, are at bottom only questions of might." So rise and fall the mightiest governments.

8

V For Victory

"War is on its last legs; and a universal peace is as sure as is the prevalence of civilization over barbarism, of liberal governments over feudal forms. The question for us is only—how soon?" These words might have been uttered yesterday instead of in the nineteenth-century lifetime of Ralph Waldo Emerson. It only magnifies man's enduring and futile quest for lasting peace—a will-o'-the-wisp.

Twenty-three years later W. Winwood Reade thought in amazingly modern terms; "It is not probable that war will ever absolutely cease until science discovers some destroying force so simple in administration, so horrible in its effects . . . that mankind will be unable to endure."

We know Mr. Reade couldn't have foreseen the atom or hydrogen bombs, yet it seems he was describing them.

The event to set worldwide war wheels turning happened September 1, 1939, when goose-stepping soldiers and rumbling war machines clattered into Poland. Two days later England and France declared war on Germany.

DRIVE AGAINST WAR IS BEGUN BY V. F. W.

Veterans Start Circulating Petitions Seeking 25,000,000 Signers to Assure Peace

PLAN PLEA TO CONGRESS

At first, Americans were opposed to any involvement in the European struggle, as this New York Times headline proves.

For the average American citizen this news seemed far away—not likely to be an active concern of ours. However, as Hitler's well-oiled mechanisms steamrollered over more and more European countries and Russia began to rumble, everyone became worried from President Roosevelt down to the smallest man on the smallest American street.

Everyone speculated or brashly said, "We simply won't get into it!" Anyone who'd just come back from Europe was avidly questioned. When the theatrical couple, Alfred Lunt and Lynn Fontanne, came from a play in London they said, "Europe's atmosphere is so tense you can scarcely breathe. Events abroad change everything for all of us."

There was much difference of opinion on what who should do to whom and when, but on one thing we nearly all agreed; that sympathies for our allies must not involve this country in war! We were pro-British and French all along and supplied much war material to them, but our

Goose-stepping Nazis marching into Poland to set off World War II.

self-assured neutrality received a shock following the collapse of France. We were scared into making concerted defense preparations for ourselves in 1940 when we finally realized it might not be possible to steer clear of a Europe aflame.

In the fall of 1940 the first peacetime conscription went into effect for American men. We traded old destroyers to Britain in return for long-term leases on naval and air bases in British territories. After German submarines sank some U.S. ships, we had orders to shoot any Axis boats that came near while we kept watch from Iceland and Greenland.

On December 7, 1941, one of the bitterest pills for us to swallow concerning Japan's Pearl Harbor attack was that their emissaries were at that very moment peacefully conferring with our Secretary of State, Cordell Hull. It was like a smoke screen over our eyes. The attackers bombed and strafed our closely packed Army and Navy aircraft before pilots could get them off the ground to fight.

Burning oil added to the fearsome Pearl Harbor scene of wreckage. Our flags were still flying amid the havoc around the U.S.S. "West Virginia" and "Tennessee" in "Battleship Row."

Another casualty of Pearl Harbor's bombing was the U.S.S. "Arizona," which toppled apart in the evil sea of smoke. Adding insult to injury seems a tame comparison when not more than two hours after the Japanese attack, *they* declared war on the United States and England.

In the newspapers we first read about the devastating attack from Japan. At this point most Americans felt either numb or hysterical. I must confess that the name Pearl Harbor hadn't figured in my vocabulary before and I didn't immediately realize the significance of the attack.

Our morning newspaper came out before the formal declaration of war was broadcast, but in the evening we read in a sixth extra edition that the Senate had made clear what our course must now be. Little groups of workers huddled around radios on their jobs to hear the solemn words of President Roosevelt's declaration of war. A strained hush fell over everyone.

It isn't only the big, flaming battle scenes that make up a war. These events are covered in history books. It's the personal touches, the human elements that directly affected many of our lives that we may recall—or have nearly forgotten. The police force helped to summon servicemen on leave, to be sent immediately back to their posts.

Pearl Harbor, December 7, 1941. (Department of Defense Photograph)

90

The "Arizona" goes down in a cloud of smoke. (Department of Defense Photo)

Japanese Ambassador Nomura and Envoy Kurusu were the men who procrastinatingly lingered over talks in Washington while our ships and planes were reduced to rubble.

Inside the front page of the December 8 newspaper, war was already creeping into many articles. Since it was the twelfth month, Christmas advertising was present but the usual holiday spirit was missing. Sports pages still told of games, but athletes were either expecting to be drafted any day or they were enlisting. Ordinary reports of accidents and miscellaneous news were crowded into far corners. The society page showed a girl just married to a uniformed man while matrons planned welcoming posts for incoming servicemen. It was prophetic that "Hellzapoppin'" was showing at our legitimate theater. There was never a time when this title so nearly matched the actual scene. Many young men were lined up to enlist before recruiting offices opened the day after Pearl Harbor.

If there was reluctance on the part of any Americans about bending every muscle toward the total war effort, wild headlines were designed to draw them into the fold of doers. Fortunately, the rumors of enemy planes on both coasts didn't materialize into stark reality.

If the proceedings weren't so deadly grim, the actions that followed might be compared to a child's game of tag. Germany and Italy declared war on the U.S. on December 9. The following day we declared war on them. An editorial stated, "Well, fellow Americans, we are in the war and we have got to win it. There may have been some difference of opinion among good Americans about getting into the war, but there is no difference about how we should come out of it."

The United States Government was glad to have any optimistic headline for the December 10 papers, but there were many reverses ahead of us.

Five days after Japan's sneak attack, she turned tail when confronted by our Navy. We could only take cold comfort from this as the enemy captured Hong Kong and Singapore, then cut the Burma Road in the ensuing weeks.

Amid the bare-bone gauntness of total war, there had to be remarks tinged with the unquenchable American sense of humor or a light touch. After Squadron Commander John Bulkeley led a torpedo attack on a Jap aircraft carrier, he reported, "So with splashes all around us, we executed that naval maneuver technically known as getting the hell out of there."

U. S. LOSSES VERY HEAVY

Japs Attack Hawaii, Singapore, Philippines

DETROIT TIMES EXTRA

Only Detroit Newspaper Carrying International News Service and Complete Sport Dispatches

42ND YEAR, NO. 69 — DETROIT, MICH., MONDAY, DEC. 8, 1941 — 28 PAGES — 3 CENTS

2 U.S. Warships Hit

President May Ask Declaration of War By Congress Today

LONDON, Dec. 8.—(INS)—A Japanese naval force is now engaged in a "second sea battle" with a mixed American-British naval fleet in the western Pacific, the London Daily Express reported today, quoting the Japanese newspaper Osaki Mainichi.

NEW YORK, Dec. 8.—(INS)—The Japanese aircraft carrier, from which planes presumably operated to attack Pearl Harbor, has been sunk by units of the United States Navy, according to unofficial reports circulated in London tonight and reported to New York by CBS. The same sources said two British cruisers had been sunk at Singapore.

HOLLYWOOD, Cal., Dec. 8.—(INS)—A Japanese expeditionary force has landed in strategic points in the Malay States, and for a second time Japanese bombers have raided Hongkong, according to a Tokio newscast heard by the NBC short wave listening post. (See story at bottom of columns 2 and 3.)

By ROBERT G. NIXON
International News Service Staff Correspondent

WASHINGTON, Dec. 8.—The United States was plunged abruptly into total war with Japan after Nipponese bombers carried out a series of surprise dawn attacks on bases in Hawaii, the Philippines and Guam, which President Roosevelt revealed today had cost the navy and army "very heavy losses."

The war department officially stated the savage aerial bomb attacks, which apparently caught American defense forces by surprise, had taken a toll of 104 American military dead and more than 300 wounded on the island of Oahu alone.

Uncounted civilian and naval casualties, which were feared large, added to the toll.

President Reports Heavy Losses

President Roosevelt, who called his full cabinet into extraordinary session last night to consider defense measures against Japan's "treacherous attack," told the cabinet the nation must expect losses as a result of the initial attack.

After a two-hour session with the cabinet and congressional leaders at which Mr. Roosevelt also announced his decision to appear before a joint session of Congress at 12:30 p. m. today, presumably to request a declaration of war, Stephen T. Early, presidential secretary, called in the press and said:

"The President told them (the cabinet and leaders) of doubtless very heavy losses sustained by the navy and also large losses sustained by the army in the island of Oahu (Hawaii)."

A report from Honolulu, not confirmed by the war department, stated 350 were killed when a bomb made a direct hit on a barracks at the army's air base, Hickam Field. It was not

Britain to Join U. S. in War Against Japan

By GEORGE LAIT
Int'l News Service Staff Correspondent

LONDON, Dec. 8.—As Japan hurled her air and sea forces into unheralded assaults on American and British bases in the Pacific and seized Shanghai, Great Britain today prepared to declare war jointly and simultaneously with the United States on the Japanese empire.

Both houses of Parliament were summoned to meet in emergency session at 3 p. m. today (9 a. m. Detroit time), at which time Prime Minister Winston Churchill is expected to announce that Britain, in concert with the United States, has entered formally into a state of all-out war against Japan.

Seizure of Shanghai Reported

That Japanese forces have occupied the entire water front and the international settlement of Shanghai was announced in a Reuters dispatch from the Chinese metropolis.

An authorized announcement stated:

"While details are lacking, authoritative quarters admit that Japanese planes, presumably simultaneously with their attacks on Manila and Honolulu, have bombed British Pacific bases."

The announcement was issued shortly after a dispatch from Shanghai said Japanese bombers had attacked and set fire to the British naval gunboat Peterel in Shanghai Harbor.

The Peterel burned to her waterline today. It displaced 310 tons, carried a complement of 55 officers and *Continued on Next Page, Col. 7*

Japs Land Force In North Malaya

Seek to Isolate Singapore Base; British Troops Attack Invaders

International News Service Cable

SINGAPORE, Dec. 8.—Japanese troops have landed in northern Malaya above the Singapore base and are being engaged in violent fighting, the British eastern high command announced early today.

Steaming into the Gulf of Siam aboard several naval-convoyed transports and under the harassment of British bombers and coastal guns, the Nipponese invaders were declared to be pushing toward the vital Kota Bahru air base in northern Malaya near the border of Thailand.

The Japanese drive was obviously aimed at cutting across the narrow neck of northern Malaya and thereby isolating the Singapore base. Britain's mightiest Far Eastern bastion, from land connection with Thailand and Burma.

BOMBERS ATTACK

"Enemy troops," said Singapore's communique No. 1, "have *(Continued on Page 34)*

THE 'SUNKEN' BATTLESHIP

THE U. S. BATTLESHIP WEST VIRGINIA

An air view of the West Virginia, the American capital ship reported sunk by Jap bombs at Pearl Harbor. Although modernized, the West Virginia was no modern ship. She displaced 31,800 tons, did 21 knots on 30,000 horsepower, by virtue of her turning 20 years of age this year could be called obsolete.

Hundreds Die, Injured At Honolulu

Buildings Aflame Downtown, Home Sections Blasted

International News Service Cable

HONOLULU, Dec. 8 — Striking with sudden savagery out of Sunday morning skies, red - emblemed Japanese airplanes unleashed total war on America's Pacific outposts, Hawaii and the Philippines.

Shanghai also was attacked, as the Japanese imperial general staff announced the Rising Sun empire is officially at war with the United States and Britain.

Hundreds were killed and injured in Honolulu, Hickam army airfield and the Pearl Harbor navy base as the Japanese planes swooped over the city in two waves, beginning at 8 a. m., dropping repeated sticks of bombs.

The attacks came from the south, presumably from an aircraft carrier.

REPORT TORPEDOING

There were unconfirmed reports that at least one American vessel had been torpedoed in the Pacific between Honolulu and San Francisco.

At Queens Hospital, the largest civilian hospital in the city, there were at least six dead and 200 injured.

The Tripler Military Hospital reported it was jammed with injured.

There were unconfirmed reports of heavy casualties within the Pearl Harbor navy yard.

Two United States battleships, the West Virginia and the Oklahoma, were reported sunk or damaged in Pearl Harbor.

At least one woman was re- *(Continued on Next Page, Col. 5)*

WAR EDITORIAL
See Editorial
On War With Japan
Page 14

Japs Seize Shanghai, Grab U. S. Gunboat

SHANGHAI, Dec. 8.—(INS)—370 tons, was believed undamaged. The United States gunboat Wake was taken over by the Japanese and today flew the Japanese flag as the Nipponese assumed control of Shanghai's waterfront.

The U. S. S. Wake, formerly the Guam, with a displacement of *(Continued on Page 34)*

Here's how Detroiters got the grim news of Pearl Harbor.
(Courtesy Detroit *Times*)

The police rounded up servicemen, on December 8, and ordered them back to their posts. (Courtesy Detroit News)

This frightening headline fortunately turned out to be a rumor. (Courtesy Detroit News)

WAR VOTED BY SENATE

6th Extra   **DETROIT TIMES**   6th Extra

Only Detroit Newspaper Carrying International   EVENING   *News Service and Complete Sport Dispatches*

42ND YEAR, NO. 69   DETROIT, MICH., MONDAY, DEC. 8, 1941   34 PAGES   3 CENTS

3,000 Casualties in Hawaii

IN THE NEWS

WELL, fellow Americans, we are in the war and we have got to win it.

There may have been some difference of opinion among good Americans about getting into the war, but there is no difference about how we should come out of it.

We must come out victorious and with the largest V in the alphabet.

We are not completely prepared for war.

We have not got a Swiss system of universal service that we will have to have some day, since the lands are full of robbers and sea of pirates.

But we will get better and stronger every day, and we will not have to get very good and very strong to knock the everlasting daylights out of Japan.

We may have some small reverses at first, but do not let that worry you—if it happens.

It is not who wins the first round but who wins the last one that counts for victory.

And there is no doubt about the victory, folks—none whatever.

The worst thing about the ... is that it will

Jap Chute Troops on U. S. Isles

International News Service Wire

NEW YORK, Dec. 8.—Landing of Japanese parachute troops in the Philippine Islands was reported in a Manila broadcast to WOR-Mutual today. Japanese residents were said to have seized control of their own regions on the island.

763 Japs Jailed In FBI Roundup

International News Service Wire

WASHINGTON, Dec. 8.—Atty. Gen. Francis Biddle today reported that the FBI had rounded up and taken into custody 763 Japanese aliens throughout the United States during the night.

He said the number represented most of the Japanese nationals who had been under surveillance by FBI agents but added a few more Japanese might be taken into custody.

Nazis Say Japs Take Tientsin

BERLIN, Dec. 8.—Japanese troops have taken over the entire British concession at Tientsin and occupied all strategic points, DNB reported today.

According to the Rome radio, the Japanese took prisoners 63 United States marines at Tientsin.

WAR EDITORIAL

See Editorial

On Wa...

Churchill Asks British War on Japs

Prime Minister Says Nippon Talks Covered Attack Plan

By CHARLES A. SMITH
Int'l News Service Staff Correspondent

LONDON, Dec. 8.—Prime Minister Winston Churchill, fulfilling Great Britain's pledge to the United States, today announced to the House of Commons that a state of war exists between the British Empire and Japan.

The cabinet met at noon today. Churchill said, and authorized a declaration of war upon Japan. Notification to this effect has been delivered to the Nipponese government.

"I spoke to President Roosevelt on the Atlantic phone last night, with a view to arranging the time of our respective declarations," Churchill said.

"The British declaration was presented at 1 p. m. today (7 a. m. EST.)

TELLS OF TALKS HERE

The prime minister dealt at length with the negotiations in Washington carried on by Japanese Ambassador Kichisaburo Nomura and Special Envoy Saburo Kurusu.

"There cannot be any doubt," he said, "that the Japanese envoys were ordered to prolong their mission in the United States in order to keep the conversations going while a surprise attack was being prepared and before a declaration of war could be delivered.

"No one can doubt that every effort to bring about a peaceful solu..." by the J...

Nearly Half Of U. S. Losses Feared Dead

International News Service Wire

WASHINGTON, Dec. 8.—The White House today announced that the casualty list at the island of Oahu, Hawaii "in all probability will amount to about 3,000," nearly half of which are fatalities.

Simultaneously it was announced that one old United States battleship had capsized, several other ships were seriously damaged and one destroyer was blown up.

Army and navy flying fields in the Pearl Harbor area were bombed with the resulting destruction of several hangars and a large number of planes, it was announced.

Bombers Rush to Battle Scene

Meanwhile, American bombers rushing to the scene of hostilities arrived safely from San Francisco during the height of the engagement it was disclosed. More reinforcements are on the way.

Guam, Wake, Midway Islands and Hong Kong have been attacked, the White House announcement said.

Early Reads President's Bulletin

Stephen T. Early, White House secretary, read a war bulletin, an... ...President Roosevelt, as follows: ...ur forces in Oahu, in yester... ...an at first believed. ...attleship had cap... ...iously damaged.

U. S. Fleet Chases Japs; Guns Heard

Navy Acts Swiftly to Retaliate After Raid Kills Scores

International News Service Wire

HONOLULU, Dec. 8.—The fighting United States Navy moved out today to meet the Japanese, and the sound of apparent heavy gunfire indicated that the Americans already may have engaged the enemy.

What seemed to be heavy cannonading was heard at sea off Barber's Point, a promontory jutting out from the Pearl Harbor entrance. There were rumors four enemy ships had been sighted.

The navy moved swiftly to exact retribution for the devastating raids of Japanese bombers yesterday in which upwards of 350 soldiers and civilians may have been killed and in which the battleship U.S.S. Oklahoma was reported sunk, one of them the battleship West Virginia, and the other understood to be the aircraft carrier Lexing...

Assails Attack On Outposts, Sees Victory

International News Service Wire

WASHINGTON, Dec. 8.—The Senate today passed a resolution declaring that a state of war exists between the United States and Japan less than half an hour after President Roosevelt asked for a declaration of war because of Nippon's attacks on United States bases in the Pacific.

By WILLIAM K. HUTCHINSON
International News Service Staff Correspondent

WASHINGTON, Dec. 8.—President Roosevelt today asked Congress to take the United States into the Second World War by declaring a state of war with Japan.

To a historic, sober joint session of the House and Senate, he said:

"I ask that the Congress declare that since the unprovoked and dastardly attack by Japan on Sunday, December 7, a state of war has existed between the United States and the Japanese empire," he told a tense joint session.

"Hostilities exist," the Chief Executive asserted. "There is no blinking at the fact that our people, our territory and our interests are in grave danger.

"With confidence in our armed forces—with the unbounding determination of our people we will gain the inevitable triumph so help us God."

The President directly accused Japan of having planned and prepared "many days or even week ago," its series of devastating blitzkrieg attacks on America's Pacific outposts.

Indicates Possible Long War

Mr. Roosevelt also pledged the United States "l victory." He indicated it might be a lo... ...end, it would be an Amer...

The 6th Extra edition of the Detroit *Times* told of the declaration of war by the Senate. (Courtesy Detroit *Times*)

These Japanese envoys were meeting with Washington officials about possible peace while Pearl Harbor was being burned. (Courtesy Detroit *News*)

The Detroit Free Press

On Guard for Over a Century

METROPOLITAN
EXTRA

Monday, December 8, 1941. No. 218   111th Year   26 Pages   Three Cents

Army Guards Detroit Tunnel and Bridge

U.S. NAVY IS HARD HIT AS JAPAN OPENS WAR

Roosevelt Taking Message to Congress Today

War Guard Moves into City Plants

FBI Takes Action to Fight Sabotage; Workers to Have Strict Regulations

BY CLIFFORD A.

Joint Session Is Due to Vote a Declaration; Whole Nation Rallied

U. S. Swiftly Put on War Basis; All Military Personnel Mobilized

Momentous News for the Whole Nation

2 U.S. Battleships Reported Sunk

Pearl Harbor Base and Honolulu Bombed Heavily; Big Toll Feared

BY FRANCIS McCARTHY
United Press Correspondent

HONOLULU, Dec. 7—War broke with lightning suddenness in the Pacific today when waves of Japa-...ed Hawaii and the United States

The morning papers of December 8, 1941 carried the
only news of the day: War. (Courtesy Detroit *Free Press*)

DETROIT TIMES

Only Detroit Newspaper Carrying International EVENING News Service and Complete Sport Dispatches

42ND YEAR, NO. 72   DETROIT, MICHIGAN, THURSDAY, DECEMBER 11, 1941   52 PAGES   3 CENTS

6th Extra   *Huge Jap Battleship Sunk*   Night Edition

U. S. DECLARES WAR ON AXIS!

★ ★ ★ ★ ★ ★ ★ ★ ★ ★ ★ ★ ★ ★

4,000,000 Army to Draft Men, 18 to 65

A few days after Pearl Harbor, the U.S. declared war on
the Axis powers. (Courtesy Detroit *News*)

DETROIT ☆ TIMES

EVENING

42ND YEAR, NO. 71   DETROIT, MICHIGAN, WEDNESDAY, DECEMBER 10, 1941   40 PAGES   3 CENTS

6th Extra

Nazis Oust U. S. Reporters

Night Edition

JAPS BEATEN IN PHILIPPINES

★ ★ ★ ★ ★ ★ ★ ★ ★ ★ ★ ★ ★ ★ ★ ★ ★ ★

Japs Sink 2 Huge Warships

The December 10 papers told of our first triumph. (Courtesy Detroit News)

DETROIT ☆ TIMES

EVENING

Only Detroit Newspaper Carrying International News Service and Complete Sport Dispatches

42ND YEAR, NO. 73   DETROIT, MICHIGAN, FRIDAY, DECEMBER 12, 1941   52 PAGES   3 CENTS

JAP WARSHIPS FLEE U.S. NAVY

Five days after Pearl Harbor, the Japanese fleet was on the run. (Courtesy Detroit News)

The *New York Times* told of Japanese war aims.

The Chinese resisted Japanese advances with a valor that sometimes surpassed understanding. They clung tenaciously and in the spring of 1943 their morale still hadn't cracked. The time would come when courage needed a lift with something more tangible than kind words and sympathy. It was a question of getting supplies to these necessary fighters. The United States was more than sentimental about aid for China; it was helpful to us for that country to continue fighting.

Out of nearly eight billion dollars worth of Lend-Lease materials sent to our Allies in two years, a small portion was allocated to China and it didn't actually receive all of that allotment. There was the problem of transport which was eventually solved by the New China Road; it was built, with the bare hands of coolies, through the rugged Himalayan Mountains, from Sadiya, India, to Chunking, after the Burma Road was cut by the enemy. Later, air-drops by the Flying Tigers under Brigadier General Chennault helped the cause.

Ahead of the Allies there still lay the battles after the fall of Bataan. The fighting was hindered by jungle terrain in which it was difficult to find the elusive and fanatical enemy. The famous words of General Douglas MacArthur, "I shall return," were bitingly repeated after Corregidor surrendered. In the years 1943 to 1945 we lost some and gained some in places whose names had previously meant little or nothing to the average American. These sites now became daily words in our newspapers and on radio. The Battle of the Coral Sea was our first major engagement with the Japanese air force. There was the Battle of Midway, our landing in the Solomon Islands, where we finally won, only to have ahead the Battle of Guadalcanal. Do these names sound too painfully familiar even now?

Meantime, the European struggle was still with us. War had been declared on us by Germany and Italy in 1941. We sent troops to Europe. They landed in Ireland. By now Mexico had also declared war.

A German Field Marshal we heard much about was Erwin Rommel—"The Desert Fox." He so successfully pushed the British around in Egypt that he drank a toast to his feats, but he misjudged the immediate victories of his Afrika Korps for total victory. American forces landed in North Africa and Rommel's cocksure men began to be routed and battered as the Germans fled across Libya.

In the early part of 1943, President Roosevelt called for increasingly more movement toward the key goals of Tokyo and Berlin.

From time to time another country declared war. Brazil did it in August of 1942, to be followed in the spring by Bolivia.

The news was looking much better for the allies by 1943 —six days before the historic meeting of Roosevelt and Churchill at Casablanca. (Courtesy Detroit *Free Press*)

Planes discharged their men in Europe . . . then they went to the battlefield in Jeeps. (Courtesy KAISER Jeep CORPORATION)

German U-boats sank an alarming number of Allied ships in the North Atlantic. (Courtesy Detroit News)

It must have been a refreshing sight when American planes opened up to discharge their men loaded in Jeep Vehicles in the European War Theater. The sturdy Jeep Vehicles made an indispensable contribution to the war and built a solid niche for themselves after peace came.

We had to tangle in a beastial, wet battleground—the North Atlantic, where German U-boats were sinking an alarming number of Allied ships. The enemy subs worked in packs that struck and ran, luring the escort vessels away so that another pack could come in for the kill of the main ships.

American civilian workers were warned on every side about the dangers of loose talk or of permitting security leaks that had insidious ways of getting into enemy ears. Many top illustrators were engaged in designing posters to point up the hazards. "Even the walls have ears."

Italy. It wasn't uncommon for knots of Italians to happily surrender to the Americans, glad to be out of the fight. Italy's surrender was imminent in the early fall of 1943. War is never a joke, but there was a humorous twist when barely over a month later Italy declared war on her partner, Germany.

It was not a triumphal picture that Americans looked at in Europe. Although some thought there could be no doubt of our victory, sober consideration showed that there could be such a possibility as defeat which cockiness couldn't override. We were asked to think about the critical situation. The Nazi submarine force could make it impossible for us to launch a large-scale offensive on German-held Europe according to our timetable. China might not hold out against the Japs, or we might not win back Burma. There was worry of a stalemate that could

Signs everywhere warned us against accidentally giving away secrets. (Left: painted by Steven Dohanos; center: painted by Adolph Treidler; right: painted by John Holmgren—all for Office of War Information)

The weak sister of the Axis was always Italy. She was no aid or comfort to Hitler's cause. It was like having the youngest boy in the neighborhood spoil a good game on the sandlot by wanting to play with the "big boys." Many Italians were opposed to Communism, but they had little heart for fighting. When Mussolini's troops entered Greece, Hitler had to bolster them. Again in Libya and Egypt, Hitler was obliged to throw a lifeline of soldiers to the inundated Italians to help them fight the British. In July of 1943 the Allies invaded Sicily and soon the Americans bombed Rome. The reverses were too much for Mussolini; he resigned the following week. Rome became an open city to save itself as the Allies took Sicily and pushed doggedly deeper into the body of

drag on so long that the Allied block would run into disagreements. We had a fierce fight in the North Atlantic with Hitler's U-boats.

An industrial giant who arose among us with wondrous works was Henry J. Kaiser, when his first "Liberty Ship" slid down the ways after only five days a-building in 1942. There was great need for his rapidly produced ships. Don't forget that while we were at war, all of the union's pleas could not forestall some strikes and certain plants weren't producing shells speedily enough. In at least one instance, soldiers were sent in as factory workers to speed up production. The factoryman was every bit as vital as the soldier with a gun.

The heavy air raids on Berlin started in the fall of 1943

Cooperation between the factory worker and the soldier is symbolized in this drawing. (Courtesy Fleischmann Yeast Division, Standard Brands, Inc.)

The German *Luftwaffe's* famed blitzkrieg in action.

after the German Luftwaffe had battered London with its blitzkrieg all too long. By January of the next year we were organized into the repetitious and relentless bombing raids over Germany's industries, railways and airdromes.

There was still much fight in Hitler's men, but many events occurred as the Allies went forward and the Russians crossed onto German soil in East Prussia, entered Bulgaria and invaded Hungary and Czechoslovakia. Finland signed an armistice with Russia, as did Bulgaria. In

General D. Eisenhower (left) with Lt. General George S. Patton at the Palermo Airport in Sicily. (U.S. Army photograph)

Meantime, Roosevelt, Churchill and Stalin met at Teheran to make plans for the invasion we were desperately awaiting. General Eisenhower was given the supreme command over the invasion.

This was the day a reverent hush fell over our country and many prayers of all faiths were sent up for our boys— D-Day! There were over four thousand ships, protected by eleven thousand planes, as the American, British and Canadian troops splashed up on the Normandy beaches. Little enemy resistance was offered.

The following month a group of German generals unsuccessfully attempted the assassination of Hitler. It appeared that all Germans did not revere *der Fuehrer.*

It took from June 5th until August 25th to liberate Paris. Do you remember the wild jubilation at this event? Aside from an end of the War and going home, the best an American soldier could hope for was the relief of a few days in Paris after the liberation.

the late fall of 1944 Greece was liberated and by the end of December, we were engaged in the tough "Battle of the Bulge."

As our men slogged on, short of shells and suffering reverses in the Battle of the Bulge, an eager German officer asked one of our officers if he and his men were ready to surrender. The immediate and brief reply was, "NUTS!"

It was getting into 1945 and everyone was war-weary. There were many aspects not yet apparent to Americans. We were praising the Russians' bravery and aid in "liberating" many places that Hitler captured. They were our Allies as well as Britain, Canada and France—the main members. We didn't foresee a time when they would be a threat to us and the free world.

We also didn't know that the Yalta meeting to plan the war's final phases would be the last major meeting that President Roosevelt would have with Churchill and Sta-

This postal card was picked up in a French school as our troops pushed on with the invasion. It is a well-executed drawing of the fearsome-looking Field Marshal von Rundstedt.

On June 6, 1944, Americans read of the successful invasion of Normandy—D-Day. (Courtesy the Detroit News)

General Dwight D. Eisenhower, Lt. General Omar Brad-
ley, and General J. Lawton Collins during a conference
at French headquarters. (U.S. Army photograph)

Headlines such as this made the homefolks feel that our
boys might soon be home. At least, the Germans were
aware of our presence. (Courtesy Detroit News)

lin. By April 12 the country was stunned with the shocking news of Franklin Roosevelt's death.

The next day's papers contained little else than memories of Franklin Roosevelt, tributes from heads of state, lesser officials and plain citizens, plus prayers for Harry S Truman, who was immediately sworn into office. We wondered—was the new chief executive capable of carrying on to a decisive victory? The terrible toll showed in photos of Roosevelt taken at Yalta; he seemed to have been ill then.

On Friday, April 13, 1945, newspapers carried the story of the death of President Roosevelt.

ories of Franklin Roosevelt, tributes from heads of state, lesser officials and plain citizens, plus prayers for Harry S Truman, who was immediately sworn into office. We wondered—was the new chief executive capable of carrying

The picture page showed Franklin Delano Roosevelt from infancy through the many phases of his public life. The sports page ran a photo of the late President as he threw out the first ball for a new baseball season. There

Recall FDR's
3 Visits to City

1936 Crowd Greatest
in Detroit's History

City Mourns
Mr. Roosevelt

City Pays Homage to FDR

By VERA BROWN

PRAYER OF MOURNING

Aged Mother
Offers Prayer

SENATOR BARKLEY, majority leader of the Senate—The death of President Roosevelt is the greatest tragedy that has ever happened to this nation.

SECRETARY OF THE TREASURY MORGENTHAU—It is a tragedy he did not live to see the unconditional surrender of Germany and Japan. I am confident that history will recognize in him a great force for democracy and human rights.

SOVIETS SHARE GRIEF

SOVIET AMBASSADOR ANDREI A. GROMYKO—Mr. Roosevelt's merits in the task of mobilizing the forces of this nation for war against our common enemy, Nazi Germany, are enormous. The Soviet people share this great national grief which has befallen the friendly American people.

SECRETARY OF INTERIOR ICKES—We know what his ideals were. We are, as we have been, in full accord with his aims. President Roosevelt has died for us. President Truman will take up where President Roosevelt left off.

FORMER SECRETARY OF STATE HULL—No greater tragedy could have befallen our country and the world at this time.

SECRETARY OF STATE STETTINUS—Mr. Roosevelt, like Abraham Lincoln, has truly given his life that America might live and freedom be upheld.

SECRETARY OF COMMERCE WALLACE—He was a gallant world citizen who so unerringly acted to save democracy.

Tributes to Roosevelt poured in as Chief Justice Harlan F. Stone administered the oath of office to Harry S Truman.

When President Roosevelt met with Winston Churchill at Casablanca in 1943, we little knew that he would be gone before the War's end. (Courtesy Franklin D. Roosevelt Library)

President Roosevelt

THE greatest calamity to which any nation is subject, the loss by death of its leader upon whom the mantle of power has been bestowed and in whom the affections of its people repose, has befallen the American nation in the death of President Roosevelt.

The shock of this tragic event is not in its suddenness, although that is severe.

The delicate health and impaired physical condition of Mr. Roosevelt have long been well known to the American people, for their prayers attended him throughout the long years of his struggle in the shadow of death, and the indomitable courage and indefatigable spirit with which he endured and finally triumphed over his affliction have been of such example and inspiration to the people that they have seemed of providential intention.

The tragedy of the event is not in the loss of his leadership at the time of his greatest responsibility and power, although that is indeed great.

The leadership of such a man does not end with his life, no more than his name passes from the memory of his countrymen.

★　★　★

THE work and name of Franklin Delano Roosevelt will live on, not only today or tomorrow but in all the annals of recorded time, attesting all the things he achieved, all the things of which he dreamed—in keeping with the great love in which he was held by so many of his people, and with the high trust they placed in him.

The greatest shock and tragedy of this calamitous event is in the manner in which it symbolizes the whole cost and price of war.

Mr. Roosevelt has fallen as a casualty in this terrible war, even as the unknown boy whose life ebbs out on a distant battlefield.

He has given his life for his country.

He loved his country above all else and labored in its service with utter disregard of his own well-being, of his own comforts and conveniences, of life itself.

This is what the death of President Roosevelt means to the American people—as the deaths of so many thousands of beloved Americans have come to mean in so many homes.

★　★　★

ALL of those who die in this war make the meaning of these facts clear to us.

They do not die in vain.

They do not leave tasks undone.

Those who have given their all have lost nothing, but gained the fulfillment of deeds and dreams.

President Roosevelt is among these exalted and immortal dead, a leader and honored among them—tried by the same tests of loyalty and devotion as the least of them, and proved by these tests as the most heroic and faithful of them.

America has suffered an incalculable and irreplaceable loss in the death of President Roosevelt.

But in being a nation so faithfully served as he and all the other casualties of this war have served, so gladly served and so worth serving, it measures up to their sacrifice.

 **1882**　　　**1945**

This solemn editorial appeared in the Detroit *News* the day after the President's death. (Courtesy the Detroit *News*)

These three pictures show F.D.R. at different stages of his career. (Courtesy Detroit News)

were stories of his friendship with the sports world.

Nine days after the President's death, Russia reached Berlin. We were forcing our way along and across the Rhine River in several locations. Americans and Russians finally met face-to-face near Berlin, and it was cause for celebration.

On April 28, 1945, another startling event came with the rapid turn of the times; those who had been loyal to Italy assassinated Mussolini. Somewhat as Shakespeare said . . . "the evil that men do lives after them, the good is oft interred with the bones . . . " *Il Duce's* dream of empire had come to an infamous close as his body was desecrated in the streets.

Only the third day after Mussolini's assassination came the announcement the free world had prayed for—an end to the insane Hitler regime. Mystery shrouded the actual death and there were conflicting reports. But Adolph Hitler was seen no more—dead or alive. Admiral Karl Doenitz replaced the evil dictator.

In the evening paper, the day after Hitler's presumed death, we read of the unconditional surrender of Nazis in Italy. The Reds in Berlin launched a final, bloody assault on the shambles of the German Chancellory.

I shall never forget V-E Day! There was only one radio that still worked and it had been spared so it could be heard on the day of victory. New tubes weren't available

On April 30, 1945, it was revealed that Mussolini had been assassinated by his own countrymen. (Courtesy Detroit News)

The Detroit Free Press

WEDNESDAY, MAY 2, 1945   On Guard for Over a Century   Vol. 114—No. 363   Five Cents

Germans Announce:

HITLER DEAD

Hitler's death was revealed on May 2, 1945.

NAZIS IN ITALY SURRENDER!

On the same date that Hitler's death was announced, his followers in Italy surrendered. (Courtesy Detroit *Times*)

DETROIT TIMES 8 STAR

45th Year, No. 214   C   Detroit 31, Mich., Wednesday, May 2, 1945   5 Cents   COMPLETE WANT ADS

Nazi Radio Announces:

WAR ENDS IN EUROPE

LONDON, May 7 (INS)—Amidst general expectancy that formal announcement of the end of hostilities in Europe

The headlines screamed out the happy news: V-E Day had arrived! (Courtesy the Detroit *News*)

and radio repair was almost non-obtainable. This Monday started like the other bleak wartime days, but suddenly neighbors ran into the streets and yards laughing and shouting. I turned on the precious radio and the surrender news tumbled out . . . still unofficial. They said the air in New York was so full of paper that people could scarcely see. I ran outside, giggling and shouting to the assemblage, happier than any of them because I'd been the only war "widow" on the street. With a small baby to tend, I couldn't celebrate further from home.

On the 8th, V-E Day was official. I turned the radio on at six o'clock in the morning and the faithful old set ran steadily until midnight. Regular programs were off so that interviews with a cross-section of people in cities across the United States could be aired. The celebrations in Europe's capitals were also reported. President Truman

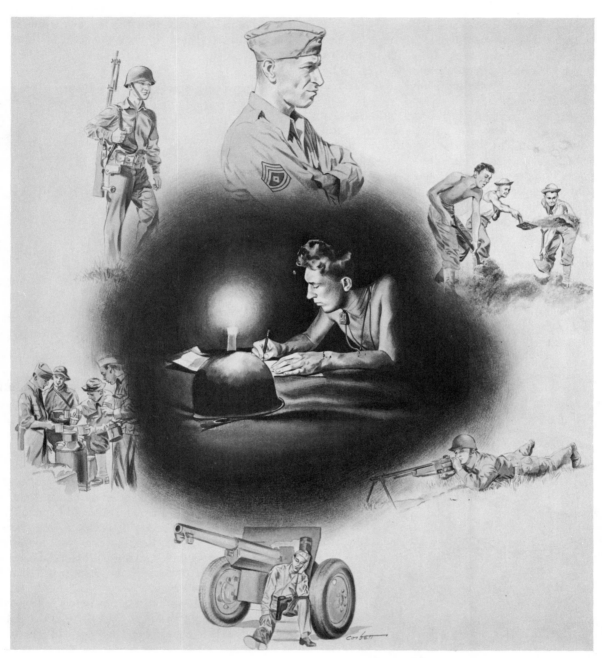

A routine day in the life of an American soldier. The "top kick" was tough, the work hard. Who could blame the sleepy soldier for napping, except maybe all of the top brass? After walking, digging, guarding, shooting and eating, GI Joe still wrote home, "Dear Mom . . ."

read the Armistice Proclamation while we thanked God that it was over.

In spite of the joy at the conclusion of the European war, we still had a formidable foe in the Pacific, and he hadn't shown signs of surrender.

During November of 1943, the United States Marines took Tarawa and Makin in the Gilbert Islands. The 1944 winter brought reports of the atrocious treatment that brave defenders of Bataan and Corregidor were receiving from the Japs. This was the kind of news that sickened our souls but doubled our determination.

Do you remember the most famous example of brevity in a dispatch? "Sighted sub, sank same!" There were other words of the War that caught the fancy, even to being enshrined in a popular wartime song, "Praise the Lord and Pass the Ammunition."

While we gained control of the Marshall Islands, attacked the Japanese fleet and airbase in the Caroline Islands, and seized bases in the Admiralties, necessity accomplished amazing feats elsewhere. The Alcan Highway, built in 1942 by the United States Army Engineers, was a prime example of work done under extreme difficulties. The following year this 1523-mile road was renamed the Alaska Highway and served as a supply route during the War. As well as the northernmost section of the Pan American Highway system which would extend into South America.

The Pacific Theater was so vast, dotted with numberless islands, that the mere geography of the situation was staggering. Our forces were taking, invading and overcoming the enemy in many far-flung places, but with our

landing on Leyte, General MacArthur was back in the Philippines, and engagements here broke the back of the Japanese fleet.

By January of 1945 MacArthur reached Manila. Bataan was soon retaken and as promised, he indeed did return. Paratroopers swarmed over Corregidor. Some of the names that would become most familiar were about to be bloody battlegrounds—Okinawa and Iwo Jima.

The British broke the stranglehold and liberated Burma from the Japanese. We had enough bases, plus carriers, to enable us to bomb industries in Tokyo, but it took from the first of April in 1945 until the sixth of June to finally gain Okinawa.

The mushroom cloud over Hiroshima: most Americans were unaware their country possessed such a terrible weapon.

The Potsdam Conference dealt not only with peace terms in Europe, but surrender demands were made to Japan by the United States, Britain and China. The course of history might have read differently if Japan had heeded this ultimatum. A little less than two weeks later the atom bomb was dropped on Hiroshima. Most Americans didn't even know what this ferocious weapon was—so secretive had been the work on it.

Three days later another atom bomb fell on Nagasaki. It quickly brought the Japs to their reluctant knees. The world couldn't comprehend reports of the extent of devastation.

The day after the Nagasaki bombing, Japan offered to quit the war. Radio Tokyo said, "Indiscriminate use by the United States of such atomic weapons as the atomic bomb, constituted a new crime against the whole of humanity and civilization."

Dinner wasn't very fancy fare for our boys who labored in the Pacific jungles.

After the second bomb fell, on Nagasaki, the Japanese offered to surrender. (Courtesy Detroit News)

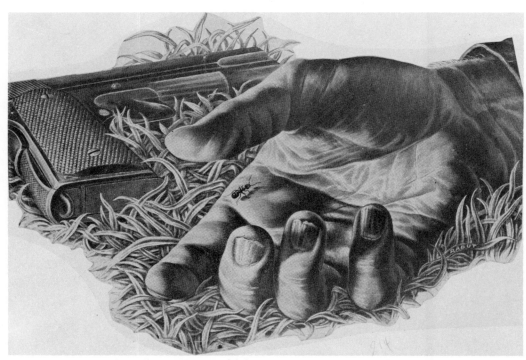

What illustration could better attest to the futility and waste of war than this award-winning painting by Paul Rabut. (Used by permission of the artist)

Discussing the use of this bomb, President Truman said; "It had been unleashed against those who attacked us without warning at Pearl Harbor . . . against those who have starved, beaten and executed American prisoners of war, against those who have abandoned all pretense of obeying international laws of warfare."

"This solemn moment of triumph, one of the greatest moments in the history of the world . . . is going to lift up humanity to a higher plane of existence for all the ages of the future." So uttered David Lloyd George in 1918. If it failed then, was it proven in 1945—will it be proven by 2000? Who will know the answer?

9

Soldiers Without Uniforms

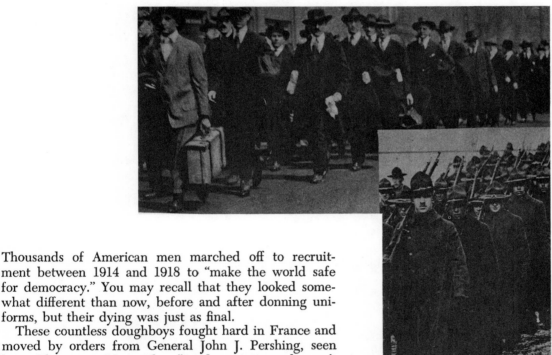

Thousands of men marching off to war, 1917. (Courtesy the Detroit *News*)

Thousands of American men marched off to recruitment between 1914 and 1918 to "make the world safe for democracy." You may recall that they looked somewhat different than now, before and after donning uniforms, but their dying was just as final.

These countless doughboys fought hard in France and moved by orders from General John J. Pershing, seen here. They sang "Over There" and patriotic zeal wasn't out of style in American homes. Women knitted with much khaki yarn and the men who weren't fighting made the homefront buzz for the cause. We sold Liberty Bonds and stamps; Elsie Janis was the "Sweetheart of the A.E.F."

Those old enough to remember believed that our efforts, whether at home or in service, were going to make a world order better than any previously experienced by humankind. Great heroic paintings were made, showing the Allied forces triumphantly marching under the Arc d'Triomphe and angels with unfurled flags, lighted torches, golden swords and all of the storied trappings due a victorious army that had battled for a noble cause. There was something about it that swelled the breast and made civilians proud if they'd done their utmost.

Something went wrong because the world wasn't safe for democracy when alien ideologies began to push their weights against those who loved peace and minded their own affairs. Europe was again embroiled with Germany, but instead of a militaristic Kaiser, it was caused by a maniac paperhanger named Hitler.

America nervously eyed and eared the situation and determined to stay out instead of learning the lyrics to "Over There" again. Like most plans, they were subject

"Black Jack" Pershing. (U.S. Army Photograph)

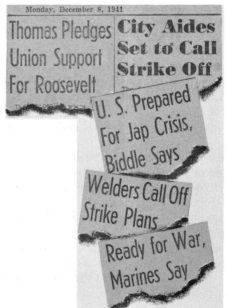

On the homefront, Americans immediately geared themselves to the war effort. (Courtesy Detroit News)

to change without warning when the quiet of a Sunday was shattered on December 7, 1941, with news at home of the general carnage in Pearl Harbor. Like it or not, we *were* in a war again. Now World Wars became numbered—I and II. There was only one way for Americans to go, straight ahead with sleeves rolled up and machines a-roar. It is good to let the unhappy memories of war moulder into forgetfulness, but since it was reality, we should be jogged to remember what the American public did as soldiers without uniforms.

One class of fighter who was pressed into many new duties overnight was the housewife. One ad read, "When a nation goes to war, many must serve at home. Meals must be prepared from less food. Clothes must be provided, but fewer new ones. These are your problems and you've buckled to them with the courage and patriotism of the fightingest soldier."

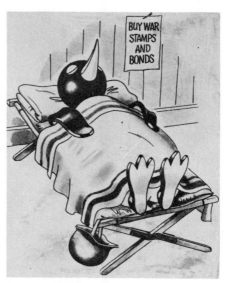

Those with green thumbs were urged to grow "Victory Gardens."

One urging that bore some fruit and vegetables, if you had a green thumb, was the "victory garden." Mom was given credit for helping the food supply by preserving the yield. Pop and the kids could grow and hoe. There was a Victory Garden Committee to help those who had

probably never touched a hoe before. Some of my neighbors either replaced flowers with vegetables, or planted in vacant lots where in some cases seedlings drowned from heavy spring rains. I planted tomatoes between the ornamental evergreens and they fared better than the trees. There was jubilation when a neighbor boasted of his first radish, worm-eaten though it was.

Willy the Penguin switched from cigarettes to the war effort. (Reprinted by permission of Brown and Williamson Tobacco Corp.)

Multitudes of advertisers quit their usual selling in magazines and newspapers since many had little civilian merchandise to sell after peacetime plants were pressed into war goods manufacture. They ran institutional advertising to keep their names alive while also giving pep talks and victory propaganda to those at home. One ad said, "You can't work like a horse if you eat like a bird. Give that warworker husband of yours a breakfast that a man can really sink his teeth into."

We were asked to save many things that had before been waste material. Boy Scouts came to our doors to collect flattened, de-labeled tin cans that had contained food. We turned in paper—newspapers and magazines—and kept rolls of foil by adding every scrap we found on packaging or even along the street. Some rolls became so heavy we could scarcely lug them to the gathering agencies.

Everyone was attuned to the community effort. Even Hart, Schaffner and Marx urged us to shorten the war to "save 100,000 lives a month and $300,000,000 a day."

Stores urged women shoppers to carry their parcels instead of having small purchases delivered.

Rationing was one of the starkest war reminders for civilians. Fleischmann's Yeast ran ration-easing recipes

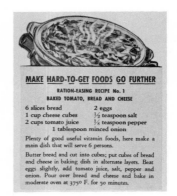

Ration-easing recipes appeared. (Courtesy of Fleischmann Yeast Division, Standard Brands, Inc.)

We were suddenly asked to save our scrap paper. The newspapers spread the word. (Courtesy Detroit News)

Hart, Schaffner and Marx appealed to our patriotism. (Courtesy Hart, Schaffner and Marx)

in their ads. They said, "This war won't be won by the driving force of fighting men alone. The way you eat has a lot to do with the way you discharge your part in the war job."

Have you forgotten about V-Mail? It was onion skin paper, but the lightness of it promised to speed your letters to relatives and friends in service. Considering the bulk of mail added to the regular amount, anything to lighten the load was desirable.

There were not only pleas to win the victory, but talk about the necessity of winning the peace. From every side we were reminded of the urgency of buying War Bonds. Stromberg Carlson devoted a full page magazine space to a helmeted soldier's wishes in the civilian world when he returned. "Promise to have a good America waiting when I return . . . this time I'll want a peace which is lasting . . . a world that's designed for living together. I'll want freedom and bread . . . justice and plumbing

. . . equality and a stout pair of shoes! It's up to you thinking people back home to see that I get 'em." So hundreds of thousands of us had War Bond money deducted from our paychecks. Others bought them as they could. Too many didn't appreciate their purpose or the wisdom of saving, so bought them one week and cashed them the next.

There were transportation problems. Maybe you have memories of the wartime car pool. It had good and bad aspects. There were people who'd never been punctual in their lives and meeting the car-of-the-week late caused friction. In some pools, illicit romance developed when

Women, accustomed to having parcels delivered, were urged to carry them home instead. (Illustration by the author for the Ernst Kern Co.)

FAST! CLEAR!
CONVENIENT!
TICONDEROGA WRITTEN
V-MAIL

Write your V-Mail with a pencil — a Ticonderoga pencil! Ticonderogas are fast convenient, dependable. V-Mail itself. Just as Uncle Sam gets your V-Mail there in half the time, a Ticonderoga pencil enables you to write it with half as much energy as with an ordinary pencil.

And remember, your fighting man will write more often if you send him a box of Ticonderogas.

A fine American Pencil with a fine American name..

TICONDEROGA

Pencil-makers urged the use of their product when writing "V-Mail." (Courtesy of Joseph Dixon Crucible Co., makers of Ticonderoga Pencils)

mixed groups shared the ride. Some were willing riders until it was their turn to drive. An inventive housewife saved gas ration stamps by carrying her child in a back seat installed on a bicycle.

Not a bit of space was wasted in newspaper columns. Niches could be chinked in with such suggestions as "Every soldier has his duty—Buy War Bonds!" Or, "Lights? Obey dim-out regulations."

In newspaper retail advertising, no heading or copy was right without some mention of the "effort" no matter what was being sold. "It's every woman's wartime duty to keep fit" might sound like a patent medicine ad, but in reality warm robes were advertised. Charge accounts by mail were offered to busy patriots. These patriots were everyone directly or indirectly contributing to our national output. It didn't matter whether the firm you worked for made battleships or breakfast food.

Wars always cause appeals for woman power. There may have been complaints from men and some women about the postwar times when more women wanted to continue working after war needs passed. They liked the additional income and the luxuries it could buy. This full page bought by Macy's Department Stores ran in the New York *Sun* in 1942 to announce many new job opportunities for women. These included previously male jobs like crane operation, steel plant work, mechanic's apprentices in the Brooklyn Navy Yard, machinist's helpers, electricians and shipfitting helpers. A predicted five million women would be working for the war effort, including the women's military auxiliaries.

"Whistle While You Work" was a good theme song for female factoryites. Some Detroit war plants piped in music from a central control to help workers along.

"Rosy the Riveter" was a common tag for girls doing such work as riveting seams on sections of planes. If there was a derogatory connotation to the title, it should be remembered that girls from all classes and walks of life entered into the total effort. Many so-called white collar

This Macy's ad was a hymn to American womanhood.
(Courtesy Macy's Herald Square, New York)

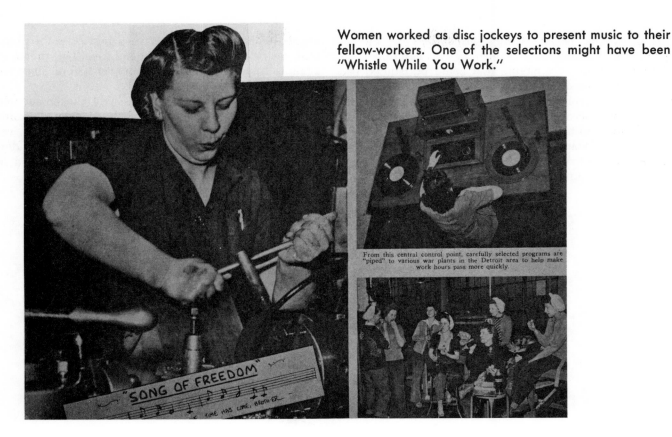

Women worked as disc jockeys to present music to their fellow-workers. One of the selections might have been "Whistle While You Work."

"SONG OF FREEDOM"

THE TIME HAS COME, BROTHER

From this central control point, carefully selected programs are "piped" to various war plants in the Detroit area to help make work hours pass more quickly.

workers donned factory overalls and identification buttons to do entirely different work than they'd known behind office typewriters.

We called it the battle of production as the machines whirred at top speed. Many plants were converted to products quite different from those made in peacetime. An example: the American Type Founders changed from making type faces for printing to the manufacture of shells.

Typical civilian soldiers saved gas by peddling bicycles to and from war jobs. Such emergencies as war created changed living patterns for civilians as well as soldiers—only the design was less dangerous.

It wasn't only in factories that the home front labored. Young and old volunteers filled vacancies among crop harvesters. Football teams and high schoolers aided in harvesting all over the nation. In spite of black marketeers and the "fifth column," the image of a united America was everywhere.

Newspaper articles about our food supply or lack of it were frequent. In May, 1943, we read of empty meat counters. In case you remember those dreary days, the bare meat counters were widespread before rationing went into effect. The shy person didn't have a chance with the aggressors or butcher's friends. Complaints were heaped on the OPA (Office of Price Administration) for the way the meat stamps were issued or timed. Some hoarded red stamps so a large meat purchase could be made all at once.

It was not uncommon to invite guests with a request for ration stamps as an "admission fee." Some hostesses

fared well on this basis. I attended a spaghetti dinner for fifteen guests, and the entire pot of spaghetti contained no more than a pound of precious ground meat in marble-sized meatballs. There was one shrunken marble on my serving but the stamps I'd contributed would have bought my meat supply for a week. Good news was an occasional announcement of a reduction in points for a given item; thirteen varieties of Kosher meats were reduced one point.

The apprehension of a food thief caused a judge to put his crime in the same category as that of a saboteur. One culprit got a year in jail for stealing 540 ration points worth of canned goods. The point value was so high on canned fruits that many people didn't taste them all through the rationing period. Alongside the price tags on grocery shelves was the ration point value.

There was plain talk in editorials by the end of 1944, aimed directly at the home front. How large should our Army be? We were warned that Adolph Hitler had taken many gambles to accomplish his goals. His last and biggest gamble was that the Americans at home wouldn't be willing to make war as the Russians and English did. If we became as inspired as the boys of Guadalcanal, Hitler had no chance in the long run. However, if we stayed in a state of confusion, ignorance and apathy, he could succeed. There were arguments about the size of armed forces the Joint Staff wanted. Some thought that American civilians would be too few to support such an army. Either those at home wanted to make the total effort or just to talk about it.

We had to think beyond grocery store shelves and

black markets, beyond labor's wishes and the internal politics of Washington. The meaning was painfully clear. All was not the best picture that could be painted of a completely united, impenetrable front. There were hoarders, cheaters, profiteers and those who wanted the continuance of war because they'd never earned so much money. People still had the vices and virtues intact.

If we grew war-weary at home and abroad, there were songs and ads to occasionally remind us that there would someday be a dove of peace winging our way. We dared yet to dream. Science had learned how to make plastics from soy beans, peanuts, wheat and trees. One dream was again to travel, maybe more than ever before, since we'd been home-locked for so long.

Peace finally came! There was wild excitement when radios blared the cease-fire news. Even in small hamlets everyone broke into smiles at everyone. In cities, celebrations were unrestrained. Maybe we hadn't shouldered guns, but the soldiers without uniforms felt they'd had a real part in the victory!

Wartime ads occasionally reminded us there would be peace again some day. (Courtesy Delco-Remy Division of General Motors)

10

Three Thousand Dollars for a House?

A roof over our heads is as important as a good cave was to early man, but how that roof has changed! We used to call an elegant house a "palace" but whether impressive or modest, it's still "man's castle," the biggest single investment of a lifetime.

The evolution of home architecture has kept pace with all changes, but whereas some styles are ageless, others become freakish within a few years. The attempt to popularize Spanish architecture in the Midwest about thirty-five years ago left a few bad examples strewn conspicuously on the landscape where they were not "at home."

The "modern" home. (Chester Janczarek Photo)

When the "modern" house first appeared, designers seemed to be lost. A few people braved the derision of neighbors and friends by erecting the flat-topped, boxy structures. Some looked like small factories.

One standard style that was built by the thousands was a "square" house. Its hip-roof went up from four sides to

A Dutch Colonial Home. (1931 *Pictorial Review*)

The gambrel-roofed Dutch Colonial tried to be popular but the roofs always reminded one of barns.

The "square" house. (*Women's Home Companion*, c. 1925)

a point at the top center. The outer material and trim varied, but underneath it was unmistakenly square—offering the most inside space for the money with no fancy furbelows.

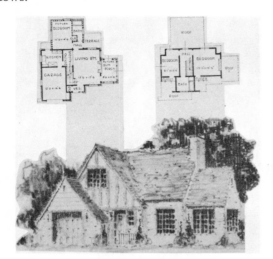

The English influence. (*Pictorial Review*)

The English influence showed in adaptations small or large, especially in the thirties. Above the brick veneer of the lower half was the "half-timbered" effect over stucco.

The Colonial. (*Pictorial Review*)

The Colonial pictured was called "the ideal small house," but it achieved the illusion of size. It wasn't especially individual because of the limited room arrangements possible: a central hall with the living room on one side and the dining room on the other. The sun room added size and elegance to break the regularity, plus providing a place for the wicker furniture.

This cottage bears the French influence. (*The Pictorial Review*)

Prior to the Depression the attentions of many architects were not directed to small, modest cottages. Pictured is one with the French influence. The copy says that "this distinctive cottage proves that good design is possible, *even* in two-bedroom houses." Indeed! If they hadn't left the mansions and learned to design two-bedroom homes, starvation could have lurked among the turrets when the Depression came.

Compactness was stressed in all of these small house styles but they still managed to fit in three bedrooms and two baths.

The design of the mansion explains why architects didn't enjoy planning small rooms inside "cracker boxes." Shown is an English home built near Rochester, Michigan, in the twenties on beautiful, rolling countryside. It could be mistaken for a university or other organization such as a country club. The lady of the house could scarcely do her own housework.

During the upheaval of size and style in forty-five years, some went completely out then crept back in—updated. The mansard roof became a museum piece until it recently reappeared as a sort of "falsie" trim on apartments, stores and some homes.

The low-pitched hip roof has looked modern for over thirty years. (Chester Janczarek Photo)

Ageless styles that have gracefully weathered the years are farmhouses, Cape Cod cottages, Colonials and the low-pitched hip roof with a wide overhang. The latter has looked modern for thirty years or more. "Face-lift" remodeling has progressed to the point where a weathered monstrosity can feel snobbish on a street with new houses.

This mansion could have been mistaken for a country club. (Courtesy Detroit *News*)

The mansard roof was a museum piece for awhile, but it has recently reemerged. (Janco Fotos)

Do you remember the stuccos of the twenties? One was wet-cement gray with nubbly little stones embedded like peanuts in chocolate candy. Another finer textured stucco had sparkly particles in the mixture Stone houses were solid for the ages with rounded, uncut rocks and deeply raked joints for an extremely bumpy appearance. An unusual roof had edges that rolled under like a "page-boy bob," with wood shingles laid in waves like the ocean. It was an expensive way to achieve the look of an old thatched roof.

Landscaping doesn't need to go in and out of style much, since trees, shrubs and plants still have varying green leaves, flowers, branches and runners. However, man has devised ways to divert natural forms. Do you remember the trees cut into geometric and animal forms? Formally balanced arrangements were popular around large homes.

If you hankered for a fair-sized formal garden covering an acre, an itemized list showed what this might cost. Plants, statuary and installation could run from $30,000 to $40,000. Then, like ladies in evening dress, gardens had to be meticulously groomed. A head gardener got $2000 and up per year, with undergardeners, one for each type of garden, $1200 annually. Laborers expected $3.50 per day. If economy was an issue, green-thumbers could coax cuttings thrown away by greenhouses into vigorous growth.

Outdoor living was expressed by a swing of a familiar design. It was likely that your front porch in the twenties

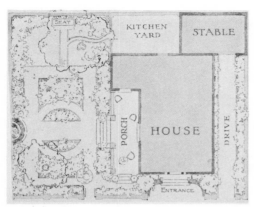

A floor plan for a house, with formal garden. (*Woman's Home Companion*)

heard the squeaking of a wooden swing, suspended from the porch ceiling by chains. It was a perfect place for young lovers to say goodnight.

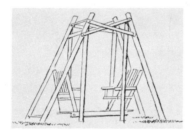

The familiar design for an outdoor swing.

In the "modernized" thirties you graduated to a gaily striped glider. Add another decade and home barbecues sprouted in back yards. They were usually of brick or

Everybody seems to be having a good time at this outdoor barbecue, 1938 style. (1938 *Homes of the West*)

stone masonry with iron grids and plates that saw more rust than usage. It's assumed they were located at the back corners of lots to keep smoke from the house and the housewives in training for the hundred meter dash. By the time a meal was ready the neighbors got ninety per cent of the smoke and the little woman sank from exhaustion.

If outside house styles weren't exactly what we'd choose now, neither were many of the interiors. Some houses remain mellowly fine and rooms may have the same quality. The pictured examples are attractive today because of warm, friendly gaiety and our continuous passion for Early American furnishings. Flowered cretonne popped out to greet you in doorways, at windows and on slipcovers, but cheeriness prevailed. Dropleaf, gateleg tables were "musts"—pictures showed their hanging wires and bridge lamps lighted the scene. Window seats have all but gone—alas.

No proper living room was complete without a piano, the baby grand being more aesthetically pleasing than an upright. Note the archway drapes that fluttered with every passing breeze.

An idea that boomed into big business was to send old rugs to the Olson factory, and in return receive a "new" rug, woven from your old material. All were in solid colors with lighter-toned plain border bands. You could order the dye color to be used, but no matter what you chose, the rug was distinctively recognizable as an Olson.

Every few years there's an ugly period when taste is lost and grace of design is swallowed by garish, over-exaggerated form. You recall the disdain for Mid-Victorian gingerbread and furbelows. In the twenties and thirties none of us were contented until we had a set of "overstuffed," an understated name. The set consisted of a davenport, rocker and lounge chair—each sticking out its cheeks as if inflated and about to burst. Bristly mo-

An interior of forty years ago. (*Pictorial Review*)

Olson would reweave your old rugs. Here is an example of one. They would use your original material, and dye it to suit your convenience. (Courtesy Olson Rug Co.)

The garish, overexaggerated, overstuffed furniture of the thirties.

hair was a popular upholstery material. Sometimes the mohair or velour had cut designs or tapestry seats would break the mohair monotony.

Our first self-conscious tries in the new age of furnishing got off to a slow, uncertain start. There were variations to the name: modern, modernist or modernistic. What the "istic" added to the meaning is a mystery. Three characteristics dominated the trend—heaviness, flamboyant color and violent geometric patterns, some resembling jagged lightning. Throw rugs were treacherous on highly waxed floors.

The "modern" period featured heaviness, flamboyant color, and violent geometric patterns.

In the thirties, color invaded the previously all-white bathroom. (*Pictorial Review*)

The size of yesterday's homes was evidenced in this spacious bathroom, divided into compartments for each function. It invited you to spend the day under the vaulted ceiling.

If revolution was apparent elsewhere in the house, the bathroom wasn't forgotten. Color invaded the heretofore white fixtures. Sometimes it would even be black. Did you strain your back trying to get the last hint-of-lint from a black tub?

The card was hung so that the amount you wanted was the figure the iceman could read. Our icebox was loaded through the top with a door that lifted up. We stooped low to fish for the foods wanted in the "generous" five cubic foot box. Where was the frozen food compartment?

The kitchen of the twenties. (Courtesy the Hoosier Manufacturing Co.)

Do you have pleasant memories of your 1920 "dream" kitchen? It was large, with plenty of space for those extra steps we hadn't thought of saving. Your separate kitchen cabinet had a niche for everything: ingenious flour and sugar dispensers, room for dishes, utensils, staples and glassware within its confines. The working shelf pulled out for more area. If you had the latest stove (a gas range), it was hoisted to working height on metal legs. The non-integrated hood wasn't especially effective, but it was a step in the right direction. A single sink was hung in space on the wall with no thought of built-ins below or around. We had no stoppers like today. If you were thoroughly modern a rubber suction disk could be bought at the hardware to hold water in the sink.

Let's suppose the modern trend hadn't caught up to you yet. The kitchen you recall might have been more old-fashioned. Instead of "work islands" in the center, the old wooden kitchen table covered with oilcloth was where goodies were concocted, non-company meals were eaten and everyone congregated. The mistress of this room was indeed fortunate for those days because she had a good, solid, "icebox" and didn't have to go far to pump cistern water—even though the pump always needed priming before it would work.

In case you've forgotten the details, here's how the interior of your icebox might have looked. The size was determined by the ice-holding capacity—fifty, one hundred or more pounds in the chunk. The ice company provided a window card that was used on delivery day. The card had four large numbers printed on it, one for each side.

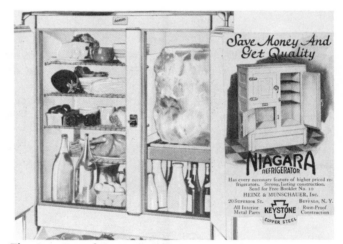

The interior of an icebox. (*Woman's Home Companion*)

The 1920 lady would look at you astonished, "What's frozen food?"

If you were progressive and prosperous, you bought a mechanical refrigerator as soon as they appeared. This might have been earlier than you think—1915! It was a modern miracle even though it eliminated the friendly iceman and the pan running over with ice water. The guardian refrigerator was the first self-contained household unit, the forerunner of the present-day Frigidaire refrigerator. The cabinet was of solid oak and insulation

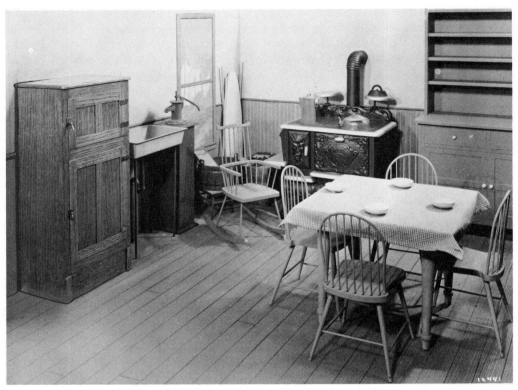

The old-fashioned kitchen: note the wooden icebox and the pump. (Courtesy of Frigidaire Division of General Motors Corp.)

was dried seawood. Freezing space consisted of slots for two ice trays, the removal of which was left to the ingenuity of the homemaker.

If you were up-to-date you had many small appliances, but electric toasters didn't pop the bread up and you had to be the timer on the electric percolator.

In 1925 public school eighth grade art classes were given color plates, as an ideal to follow for proper ar-

Small electrical appliances of yesterday: the bread didn't pop out of the toaster, and the coffee pot didn't turn itself off.

rangement of living room items. Fancy runners on tables and antimacassars on chair arms and backs were the norm. Fine lampshades were of thin silk gathered tightly over wire frames and edged with silk fringe. Beaded lampshades grew popular—small, round granules of glass were embedded in an adhesive painted on a parchment base.

Wallpaper couldn't be overlooked. We used to pore over wallpaper catalogues for an evening's entertainment and hold the small samples to the wall to imagine how a roomful of it would strike us. We hadn't heard of doing just a wall or two; all four walls and ceiling were always papered and all designs included a border trim, usually floral. As a child, I loved the ceiling paper with silver stars—just like in the sky.

Picture-hanging was an exact science with do's and don'ts in the rules. The subjects must be appropriate to the room and its furnishings; *never* have white margins around pictures unless the walls are white—or one large picture can be balanced by two smaller ones. *Never* have a triangle of wire showing above a square picture; *never* try to make a home into an art gallery!

The house of our dreams has always been our heart s desire in any decade. Can you imagine: a family with an average income (1929 to 1939 average was $2500) could build a home planned from the inside out for convenience to the housewife that would cost only $4000 to

The first refrigerator. It appeared in 1915, believe it or not! (Courtesy Frigidaire Division, General Motors Corp.)

A page from a 1920 wallpaper catalog.

A color plate like this would be given to eighth-grade art students as an ideal arrangement of living room items. (Courtesy Arthur L. Guptill, Jr.)

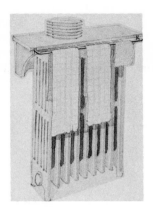

The unsightly steam radiator was a decorating problem. Here was a solution for dressing it up and also drying towels with the heat.

In the twenties you probably did not have a steam or hot air furnace yet, especially if you lived in a rural area. Here were bargain models for living room and kitchen—and guaranteed to burn you! (Courtesy Detroit *News*)

3-Pc. Lloyd Fibre Suite

$43⁹⁵

If you were tired of staring at shabby sunroom furniture, here was an opportunity to get a new set cheaply. (Courtesy Pontiac *Daily Press*)

This make-it-yourself vanity added charm to bed or dressing rooms. Two orange crates were joined by a plank, the ruffles were added . . . no one was the wiser.

$4500? A group of architects, landscape designers and decorators planned a series of small home plans for a nominal fee. These houses were scaled to your income unless it was under $2500, in which case you were advised not to build. If you earned $10,000 per annum, you could afford seven or eight rooms in a $16,000 house. All incomes and homes were scaled accordingly.

What sumptuous choices you had in the plans! You could have ceiling lights and an arrangement for connecting movable lamps. Today we'd say outlets or plugs. Floors could be hardwood—far superior was oak to pine. A fireplace wasn't only for the living room, but the dining room too. A sleeping porch? It was optional, as was the placement of the water closet (toilet) in a separate room from the tub. Many wanted pantries between dining rooms and kitchens. You could even have a rest corner in the kitchen—bargain luxury!

An economical house could be built for $1200 to $3600 that had an ingenious stove. It looked like a sleek gas range, but it not only cooked—it heated the house and water supply too. This marvel was insulated so only lids were hot to the touch. Coal was received through a vent in a kitchen bin, convenient to the stove, with no scuttle needed. Much better than an empty woodbox!

A cost breakdown of pioneerings into prefabrication showed the most expensive item was $865.30 for walls, windows and exterior doors. Kitchen cabinets were a mere $40. The total bill ran to $3500. One room added

This late-twenties dream house was in the $4500 price range. (Courtesy Woman's Home Companion)

would cost that much now as against a five hundred dollar difference between four or five rooms then.

The building trades were extremely hard hit when the Depression came. In the beginning, advertisements pleaded with prospective customers to take advantage of rock bottom costs. The ads warned it wasn't a time for pro-

crastination, but little did anyone know how long the Depression would linger. If 1931 home prices make us weep today, consider the lower incomes or unemployment that had to be faced for an indefinite time. As always—when bargains are about, we don't have the money.

In 1933 there was a property in an exclusive, hilly suburb of Detroit that begged for a buyer who would pay $29,000 for a ten room house, rolling small acreage with a natural pond, large swimming pool, (unusual then), tennis court and greenhouses. There were no prospects for this unbelievable bargain until the Depression faded.

When our entrance into the War was reality, the real estate and building pictures changed—never to be the same again. Just before our guns roared, some areas mushroomed with new houses, modest two- and three-bedroom dwellings in huge suburbs "in the sticks" that had been fallow fields before. By 1942 not a hammer was raised for houses because materials were unobtainable and our men had gone to fight. Building didn't resume until about 1946 and never again at prices resembling those we'd known. With unionization of workers and inflated material costs, the ownership of a home was like tagging onto the tail of a comet.

11

Down at the Corner Store

Housewife of days past chats with her friendly grocer; he knew her by name, and gave her personal service.

We had no supermarkets such as today—baffling arrays that can be measured in acres or miles. We even *knew* our grocer and butcher. He called us by name, passed the time of day and asked about our family. It was helpful to take a memorandum to the store because we stood in front of the counter while he trotted around behind it to gather the requested items. We could charge grocery and meat accounts and phone in orders that were delivered the same day. It may sound luxurious, but shopping has changed considerably.

It was handy to have children old enough to send to the store, with the correct change and full instructions or a note. One of my childhood tragedies was falling on the way home from buying milk. I entered the kitchen with sobs, skinned knees, but still gripping the neck of the bottle—the only part remaining. Yes, all milk came in breakable bottles.

The grocer could be a family friend for he'd point out good buys, stick a few extra stalks or pieces of something

in the bag, save choice, off-season delicacies for you that were "shipped in." Dingy glass might not make the baked goods in the case on the counter look inviting, but we ate the pastries anyhow, not being particularly germ-conscious. Some diligent housewives scoffed, "bakery stuff," but as you see, commercial baked goods have survived. Cheese was dispensed from under a big round glass or celluloid cover that kept the inevitable flies out. How good the free sample sliver of cheese tasted in comparison to the piece you took home. An attempt to rid markets of flies was done by suspending long, tape-like rolls of sticky flypaper from ceilings. It was almost as hard for humans to get loose from the gripping mess as the flies, especially if it touched your hair.

As a child, my favorite place in the grocery was near the coffee-grinder. I inhaled the fragrant aroma as the grocer ground customer's coffee. Many people preferred to buy the beans that came in a heavy paper bag, then have it freshly ground to the desired fineness.

A few chain stores began to appear in our area in the twenties—A&P, Kroger's and the C. F. Smith Company—but it didn't seem that they'd make great inroads on our corner store. Many customers scorned those "octopus chains," as did the little independent storekeepers. Each had to eventually admit that the chain could sell cheaper with quantity buying. The friendly store down the block could only combat the lower prices and bigger stocks by remaining open eighteen hours per day, seven days a week. It was pitiful to see them give up like a man dangling from a trestle by his fingertips.

If all refrigerators weren't sold from palatial palaces with arches and vaulted ceilings, at least the advertising artist felt it was a proper setting for the revolutionary mechanical ice-making invention. If the present generation thinks these pictured marvels weren't special alongside today's gleaming, sleek boxes, then they've never stooped to the overflowing ice water pan under the old "ice box." Everyone in the family always regarded this

A grocery store of the twenties. (Courtesy General Electric Co. Housewares Division)

as a job for "George," except that some families had no one named George. With the advent of this electric, wife-saving device, out went one of the children's cherished pastimes—chasing the ice wagon or truck down the street to wheedle or swipe a sliver of ice from under the canvas cover.

It wasn't only refrigerators that were displayed and sold in spacious shops. One of the early big names in the new radio industry had the same idea. Instead of loading its stores with many console radio sets, Atwater Kent left generous walking space, and would invite prospective customers to sit while listening to music from the marvelous mechanisms that were almost free of static. Think of the number of color television sets today that would be sandwiched into the wasted floor space! Also, think of the amount of rent today for said space.

When the "new" modern decorating came to the retail business, it revolutionized stores inside and out—providing they succumbed to modernity. Many did, and it appeared that some had gone berserk with color, mirrors, drapes and pipe railings. Good modern décor was yet to come in a tastier interpretation. Baked enamel panels with gaudily colored designs were installed as false fronts on many old buildings, giving streets a comically incongruous mixture of old and new.

Gone now are all but a precious few of yesterday's little bakeries, wafting their taste-tingling perfume onto the street. You could see the flour-dusted baker at work in the back room.

Have you been lately in what was called a dry goods store? Or was it a yardage shop? A fascinating feature

was the cash carrier that was propelled on cables up to a mezzanine where a cashier made change then sent it back down the cable. Later, vacuum tubes were used in department stores.

Once in a rare moment you might be traveling through a small town and chance upon an apothecary with clear red and green liquids in ornate jars hanging in the window. It was as much a part of earlier drugstores as barber poles by barber shops and wooden Indians in front of cigar sellers. The drugstore might also still have a marble-topped soda counter and a table or two with real "ice cream" chairs.

If you've a yen for nostalgia, you might somewhere find a restaurant with a ceiling fan turning lazily near the entrance, and old Coca-Cola girls smiling from the walls. Add to this a high ceiling with fussily embossed metal sheets painted white, and lattice work intertwined with imitation vines. The booths were high-backed and finished with dark stained varnish.

Near schools was the inevitable candy store where a few "coppers" could purchase wondrous goodies. Some boys anticipating jelly beans, but jawbreakers, licorice sticks and Tootsie Rolls were also popular. Few of us had enough money for packaged candy bars, and there were plenty of bulk delights.

The store I was first intimately acquainted with was the "five and ten." The name meant just that. My first Christmas shopping money, fifty cents, was spent there after carefully examining every counter. I invested the whole amount in paring knives for my mother. It seemed most practical at the time. Of course the woman who

In the days before television, the radio was sold as an item of furniture in an elegant setting. (Courtesy Atwater Kent Radios)

played jazz on the ricky-tick piano to plug sheet music was the world's greatest pianist—to me at age nine.

We'll have to admit that shopping today is different. We don't walk downtown in big cities unless we're long distance runners. If you drive, there's usually a parking problem. The decentralized shopping centers, plazas and malls have had to take care of the situation. You may never see the same face twice behind a counter, but there's always a glittering choice of merchandise—if you can afford it, after taxes!

A friendly candy-store owner ladles out a bag full of jellybeans.

Modernity came to store interiors in the thirties.

12

Look Ma, No Bones!

A 1920 recipe folder.

You may think that food is food, so what could be done to make pork chops into steak, bread into cake, celery into artichokes or bananas into passion fruit? You're right because we have just so many kinds of edible animals, birds and fish, grains, fruits and vegetables. But there have been changes in the business of eating. Science dipped into our dinnerpails and we eat differently in spite of ourselves. Or, if the eating isn't so changed, cooking and products to cook are.

A busy housewife of yesterday kneads the dough, in preparation for baking her own bread.

If bread is the "staff of life," there's a lot of variety in that staff today. Did you formerly make all of the bread your family ate? The fifty pound bags of flour were a common grocery store sight. How many do you know now who buy this amount, then struggle to empty it into the flour bin built in your modern kitchen? It was a standard fixture in the twenties. The perfume of slowly baking bread filled the house and tickled the palate. We

didn't erase the aroma with aerosol sprays for obvious reasons; we didn't have them.

Old-fashioned baked goods go into an old-fashioned stove. (Courtesy of Libby McNeill & Libby)

Baking day was great for the children as luscious big sugar and molasses cookies were laid out on waxed paper to cool. It took a certain knack to snitch one and not leave telltale empty space where it had been. Baked goods were made from scratch every week.

Have you counted the numbers of mixes now on grocer's shelves? The variety for foolproof, jiffy-baking is staggering and still growing. When mixes first appeared, one company soon learned that there was more than the newness of their product to overcome in order for sales to increase. There was a psychological quirk in women who liked to feel they had more to do with baking than adding liquid and popping a mixture in the oven. Some had an aversion to dried eggs; others felt guilty when accepting compliments on pastry they'd had little to do with. Mixes therefore began to require your own fresh eggs, milk and maybe additional shortening for a more nearly "your own" accomplishment.

135

This ad for Pillsbury cake mix stresses the idea that the housewife adds the milk. It was discovered that women like to feel that they have added something to the making of the cake. (Courtesy of The Pillsbury Co.)

Our mothers made biscuits from scratch; they took to Bisquick very slowly indeed. (Courtesy of General Mills, Inc.)

ing returned for more solid, coarser-grained bread that more nearly resembled what grandmother used to make. We were gradually becoming more nutrition-conscious and espoused whole grains and wheat germ. One of the first additions I recall was cracked, whole wheat grains that made a crunchy texture. We began to eat darker breads instead of highly bleached loaves. The wide choice is now confusing.

My mother received countless ohs and ahs for her baking powder biscuits made from scratch. She always made crumbles of flour and shortening with her fingers, a pinch of this and that, so you can imagine how slowly she took to Bisquick. But change she did eventually, and grudgingly admitted it was so much easier and you could scarcely tell the difference in taste. This was a real breakthrough for Bisquick!

In the forties another twist came into our baking habits; the partly finished bread and rolls that we put in our ovens to brown. Some innovations come from deliberate striving for a preconceived result, while others are by accident. A baker who loved to chase fire engines heard sirens pass when he had a batch of rolls in his oven. He thought to turn off the heat and left the rolls partially baked. The fire he chased must have been a large one because the rolls were nearly cold when he returned. For some reason he decided to turn the heat on again, and was rewarded with fine rolls. Since he was a discerning man, the chance happening grew into a deliberate technique. Many people prefer the fresh-from-the-oven breadstuffs.

This reminds me of the story of how pork roast was discovered: it seems a building housing pigs burned down. Luckily, a better way was devised for roasting meat—otherwise, we'd be short of buildings!

In some ways the art of breadmaking has come full circle. After supposedly preferring ever-softer loaves, the centers of which could be rolled into bullets, a yearn-

A palatial showroom was the setting for the Frigidaire. (Courtesy Frigidaire Division of General Motors)

Cracked wheat bread. The texture was crunchier than in today's breads.

If you go to a garden before a meal to pick peas, beans, lettuce, pull radishes, carrots and beets, or even dig potatoes—you are in a select, small group that knows the joys most of the population has either forgotten or never known. Then you have to know how to shell peas, snap beans, wash other items and prepare to savor flavors that vegetables were meant to have.

By the middle twenties Clarence Birdseye was turning out frozen products like these strawberries.

We would have given the words "frozen or frosted foods" a blank stare in 1920, since we had no knowledge of them until Clarence Birdseye worked several years to perfect his history-making quick-freezing method for meat, fish, vegetables and fruit without altering taste or vitamin content appreciably. In 1925 Mr. Birdseye was producing packaged, frozen haddock in the new General Seafoods Company of Gloucester, Massachusetts. In 1929 he sold the Birdseye process to the Postum Company with Goldman Sachs Trading Corporation acting as agent for the $22,000,000 transaction. The General Foods Corporation dispensed Birdseye Frosted Foods to the public in 1930 in Springfield, Massachusetts, for the first time. In 1945 Mr. Birdseye developed a better method of dehydrating foods known as "anhydrous."

At first we tried these boxed, icy things with skepticism, as with many new ideas. There wasn't a wide choice at first, but once accepted, the new merchandise gradually enlarged until today's gourmet fare, which is complicated to make at home, can be bought as frozen food.

No restaurant or kitchen was without a squeezing device. There were several styles but orange juice always meant cutting the fruit and messing with juice extraction by our own efforts. Canned orange juice wasn't a good substitute for the fresh. It wasn't until quick-frozen pulp appeared that we had a fast, unmessy solution to seedless orange juice which tasted real.

Our memory of meat markets included sawdust on the floor, white enameled trays of various cuts in a glass-windowed counter. Perhaps the butcher was about to cut up a half of beef on the heavy wooden meat block after struggling under the weight of the deceased animal. We would have sniffed and snorted if anyone in the

Today, the Green Giant turns out ready-made frozen products which would have been difficult to make at home. (Courtesy Green Giant Co.)

In the twenties, restaurants always served fresh orange juice. (Courtesy of Sunkist Growers)

twenties suggested that meat would someday be pre-cut, packaged in cellophane, marked for weight and price, then put on self-serve counters. Many housewives rejected the idea, but it has come to pass as predicted. To be sure, you may still see what a butcher looks like if you ring the bell for him—but please, he's now a meat-cutter.

What about the meat itself? We used to only buy hams with the bone inside and tough hide still intact around the outside. Now we can get pre-cooked, boned hams without waste. How many times did you slowly cook the oldtime hams, thinking you had enough for company, only to find, after skinning and serving two or three lush slices, that nothing but partial-piece tidbits remained around the bone?

Frozen orange juice soon came along; it tasted like the real thing. (Courtesy Minute Maid Co.)

Bacon was also bought with a heavy rind and in a slab. It was a detestable task to cut slices thin enough to fry decently. I had no taste for bacon until we got the professionally cut, uniformly thin slices.

Bacon was purchased with a heavy rind and a slab.

Consider the fancy variations we now have in cold cuts. We used to eat bologna, boiled ham, a few sausages, perhaps of European style. We ordered from the long piece and designated the thickness and the number of slices. The butcher put the chunk on a manually operated machine and turned the crank. Or we'd buy a chunk and slice it at home as best we could. There weren't varieties with cheese checked through, sprinkled with pickles or stuffed olives, or several kinds in one loaf.

Turkey was for holidays only, because no one had yet developed the "junior" bird.

We thought of chicken as the fowl for Sunday dinner, and turkey, duck or goose was for holidays. Turkeys were king-sized because no one had developed the "junior" bird. We'd always quip after Thanksgiving about eating turkey for a week. Bless the one who thought of severing the parts of birds so we could indulge in favorite pieces! We used to bemoan the fact that fowl was designed with only two drumsticks.

Do you remember when cheese was cheese—a big, round chunk under a glass cover to protect it from flies, drying out and fingers? Its flavor was usually sharp, the texture crumbly and it dried quickly after you brought the slice home. Was there a grocer who didn't guess over the amount you ordered?

There was labor attached to preparing big holiday dinners, including the bird that was always too big for the roaster, or even the oven. In the twenties I usually helped my mother make the dressing from stale bread she'd stowed away for several days. Out came the largest darning needle, threaded with string which she laboriously sewed through the flesh flaps. Now we add liquid to a dressing mix, skewer the bird's openings, wrap foil around to hasten cooking and are ready to do something trivial after a fraction of the time formerly consumed.

The remainder of a big dinner might have been planned or prepared well in advance—pumpkin pies that were made after hacking up a pumpkin, then cooking the flesh instead of buying a can of ready-to-use pulp. Some purist women even made their own mincemeat so they'd know what was in it. My grandmother worked for days to make an enameled dishpanful of mincemeat to which she added boiled cider, syrupy and dark. It was pure ambrosia even without the pie around it!

The pickles, relishes, conserves, preserves and jellies along with spiced fruits were brought up from the fruit cellar. No house was built without one room in which to store the rows of home-canned foods.

Most housewives "put up" enough things to last through the winter. Of course commercially canned goods were available, but many women took pride in the store they preserved themselves.

The only dehydrated foods I can remember from the twenties were my grandmother's home-dried corn and dried apple slices. We didn't make mashed potatoes from chips, flakes or granules; we didn't season with onion, garlic or celery salt; and we didn't brew coffee by adding hot water to powder.

Coffee was made by slower methods, with different equipment than now. There weren't any glass coffee-makers that worked on the vacuum principle, nor were there automatic pots plated with gleaming chrome. Often the utensil was an enameled pot heated until the water just came to a boil. Sometimes eggshells went in with the grounds. Some believed good coffee resulted from a shake of salt added. At any rate, there were pet techniques for achieving an acceptable brew. One of my grandmothers left a battered old enameled pot on a little iron stove used for room heating. When the fire was

hot, the coffee simmered until you could "cut it with a knife." Instant coffee wasn't readily accepted and many still turn down a cup suspected of instantaneousness. All companies eventually improved the product and vied with the competition in trying to achieve the natural coffee taste in instant makings.

A 1920 recipe folder.

In the twenties we began to hear of a mysterious element called a vitamin; I studied about them briefly in the eighth grade. The study had to be brief because information was scanty. Now you can't avoid vitamins and everything's "enriched." There are arguments on both sides of the enriching subject. Some nutritionists believe that if the natural nutritive qualities of foods weren't tampered with by too much processing, it wouldn't be necessary to add synthetically what was stolen from the foods. They also argue and scold about the condition of soil in which food grows. Numbers of large markets now have sections for organically grown produce. Do you remember health food stores in the twenties? You could have starved while looking for one.

Selling vitamin products as dietary additives has grown into big business, and although many couldn't tell you what they're taking or why, they've become faithful adherents to the one capsule per day.

The other argument is that manufacturers know that customers like bread that keeps reasonably long, grocers like items with longer shelf life and label-readers like to know they're getting every known minimum daily requirement of vitamins and minerals.

Our milk is pasteurized to save us from tuberculosis,

Many of us got our first view of Niagara Falls from a Shredded Wheat Box. (Courtesy of National Biscuit Co.)

Margarine used to be white; you added color to it yourself. (Courtesy Cudahy Co.)

PINCH THE COLOR BERRY!

KNEAD BAG

CUDAHY'S DELRICH E-Z COLOR PAK VEGETABLE MARGARINE THE CUDAHY PACKING CO.

vitamin D is added to aid calcium absorption by the body. The round milk bottle with a cream line showing has become a memory. Do you remember milk bottles in winter, setting on front steps with caps lifted out of the bottle, lying atop a column of frozen cream?

In the matter of preservation, much has been done under the title of hydrogenation, especially in regard to our fats and oils. We used to buy a paper dish of lard at the meat market. It was our shortening and old-fashioned housewives took slowly to the cans of refined vegetable shortening or bottles of oil that could be stored without refrigeration. At that time we hadn't become conscious of cholesterol in relation to arteriosclerosis.

If you haven't noticed the changes in the cereal departments, then you haven't been in a food market. We used to have cornflakes from the Kellogg or Post Companies—or Shredded Wheat biscuits from Nabisco with Niagara Falls on the box end. That was my earliest viewing of the Falls. There was Puffed Wheat and Puffed Rice from Quaker, All-Bran a little later from Kellogg. The latter product made us aware of "regularity" and various other makers came along with bran flakes which were also beneficial. Competition knuckled down and now it's amazing to see the shapes that grain has been pressed, stamped, blown and squeezed into . . . plus sugar-coating. Grain nutrition was recommended for growing children, and they were coaxed to insist that their mothers send in boxtops for intriguing items.

Quaker Oats and Mother's Oats were breakfast favorites, then as now. (Courtesy the Quaker Oats Co.)

We had many less hot cereals too, the standbys being oatmeal from Quaker, Cream of Wheat, Ralston's and Pettijohn's. You may have had a few others. In the early thirties we tried that new taste treat, Malt-O-Meal. The cereal scientists may have new shapes and tastes in store

for us by combining wheat, rice, oats and corn into one flake, plus fruit-in-the-box!

Did you have a regular "butter and egg" man? He didn't represent big business in today's sense. He came by every week to fill our standing order for earthen crocks of "dairy" butter—contrasted to creamery or commercial butter. His wife churned it. He brought big, brown eggs, sometimes with a bit of straw or a feather clinging to the shell, but they were really fresh!

Oleomargarine makers had a struggle. We used to call it "oleo" instead of "margarine." It was white, like lard, and a color capsule was included in the package. It was a miserable job getting that color mixed evenly into the white mass. Manufacturers wanted to help us, but a long-enduring court battle ensued between oleomargarine makers and the butter interests before coloring could be pre-mixed into the "less expensive" spread. Before the affair was settled, an enterprising fellow got the idea to put the product in a pliofilm bag so the color could be easily kneaded into the contents. A handsome sum of money was realized from this simple innovation.

141

Aunt Sarah's Oven promised easy baking, broiling, browning, or toasting, over the single flame of a stove. (1926 *Woman's Home Companion*)

In forty years, changes were bound to come to cookware. We used to have mainly enameled pots and pans that would get chipped, then develop rusted holes. Wagner Ironware has been with us probably longer than anything and hasn't been beaten for cooking qualities, once it's well broken-in. Aluminum was big in the earlier two decades, but real competition arrived with the postwar advent of stainless steel cooking ware, some with copper bottoms. Some interior decorators liked to see these hung in the kitchen as part of the décor, instead of relegated to cupboard shelves.

Most stoves used to have a copper teakettle for fast boiling of water. My mother's first official meal-getting act was to "put on the teakettle." We had no dishwashers so boiling water was good for dish rinsing as well as brewing tea or speeding vegetable cooking.

matic gadgets, all in gleaming, non-tarnishing chrome. We used to have wire and metal toasters that sat on the gas burner of the stove. They held a slice of bread nearly upright on each of four sides. You had to keep a close watch or you'd be eating buttered charcoal for breakfast. Your fingers could also burn as easily as the bread. Waffles were also made on the stove-top and the irons had a ball joint at the hinge so the waffle could be whirled over to brown both sides.

On festive occasions we'd make a batch of buttery fudge that bubbled tantalizingly in the iron frying pan. We'd crack English walnuts and pick out meats to stir into the candy that was cooled in a square cake pan. We often popped corn in the evening to eat with cold, crunchy apples. Again the trusty iron frying pan came into use as it was kept in motion over the stove burner. There were no automatic electric corn-popping appliances.

A never-to-be-repeated taste of long ago was a four-layer feather light cake slathered all over with real whipped cream and generously sprinkled with hickory nuts. Since many people resoled shoes at home, it wasn't uncommon to have a shoe iron that doubled as a surface for cracking nuts. It was placed firmly in the lap, then the small, unwieldy, hard-shelled nuts were held on the iron and hit with a hammer. Of course, fingers were also often cracked. It required a deep love of hickory nuts to stick at the picking-out chore long enough for a sufficient amount of meats. Let's compare; now we'd get a box of cake mix, an aerosol can of synthetic whip, a cellophane bag of nutmeats, and minutes later we'd have a replica. But the same?—Never!

Fudge, served in an iron frying pan, was a treat.

Undoubtedly table offerings are presented more artistically now since we're exposed to beautiful color photos of food in ads and women's magazine articles. This wasn't always so. In the twenties many artists specialized in food painting. It was an exacting field because colors had to be true but brighter than life, and every curl on a lettuce leaf or bean in a bowl had to be respectfully treated. A food artist I knew said, "Every bean must be a portrait!" As color photography improved, the army of food artists had to find other items to paint.

Let's consider some of the food aversions we've had. When pascal celery first came on the counters, it won

An early pop-up toaster. (Courtesy Libby, McNeill & Libby)

There were fewer dishes that looked presentable enough for table service. The chafing dish wasn't new, but they weren't found in many ordinary people's homes. We take for granted our pop-up toasters and other auto-

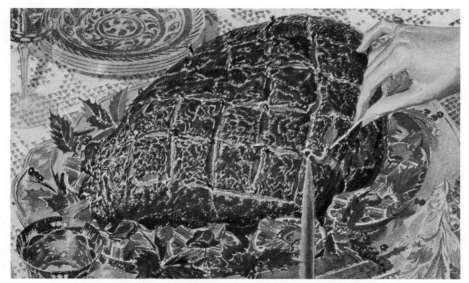

The artist probably got hungry doing this illustration. Before color photos became common, artists used to specialize in painting food. (*Pictorial Review*)

no popularity contests. Women had no use for green celery when everyone knew the choice parts were the white celery hearts. Most markets offered hearts separatly for the discriminating buyer who paid more for them, even though the new variety had less resistant strings and a greater supply of vitamin A. We also bought calf's liver if we could afford the higher price. It had no more nutrients than the lower priced livers of other animals, but it was the preferred choice.

Our introduction to grapefruit was not a happy one. We'd been instructed to cut them in half, remove the seeds (hundreds of them), pour on sugar generously then let them set overnight. There was only the strong flavored, rather bitter white grapefruit. By morning, the sugar had formed a crust as it mixed with the juice. It was years later before the non-bitter, pink, seedless grapefruit delighted us.

Our regard for certain foods has changed. You may recall when nuts, oranges and hard candies were put in children's stockings hung up for Santa Claus. These would scarcely get by now as stocking fillers with today's sophisticated children who fish for *real* gifts.

There's been a revolution in food packaging. We formerly bought many items in bulk and not always under strictly sanitary conditions. Perhaps we had more immunity to germs. If the style of containers has remained the same, surely the label has been updated. Heavy waxed papers, aluminum foil and plastics have contributed much to the changes. We didn't always have fruits in glass jars, coffee in vacuum-packed cans or soft drinks in no-return bottles. Coffee was bought in-the-bean and ground while we waited; then it was put into a heavy bag to seal in the flavor. Pull tabs, pouring spouts, trick perforated openings, waxed paper milk cartons and elec-

tric can openers didn't come until the period we call "lately."

Salt and sugar came in cloth bags and if you were clever you'd get the right thread—the one that allowed the sewn top to unravel easily. But I never got it. If the bag was near moisture, you could expect lump trouble. Someone had a brainstorm when he invented salt that could be made to pour in the rain and added iodine to prevent goiter.

We're concerned with noting the food differences rather than condemning either the old or the new. But a loud "huzza" should be sounded for the improved peanut butter that doesn't stick to the mouth like Scotch tape on glass.

Ice cream has come a long road since the vanilla, chocolate, strawberry and maple-nut of the twenties. There are so many flavors now it's confusing to choose one, and if you linger too long, there will be others added. Howard Johnson was in the forefront of the race for flavors. Oddly enough, statistics prove that plain old vanilla is still the biggest favorite.

It was a rare, very special occasion on the farm when the old hand-operated ice cream freezer was hauled out, someone brought ice and salt from the village, and grandmother made a batch of the rich recipe. The men took turns at the crank for the long, tedious job of turning the freezer handle. When at last we had real ice cream, it was fit for the gods! The Depression brought on the double-dip ice cream cone when dealers had more merchandise than customers had money. Some even offered triple-dips for the price of one, to wean customers from the competition.

It would be difficult to say precisely when the many changes came. The working wife and instant meals must

143

By the twenties, "quickie meals" had become common.
(*Woman's Home Companion*)

tie into the scheme. She could no longer nurse things on the stove all day. The trend toward speed hit the kitchen as well as the highways. As delicious as were the tastes of old and the memories of them, eating has changed whether we like it or not. In spite of pre-cooked, quickie meals, it's still a chore to work from nine to five, battle through traffic—then place a good meal on the table. Manufacturers always have a sensitive ear to the public needs, so the next great breakthrough may be meals in pellets, non-calorie cakes, bacon without fat and flavors without substance.

13

Anyone For Tennis?

You were the luckiest sports fan of all time if you lived through the first half of the twentieth century. The ancient Romans may have sent up a roar of cheers in the Colosseum when their games were played, but they couldn't have enjoyed a more glittering group of all-time great champs as we've been privileged to cheer.

These star athletes covered the gamut of team and individual accomplishments and their fame hasn't tarnished even when records were broken. We'll also recall games and sports that "John Public" played without the strain of competition.

Golf would be a logical starter since it has greatly

A montage of sport. (Courtesy Detroit News)

increased in popularity at the same time that competition has tightened among the devotees of tournament caliber.

Styles in golf clothing have changed and the mode of play has been infiltrated by modern devices that were unknown in my father's time—the electric golf cart for example. The so-called "working man" wasn't likely to neglect the lawn mowing to shoot nine holes at his club. The Model T might have had to travel considerable distance to place his owner at the first tee. We passed only one golf course in the fifty-two mile drive to my grandmother's, and my father never missed saying scornfully, "Look at those fools 'hitting the pill!'"

The golf bag on wheels has bettered the lot for players but worsened the summer earning capacity of the boys who could caddy. Even during the Depression, they could earn a few dollars on weekends if they had connections as caddies at exclusive and busy golf clubs.

The well-dressed golfer once wore this outfit.

For the fashion-wise golfing man, a quite acceptable outfit was plus-four trousers, socks to match his sweater and a cap. His shoes might be two-toned or oxfords with a fringed over-tongue.

Whether you're an average good weekend golfer who works to improve, or a dyed-in-the-bunker duffer, you probably have no idea of the antiquity that is intermixed

with your efforts. The game dates back to the fourteenth century, and the form most closely resembling our present game is attributed to Scotland. If you've been using the words "course" and "links" interchangably, you shouldn't be. A course runs inland while the links are laid alongside water, as the famous Pebble Beach near Monterey, California.

There has been variation over the years in regard to the material, weight and size of golf balls. Since 1921, standards of weight and size have had to be maintained. Clubs for hitting the balls have gradually evolved to today's material and identification. Numbering of playing sticks started in 1920.

Bobby Jones.

One name immediately pops into mind as that of the all-time greatest American golfer of the twenties and thirties—Robert (Bobby) Jones of Atlanta, Georgia. His record shines from winning the British Open Tournament three times, the United States Amateur contest five times. Bobby Jones's biggest year was 1930 when he won the four major competitions.

There have been many golfers tinged with fame in varying degrees. The most P.G.A. championships were won by Walter Hagen who got four of his five wins in consecutive years.

At the tender age of twenty, Gene Sarazen distinguished himself by winning the 1922 P.G.A. tournament. His name appeared again on top in the 1933 event and he was runner-up against Tommy Armour in 1930. He was the second highest repeat-winner.

"Lord" Byron Nelson won the P.G.A. crown in 1940 and again five years later. The proceeds of the latter play were given to a Dayton, Ohio, Army hospital as the largest contribution up to that time from such a source. Mr. Nelson was also runner-up in the 1939 and 1944 P.G.A. contests.

Most of the tournaments were medal play events as they are now; but the P.G.A. meet was match play. Ben Hogan won the title in 1946 and tried it again the next year.

A judge, who was a golf enthusiast, confronted a prisoner for sentencing after the man had battered his wife with a golf club. Said the judge; "I'm not fining you for

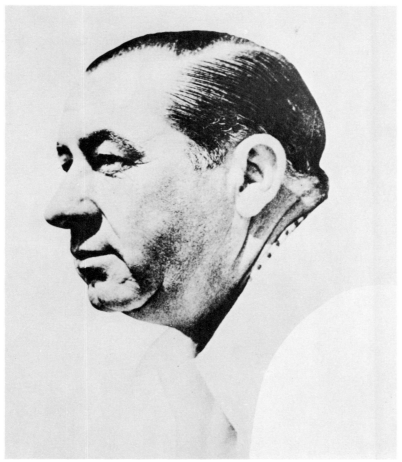

Walter Hagen. (Courtesy The Professional Golfer's Association)

Gene Sarazen. (Courtesy The Professional Golfer's Association)

Byron Nelson. (Courtesy The Professional Golfer's Association)

Ben Hogan. (Courtesy The Professional Golfer's Association)

148

New York Times headline tells of a match play event.
(Courtesy *The New York Times*)

Jimmy Demaret. (Courtesy The Professional Golfer's Association)

hitting your wife with the stick, it's for using the wrong one."

Jimmy Demaret was one of the high-rated golfers who was noted for his love of the spotlight and his ready wit almost as much as for his skill at the game. In 1940 he won nearly all of the titles except the P.G.A. and National Open.

"Slammin' Sammy" Snead is certainly a golfing name you haven't forgotten. He won the 1942 P.G.A. event and was twice the next-to-top man. His nickname came from being one of the longest hitters of this era.

A golfer who was regarded as one of the best at match play was Lawson Little. How many other greats can you recall?

A few women of the period took their games seriously enough for tourney play. Maybe you recall two early rated players, Helen Hicks and Glenna Collett. In the U.S. National Women's Amateur tournament of 1946, Babe Didricksen Zaharias won the title. Golf was only one facet of this remarkable woman's athletic skills. She was probably the greatest all-around woman athlete that America has had. She was not only a game sportswoman, but the nation had cause to applaud her courage in her long battle against cancer.

It would be unfair to ignore an offshoot of golf that was a sudden fad and as suddenly disappeared, until recent times when it was unearthed for another fling. It was miniature or "pee-wee" golf that made vacant lots

Lawson Little. (Courtesy The Professional Golfer's Association)

Sammy Snead. (Courtesy The Professional Golfer's Association)

150

L. Helen Hicks, left, and R. Glenna Collett.

bloom like strange parks with all sorts of contrivances for knocking golf balls into, over, up on, against and around. Even the children could play. A few early birds in this Depression operation probably made some profit, but latecomers were left with a weed-grown lot that yielded little interest and less money after the craze passed. It's reminiscent of the more recent sprouting of trampolines for the public; the fad arrived overnight, but died suddenly after a number of injuries to the unskilled. However, miniature golf was never known to be injurious except to pride—unless you stumbled over an obstacle after hitting your shin with a club.

Swimming is another sport or amusement (depending on how avidly you pursue it), that is widely enjoyed by the masses now as well as then. The amount of energy expended in direct exercise by the bathing beauties of previous eras is debatable, but the sun and fresh air were beneficial.

These covered-up splashers were demonstrating the latest, smart "watering place" attire. It was daring enough for the late twenties and well into the thirties. The removal of tops on men's suits came about gradually.

There have long been beauty contest winners—a bumper crop is harvested every summer—but the ultimate achievement from 1921 on was to be crowned "Miss America" in the Atlantic City-based granddaddy of all such contests.

A bathing beauty, Mack Sennett style.

Miss Chicago was a Miss America hopeful in the late twenties. (Courtesy Pontiac *Daily Press*)

Johnny Weissmuller.

that can be held as long as his lightning 100 yards in 51 seconds, which persisted from 1927 until World War II.

Certain games must be enjoyed from the spectator stands. However, you can enjoy tennis whether you are an onlooker or a participant; there are crowded courts to attest to its public popularity even though many think it too strenuous for any but the young.

The serious swimmers who battled waves, weariness, cold, distance and stopwatches will be long remembered. In 1926 the English Channel was still a swimmer's challenge even though an Englishman, Captain Matthew Webb, had accomplished the feat in 1875. But an American wasn't successful until 1926 when a girl of nineteen years not only did the difficult distance, but pared seven hours and fourteen minutes from Captain Webb's time. This feat made Gertrude Ederle doubly famous because she was the first American—and the first female—to do it. Twenty-five years later another American woman was the first woman to cross the English Channel in both directions. She was Florence Chadwick.

One of the best-remembered male swimming champions is Johnny Weissmuller. There aren't many titles

Gertrude Ederle.

"Big" Bill Tilden.

"Big" Bill Tilden's name was synonymous with tennis for many years. His championships were so numerous and his records so long-standing that there could be no doubt of his worthiness. He was the United States singles champion from 1920 to 1925, then he picked it up again in 1929. He held the title of world's best singles player in 1920, 1921 and 1930. From 1920 to 1930 he was on the Davis Cup team. When he decided to turn

Don Budge shown ready to smash a sizzler to his opponent's court—disarmingly out of reach.

Helen Wills Moody.

professional in 1931, the name of Tilden was again in the titleholding ranks. Mr. Tilden wasn't one-sided either because he wrote several books, a play, syndicated newspaper material and magazine articles.

If you were a tennis buff in the thirties and forties, you may remember such names as Ellsworth Vines, Fred Perry and Don Budge.

In the days when tennis was more popular with fans than today, there was a fine crop of women champions. They got much publicity and the man-in-the-street knew who Helen Wills was. She was later Helen Wills Moody. Mrs. Moody was the greatest winner, gaining the American crown from 1923 to 1929, except for 1926. She again won in singles in 1931 after showing England and France the brand of playing that made her great.

Miss Wills began to win tournaments when she was barely seventeen. In profile she possessed a classic beauty, with features resembling those of the Venus de Milo. The net star might have been an artist if she tired of tennis. An exhibition of her work appeared in New York in 1930. Helen Wills Moody was often referred to as "Little Miss Poker-Face" because of her serious concentration on the game.

In addition to her tennis playing ability, Mrs. Moody possessed a classic beauty. She is shown compared with the Venus de Milo. (Courtesy Detroit *News*)

Helen Jacobs.

It is not always the winners who are the longest or most fondly remembered. A notable loser who won popular respect was Sir Thomas Lipton. Before the turn of the century he started his many tries to get the America's Cup, the international yachting trophy. This cup was originally a British award of the Royal Yachting Squadron and was called the Queen's Cup. But once the trophy was captured by New York's Yacht Club, not Sir Thomas Lipton's final try in 1930 could disturb the cup's resting place. Through all of his disappointing years of

Helen Jacobs was a highly rated player in the same era and she revolutionized women's tennis court dress by being the first tournament champion to wear shorts. It certainly was a practical improvement. I still have my copy of a Helen Jacobs tennis costume that for looks, comfort and freedom of movement hasn't yet been improved on.

Versatility ran in tennis ranks and in 1939 Alice Marble was no exception. She sang in a New York nightclub, tried the movies and designed her gowns. She de-valued the concept that women athletes all looked like muscle-bound Amazons.

Undoubtedly one of the most ancient sports is skating, since it appeared in some form over a thousand years ago. There weren't many children in our young days who didn't ply skates on sidewalks or ice. In trying rudimentary figures on either wheels or blades, many a young body has been banged and bruised. I still can't understand how I kept my two front teeth when trying to emulate Sonya Henie.

In competitive and championship ice figure skating, Sonya Henie has been regarded as the outstanding woman of modern times. At the slight age of fourteen she won the title for figures in her native Norway. Within three years she'd captured the world crown. She garnered three Olympic titles before Miss Henie began to skate for Hollywood cameras and tour with her extravaganza ice shows. She did more than any other skater to get the people of this country up on blades wherever a patch of water was hard and gleaming.

Sonya Henie curtsies after finishing her performance. (Courtesy Detroit *News*)

failure, this gentleman won something even better—the love of America for his perfect sportsmanship.

It would be improbable to expect the same spectator interest for all sports, but many have survived thanks to sufficient crowds of the curiously interested. In the Depression thirties one of the consistent profit-makers was the not-too-common six-day bike race. Madison Square Garden was the best known locale for this revival from earlier days. For six days and nights thirty men "went around in circles." The most ardent fans were Europeans —Italians, Germans and French who learned the lure of cycling in their homelands, where it had long been popular. Some people found that the continuously monotonous movement and sound had a lulling, hypnotic effect, while others dropped in to watch a few minutes, then went on their ways. The cyclists ate ten meals per day, took catnaps and received massages during short rest times between the incessant pedaling.

There are few contenders in the roster of games that could come anywhere near the age of polo. Its estimated beginnings were in Persia several hundred years before Christ. It was introduced into America by the English in the 1870's. In the Cinerama production, *A Search for Paradise*, children beginning to toddle in Hunza start learning to play polo in rudimentary form.

Tommie Hitchcock is one of our renowned polo players. (Photo Courtesy *Harper's Bazaar*)

Because of the cost of obtaining and maintaining a stable of good polo ponies, it could be regarded as a rich man's game. It isn't likely that the same spectators who lose their minds over baseball would shout themselves hoarse at polo matches. Tommie Hitchcock is one of the outstanding names among polo players.

In 1922 it was said that the renewed public interest in

Six-Day bike races were all the rage in the thirties. (Courtesy K. Soldwedel for *Fortune* magazine)

polo brought this strenuous pastime to the fore this year. "While the game remains expensive and exclusive—the distinctly gentleman's sport—it is also true that the general public, discovering through the pictorial press the fascination, skill and sporting risks of the contests, has taken the keenest interest in the several matches, particularly the international one, and have discussed the points of play with an intelligent zest almost approaching that displayed for tennis and baseball." You see, there's hope for the general public if given a chance!

In the art of pugilism we've had our share of thrills, chills and notable champions. The memories of dyed-in-the-ring boxing fans must be good because of the many times that Jim Corbett and John L. Sullivan are still mentioned, even though their several fights were just before and following the turn of the century.

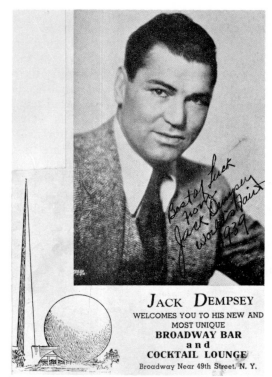

JACK DEMPSEY
WELCOMES YOU TO HIS NEW AND
MOST UNIQUE
BROADWAY BAR
and
COCKTAIL LOUNGE
Broadway Near 49th Street, N. Y.

This photo of the great Jack Dempsey was autographed by the champ in his popular cocktail lounge on Broadway in 1939, when the World's Fair opened.

Boxers used to wear tops with their trunks. These smooth fellows don't appear very lethal.

The fights of our three decades should start with Jack Dempsey who beat Jess Willard in 1919 to gain the heavyweight crown that he held until 1926 when Gene Tunney did a bit better.

Gene Tunney's start in boxing came when he won the championship of the A.E.F. during World War I. He was a Marine. Tunney retained his 1926 world title by again defeating Dempsey, but retired from the ring in 1928.

There were many names you must remember, even though they didn't make it to the top: Georges Carpentier, Luis Firpo and Tom Heeney.

Max Schmeling had the distinction of being the first fighter to put Joe Louis "on the mat." But even though he was the title holder in 1930, two years later Jack Sharkey possessed it. Also, when Schmeling fought Louis again, the latter had sweet revenge and wrecked the big German in 1938.

Hulking 260 pound Primo Carnera was a rather sad figure in fighting circles. He wasn't a brain trust and those shrewd flies who buzzed around him came out with a good share of the sugar—the earnings he didn't see. The same year that he won the heavyweight title, 1933, he had one of the bad ring experiences that happen occasionally when an opponent dies as a result of the fight. He'd fought Ernie Schaaf who was dead three days after the bout.

The next year, after Carnera had won the title by beating Sharkey, Max Baer came along to snatch the crown from Carnera. Fighter Baer also was confronted by a ring death that came a few hours after he faced Frankie Campbell in San Francisco.

Gene Tunney. (Courtesy *The Ring,* Inc.)

THE LOUIS-SCHMELING FIGHT

Joe Louis, the sensational Detroit Heavyweight fighter (the Brown Bomber) will fight Max Schmeling, former World's Heavyweight Champion, in the Yankee Stadium, New York City, Thursday Night, June 18th.

We invite you and your friends to join our big party and witness this outstanding International Sport event.

Our All Expense Trip Includes:

Standard Round Trip Transportation, Pullman Drawing Room—Bedroom—Compartments or Lower Berth Accommodations for round trip.

Dinner at the Hotel Hollenden before leaving.

All Meals in Dining Car going and returning.

Reception by Jack Dempsey, and Luncheon at his Famous Restaurant.

Best rooms with bath at the Hotel Astor, New York City.

CHOICE ELEVATED ($40.00) RINGSIDE SEAT.

Refreshments.

Entertainment.

Recreations.

Special Features.

NO TRAVEL WORRIES

Special Train Rates
(per person)

Drawing Room	(2 in room)	$100.00
Drawing Room	(3 in room)	95.00
Compartment	(2 in room)	95.00
Bedroom	(2 in room)	90.00
Section	(2 persons)	87.50
Lower Berth	(1 person)	90.00
Lower Berth	(2 persons)	85.00
Upper Berth	(1 person)	85.00

EQUIPMENT

Our Special Train Equipment will consist of the latest type of Pullman Cars—Sleeping Cars—Club Car—Dining Cars—and Recreation Car, which has proven so popular on previous trips. It is the last word in a desirable travel arrangement of this kind.

Our schedule is so arranged as to allow Two Full Days and Nights in New York City, for pleasure and business.

LADIES ARE INVITED

The New York Central advertised a three-day deluxe trip from Cleveland to New York for the Lewis-Schmeling fight in 1936. (Courtesy Penn Central Railroad)

157

Primo Carnera. (Courtesy *The Ring*, Inc.)

ing, Louis would be financially set for life, but they hadn't reckoned with the tax collector and a string of bad investments.

Another most remarkable boxer was Henry Armstrong. Do you remember that he simultaneously held three championships in different weight classes?

When the autumn air tingles and you've shouted or wailed through the World Series, football is at hand. Kicking a ball in the confines of game rules predates even the Greeks and Romans who similarly named their pastime "harpaston" or "harpastum." Even savage tribes played varying forms of football, and by means scarcely authenticated in history, the game got to the British Isles—unless the English had already invented their own version. English Rugby, named after the school, most closely resembles football as we know it, wherein the ball is not only kicked but carried by players through the lines. The Pilgrims brought the game to America, but it

Jack Sharkey. (Courtesy *The Ring*, Inc.)

Max Baer could be classed as a clown fighter who loved to play up to the audience, more like a vaudevillian than a serious athlete. Many years later he got his wish with his own television show. A man considered too old for the boxing business took the title from Baer after he'd had it only one year. This was James Braddock.

In the wings, a boxer was coming on who would surpass them all—not in being a colorful personality, a clown or anything other than a systematic fighting machine who could take care of his opposition in jig-time. Joe Louis (Barrow) won his crown in 1937 and held it securely through a succession of challengers who thought they'd figured the formula that would beat him. The last two years that Louis ruled the ring, old "Jersey Joe" Walcott tried twice to wrest the crown, but the "Brown Bomber" was too much for him. Then Joe Louis retired in 1948 after defending his title twenty-five times. It's too bad that he chose to come out of retirement in 1950—to be beaten by the champ that year, Ezzard Charles.

Some said that after his phenomenal years of title-hold-

Max Baer. (Courtesy Keystone View Co.)

Joe Louis. (Courtesy Keystone View Co.)

This pennant-waving group is headed for a football game, 1920's style. There was a difference in dress, but none in their enthusiasm.

Red Grange.

wasn't an instantaneous passion or pre-occupation. The first collegiate mention of it was about 1827 at Harvard when the sophomores played the juniors. Gradually other schools became engaged in football but the first recorded intercollegiate game did not occur until 1869, when Princeton was defeated by Rutgers.

There could be much disagreement about the relative merits of great football players in our three decades, considering the thousands who've played the game in colleges as well as in professional leagues. Sportswriters or coaches are in the best position to see and highlight individual greatnesses when they weigh values and make up All-Time All-Player lists with carefully selected names. This list-making started in 1904 and has continued. The recurrence of the same names over and over, no matter who chose them or when, would indicate the most likely best. By cross-checking and re-checking, it appears that the greatest collegiate player of all time was Walter Heffelfinger, a Yale guard who was chosen unanimously by all listers.

It is interesting to pop the question to football buffs, "Who do you consider the greatest football star?" Invariably without hesitation they will say, "Red Grange, Jim Thorpe, Bronko Nagurski or George Gipp."

This is a good beginning but it neglects many other notable names of those who toted and kicked the pigskin, or held firmly against the opposition. We, who were in Michigan, could scarcely forget Tom Harmon, the All-American halfback, Benny Oosterbaan, All-American end, or Benny Friedman, All-American quarterback.

Notre Dame's "Four Horsemen and Seven Mules" in 1924 will always be classic football memories. The Horsemen were: Don Miller, Harry Stuhldreher, Jim Crowley and Elmer Layden.

Stanford's All-Time All-American selection in the twenties was Ernie Nevers, fullback. Several listers chose California's Harold Muller as one of football's best passers. Some say he was the greatest end. Knute Rockne thought Benny Friedman was the greatest passer. But in 1944 Grantland Rice considered Harry Gilmer of Alabama the best college passer he'd ever seen. Coach Clark Shaughnessy called Chicago's Jay Berwanger a one-man team. He'd never seen a better player. Jay played in the thirties whereas Robert Odell of Pennsylvania was rated one of the greatest all-around players of all time. And so it could endlessly go. For every name we mention, you could think of a score of those you might class as better.

If football stars gained records and fames that haven't tarnished, certainly the rightful share of great team and individual accomplishment honors should go to the inspiring coaches. Again, it's easy to have one or a few top names come immediately to mind. Knute Rockne of Notre Dame has been called the coach of coaches who gave football its greatest impetus and popularity. He invented plays and speeded the line and backfield while getting a revered affection from his boys, many of whom turned to coaching careers afterward.

If Rockne earned an unforgettable place in the sport, we must reserve plenty of room for the "Grand Old Man of Football," Amos Alonzo Stagg. Lou Little was a master strategist at Georgetown and Columbia, Howard Jones had the distinction of leading a team from which nine of the eleven All-Americans were chosen in one year. Bernard Bierman produced such undisputedly good teams in 1934, 1936 and 1940 that Minnesota could permanently keep the Knute Rockne National Intercollegiate Memorial Trophy. Much in the development of football rules should be credited to Walter Camp who lived until 1924. Earl Blaik led Dartmouth to victory in twenty-one

Knute Rockne.

of Italy; Riviera Bowl in France; Poi Bowl of Honolulu and Coconut Bowl, New Guinea.

If you've wondered about the popularity of college football in terms of game attendance, the largest known crowd of fans could be credited to Soldier Field, Chicago, when in 1926 Army and Navy players struggled to a 21–21 tie before 110,000 people—infants not counted.

It was twenty-eight years after the first intercollegiate football game that professional players appeared—in Latrobe, Pennsylvania in 1897. Although colleges haven't encouraged their stars to seek professional careers, it was a natural for the pro leagues to pick outstanding college players for their teams. The farm system, which supplies good baseball material, could be compared to taking college football stars for pro ranks.

Bronko Nagurski did his best playing as a professional after his stint with Minnesota from 1927 to 1930. Many other top names decked the rosters of pro teams although they had to allow collegians to graduate before they could be professionally romanced. In 1920 the American Pro-

straight games from 1936 to 1938. Harvard owed much to Percy Haughton's inventive genius.

Each season, the nation's outstanding college player receives the Heisman Memorial Trophy, awarded in the name of John Heisman who consecutively coached thirty-seven years. The division of the game into quarters was one of Heisman's contributions. Glenn (Pop) Warner rates next to Stagg for continuous years as a teaching coach—forty-six. A dentist, Dr. John Sutherland, sent a number of Pittsburgh teams to the Rose Bowl, while Dr. Henry Williams not only gained a professorship of medicine at Minnesota, but brought the school's football reputation up to prominence. Fielding Yost etched his name with permanence and supplied one of the first two teams to play at the Tournament of Roses. Some of the most colorful names for play inventions were introduced by Robert Zuppke when he conceived the "flea flicker," "whoa back," "razzle-dazzle" and "flying trapeze."

The first East-West football classic was called simply that; it was played in connection with the Tournament of Roses in 1902. From that time until 1916 football disappeared from the event in favor of popular chariot and motorcycle racing. It was in 1923 that these football battles were first called Bowl games. They have continued for more years than any of the myriad other bowl events that gradually followed. You probably won't be rushing out to attend the Arab Bowl of Oran; the Potato Bowl, Belfast, Ireland; the Lily Bowl in Bermuda; Coffee and Tea Bowls of London; the Spaghetti and Bambino Bowls

Jim Thorpe.

fessional Football association was formed and had Jim Thorpe as its first president. Two years later it was renamed the National Football League. In the beginning of the American Association, membership cost a mere hundred dollars. By 1940 the League fee had increased to $50,000. It could be compared to the base fee of a liquor license as against the inflated price paid to actually acquire one. Dan Reeves paid seven million dollars to get the Rams team. This could attest to the increasing interest in pro football from that first game until now.

There has been much shuffling of ownership, transfers

of franchises, moves of teams' homes and high finance deals to sign desirable players. Rules have changed along with the number of players a team may carry. The line has softened enough between colleges and professionals so that coaches have gone from the former to the latter and back again—usually switching for the money involved. Even Rockne played with a pro team during vacation to earn the extra money.

Even the least sports-minded person in America would probably immediately say baseball if asked what our national game is. It's about as American as Coney Island and Cracker Jack. Colonel Abner Doubleday devised the diagram for baseball when he was in the United States Army. His concept of a diamond with bases ninety feet apart was a departure from any other bat and ball game. The first code rules were made by the Knickerbocker Club of New York. By 1857 separate teams were being organized, rules were improved, and our ears could have probably heard "Batter Up!" even in these pre-Civil War days. The oldest continuing club is the Athletics, even though their home is no longer Philadelphia. We hear much now of the fabulous salaries of stars and the amounts club owners pay to obtain them, but the 1869 Cincinnati team was the first to recompense every member of the team.

The senior major league is the National League of Professional Baseball Clubs which dates to 1876, despite disputes and other upsets. As with college football, rules were made to keep pros from pirating choice players from rival clubs. It could have ruined the whole business. The junior or American League grew out of the old Western League that was renamed in 1900.

The year 1921 saw a major change of modus operandi as a result of alleged dishonesty and other shenanigans. This was the beginning of Kenesaw Mountain Landis's reign as Commissioner of Baseball. He held this appointed post until his death in 1944. Then Senator Albert (Happy) Chandler presided for the next seven years. Organized baseball has joined businesses that are rated as *big* inasmuch as World Series receipts have passed the million dollar mark—to be divided among the involved parties.

Who among the numberless names that have streaked around the bases gave you your most exciting baseball memories? Could they be the stars of another era who congregated in Cooperstown in June, 1939, to celebrate the hundredth anniversary of that first game in the little New York town? If you love baseball you'll remember Honus Wagner, Grover Cleveland Alexander, Tris Speaker, Larry Lajoie, George Sisler, Walter Johnson, Eddie Collins, Babe Ruth, Connie Mack and Cy Young. At the time of the celebration Ty Cobb wasn't present and Willie Keeler and Christy Mathewson were dead. The celebration was held to induct members into the Hall of Fame, which is a part of the Cooperstown museum of baseball lore.

Some sports are storm centers for continued arguments about who's the greatest player, most valuable or sen-

sational. This isn't true where Ty Cobb is concerned. He's the undisputed top and hasn't yet been left in the dust. His record talks for him, after a reign that lasted but a year short of a quarter century. With a .367 lifetime batting average, his number of runs and base hits number into the thousands. There were great days for the Detroit Tigers with the fiery-tempered, bombastic Cobb aboard, but although his disposition left room for improvement, the team appreciated his performance at bat. There was never a more ferocious fighter for victory. In 1921, when Cobb was made Tiger manager, his stunning batting average was actually passed for a time by five points when Harry Heilmann connected solidly with sufficient pitches. Tyrus Cobb's name was the first selected for the Hall of Fame, notwithstanding several players who had higher averages for shorter periods.

The immortal Babe Ruth has just hit another homer.

Baseball and George Herman (Babe) Ruth were synonymous. No one ever hit further, received more adulation or established records that later players are still trying to emulate. In his twenty-one years with major leagues, he hit 714 homeruns. Slugger Hank Greenberg of the Tigers, tried to tie Ruth's 60 homers in-one-season but fell just short. Later, Micky Mantle edged up and in 1961 Roger Maris belted out 61 for the season but Ruth's blazing all-time record could still sear the hopefuls. It wasn't only Babe's famous ability to hit a home run directly to the place he'd indicated before batting, but the good he did for the game generally. People thronged to ballparks in the hope of seeing him hit a homer even if they didn't know which end of the bat did it. Their affection for him was returned by his extrovert's love of people.

Stars of baseball gathered in Cooperstown, New York, in June 1939 to celebrate baseball's 100th anniversary. Shown standing, left to right: Honus Wagner, Grover Cleveland Alexander, Tris Speaker, Larry Lajoie, George Sisler, and Walter Johnson. Shown seated, left to right: Eddie Collins, Babe Ruth, Connie Mack, and Cy Young. (Courtesy National Baseball Hall of Fame and Museum, Cooperstown)

Babe Ruth made his debut with the New York Yankees in April of 1920. It was the start of a long association which made him famous and the Yankees feared. It was a sad day in 1947 when organized baseball had a day of honor for the "Bambino" at Yankee Stadium. This once robust man acknowledged the cheers of thousands with a barely audible whisper. He was a dying man about to depart, but not without leaving his indelible stamp on the game he loved and the fans who loved him.

If you wanted to hire someone who was dependable, noncombative—someone who came through in the pinches —Lou Gehrig was your man. That is, if you'd consider that playing 2,130 games in an unbroken row is dependable. This represented nearly fourteen years of not missing a scheduled game, plus rarely a drop below a .300 batting average. In fact, until Ruth's last year, 1934, Lou was on the "Sultan of Swat's" heels and pressed hard with his record of powerful hits (four home runs in one game), and particularly the consistent number of runs he batted in. Gehrig and Ruth were sparkplugs in those dazzling days for the Yankees in the twenties and first half of the thirties. The colorful Ruth personality was not part of Lou's makeup. He had to work hard at the mechanics of the game—he was not the "King" of baseball, but the "Crown Prince."

After the Babe's playing days were over, Lou Gehrig was surrounded by such stars as Joe DiMaggio, Bill Dickey, Red Rolfe, Lefty Gomez and Charlie Ruffing, to mention just a few. In 1942 Hollywood made a picture, *Pride of the Yankees,* about Lou Gehrig's distinguished career. But he, like Ruth, was seized with a fatal illness. Ruth died of cancer, whereas multiple sclerosis crept up to lay away Gehrig's bat and the power behind it.

Joe DiMaggio was considered the greatest center fielder since Tris Speaker and his hitting was joy to the Yankee fans after 1936, at which time he was rookie of

Babe Ruth poses with Roy Brent (the author's husband) at Wrigley Field, Los Angeles, during filming the *Pride of the Yankees,* which starred Gary Cooper as Lou Gehrig.

Mickey Cochrane's plaque at Cooperstown. (Courtesy National Baseball Hall of Fame and Museum, Cooperstown)

the year. He made good the promise shown, by copping top batting records in 1939 and 1940. He broke Willie Keeler's 1897 mark by hitting safely in 56 consecutive games.

If the name Al Szymanski rings no bell in your baseball mind, we should identify him as the more pronounceable Athletics hitting star, Al Simmons. Connie Mack (simplified from MacGillicuddy), had a great and scrappy team in the late twenties and early thirties when he put together his last memorable aggregation with such as Simmons, Mickey Cochrane, Lefty Grove, Jimmy Dykes, Bing Miller, Eddie Rommel and Jimmy Foxx, along with other incendiary players. Al Simmons tried hard and came very close to Harry Heilmann's .393 and Tris Speaker's .389 when he racked up .386. After fourteen pennantless years, Philadelphia was treated to exciting games in 1929 and Simmons's crowning feat—eight hits in nine times at bat. The Athletics knew the sweet taste of success, but the best combinations age and wane. When Al's batting slump, expensive contract and the Depression forced Mack to let him go, he moved like a whirling dervish from club to club; but this didn't erase his glory as the sixty-fourth entry into the Hall of Fame.

Mickey Cochrane combined his talents as the greatest catcher and fiercest scrapper that ever brightened Connie Mack's eyes. His firebrand qualities were matched by his batting prowess. He starred in Philadelphia until the Tigers bought him in 1933 not only to play but manage.

A golden era followed for the Detroit team in 1934 under Cochrane's strong and effective direction. They won the pennant and might have taken the Series except for the opposition—the menacing "Gashouse Gang," the St. Louis Cardinals. They were sparked by Frankie Frisch, the colorful Dean brothers (Dizzy and Paul), Leo (Lippy) Durocher, Pepper Martin and others. These were my fan days when I was surrounded by ardent Tigerites. How they roared over "Schoolboy" Rowe; Tommy Bridges and Charlie Gehringer, the steady dependables; Hank Greenberg the slugger; Rudy York,

Dizzy Trout, Virgil Trucks and Goose Goslin—very familiar names! The "Goose" was the hero in 1935 when his hit gave the Tigers their hard-fought Series victory over the Yanks.

But what was so dizzy about that Dean fellow? He had all of the attributes that make star pitchers and an accident during his career's peak probably cut him from the all-time greatest crown. For colorful antics, certainly few could vie as he lightheartedly sought fun along with disposal of the opposition. "Me 'n Paul" was a winning duo, even though the quiet, modest and hard-working Paul had a personality opposite that of his cocky older brother. But even those who recoiled from boastfulness had to admit that when Dizzy bragged, he also delivered the advertised results. His greatest glory was in 1934 when he pitched the Cardinals into forty-nine wins, the pennant and Series, of course with the help of the other "Gashousers."

"DIZZY" AND HIS
GAS HOUSE GANG

The Cardinals of Dizzy Dean's era were known as the "Gashouse Gang."

Carl Hubbell pitched the New York Giants to victory. (Courtesy *The New York Times*)

It was in 1937 that this unusual career came crashing down on the man who lived it, when a hard ball from Earl Averill's bat broke the big toe of Dean's left foot. Favoring the foot, Dizzy strained his arm, and the great pitching days were done even though he stayed on a couple of years with brave attempts to show the old brilliance.

There were those who came so heartbreakingly close to the Hall of Fame that Cooperstown dust was on their shoes, while others made the grade but not from lovable dispositions. Rogers Hornsby fell in this class as his tactless honesty led to frequent moves, some resembling exile. Through all of his wrangling with owners, teammates and others, his impatience was with those who couldn't match his perfection in the game. They earned the brunt of the Hornsby fire.

Our era had great pitchers. Some would class Carl Hubbell as tops, others might argue for their favorites; Bobo Newsom, Lefty Grove, Hal Newhouser, Robin Roberts or the "boy wonder" who did a man's job—Bob Feller.

The difference of opinion about baseball and its practitioners seems to be part of the fun. Endlessly we hear, "It's the pitcher!" "No, it's the batter." "Well, what about the rest of the team?" The subject has been thoroughly dissected through the years. There are so many greats we left out and the less spectacular bulwarks whose names are heard less, but who can turn on memory lights when they're mentioned.

It's safe to say without argument that baseball was rightly called "The National Game!"

Fans attend a baseball game of an earlier era—when the game was still played in the daytime.

14

When Dad Was a Dude

This gentleman would have been equally in place on Wall Street or Fleet Street.

Paris told American women what to wear and London dictated men's clothing. The British stamp of approval was in evidence in every good magazine and newspaper advertisement, or in tailor shops, haberdasheries and department stores. If a man could walk with assurance down Fleet Street, he'd feel his "correct" best on Wall Street, New York, in the same clothes.

"Clothes make the man" has long been a platitude. Thomas Carlyle said essentially the same in 1836—"clothes have made men of us."

Although the changes have been less violent or freakish for men than for women, the differences are nevertheless definite if given the perspective of a few decades. Accessories kept pace with new fabrics and modern fastenings. Many of the same words used in women's adver-

tising popped up in ads for men without apparent loss of masculine appeal.

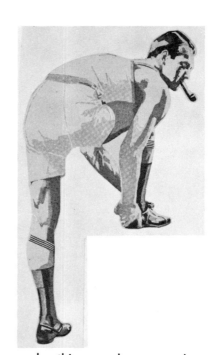

B.V.D.'s, worn by this man, became a household word.

We'll start with the "inner man"—his underwear. What was he wearing under the handsome double-breasted? It was his B. V. D.'s, for this trademark was so widely known that no one had to go on and say "underwear."

One caption with undergarments said, "Men! Isn't this the kind of underwear you've prayed for?"

The full union suit used to be a familiar clothesline sight and was amusing when it froze in winter, waving stiffly like a billowed-out ghost with more authority than

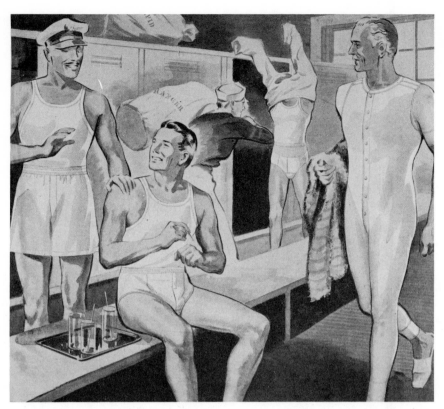

Here four chaps are locker-room congregating in 1937-approved underthings from Munswingwear for men.

substance. The words "smart style" were even used for men's shorts and union suits.

The magic of Lastex was coming into undershirts and shorts in 1937 and the miracle yarn was praised for making things fit.

Grippers were lauded as a great new type of fastener that would end all button troubles, as they wouldn't rip, break or flatten no matter how much laundered. Big League baseball players attested to their merits.

When our hypothetical man-of-the-thirties donned his socks, they might have been Interwoven, a popular brand. They made self-supporting socks that stayed up without gadgets or garters. Billie Jones and Ernie Hare, "We're the Interwoven Pair," used to sing of them on radio.

Realsilk, largely known for women's fine silk hosiery, went into the haberdashery business by peddling socks, shirts, ties, underwear and pajamas through representatives in your home or office. It was the kind of merchandising Avon has done so successfully.

The well-dressed man had to have smoothly snug socks, so he wore Paris Garters in any of several styles. There was a deplorable sloppy vogue for several years, started perhaps by college boys. to wear short socks without garters. They shuffled at will around the ankles.

The only appreciable difference in men's shoes has been today's freer use of color and easy-living shoes that undoubtedly started with the loafer. They were identical to the brown leather loafers girls wore, but for men to wear them for business instead of oxfords was a distinct departure. For golf, both men and women took to oxfords with a fringed, leather tongue that hung over the laces. Two-toned summer sport shoes were as popular for the "dudey" man as spectator pumps were for women. The brown or black standard shoe of the thirties could be worn today without giving a vintage appearance.

Our man shaved before he finished dressing, and he had to choose between the old method—with brush, cup, soap and safety or straight razor—or the new electric razor. The brush-and-cup shaver was supposedly marching off into the pages of history at the rate of ten thousand per day. The lathered man was called the "vanishing American" who could avoid cuts, nicks, scrapes and all of the mess if he'd switch to electric shaving.

Pictured is a Gillette blade ad, showing a happy man getting lathered with the faithful tools in 1937, while making ready for a heavy date for that night. He says, "I'm gonna come clean, baby!" It's a question whether today's swinger would dig some of the copy in the shaving ad. It said, "The etchings, if any, won't be on his face! Every grad on the deb list knows moonlight really puts a razor to the test. There's no point in shaving with a gadget that doesn't get you by—cheek-to-cheek . . . "

Our man continued his dress by slipping into trousers—nice, generously cut, draped pants with pleats in front.

You can't beat
Interwoven
The best wearing socks made

Interwoven was a popular brand of argyle sock in the thirties. (Courtesy of INTERWOVEN, a division of Kayser-Roth Corp.)

They gave a man room to float in and made today's styles look hilarously skimpy.

Once he donned the pants, how would he hold them up? Belt or suspenders? Some doubting souls used both simultaneously. Let's take the braces, galluses or suspenders, whichever you call them. With this accessory some men dared to sport sprightlier colors and designs. Suspenders also made the trousers hang nicely.

Meantime, he put on his shirt, and according to an English fashion arbiter, stiff collars were favored by the "carriage trade." It was impossible to overemphasize the revived importance of the white starched collar that was reachieving its long-lost standing as an established fashion. Pink came in surprisingly strong as a shirt color, even for "he-men" who first scoffed that it was sissy.

Another choice had to be made: would he wear a four-

"I'm gonna come clean, baby!"

WHEN a young man has a 'phone in one hand and a shaving brush in the other—the night is young, the girl gorgeous and they are going places. The etchings, if any, won't be on his face! Nor the prickly stubble of half-mown bristles, either. He will show up *clean*—and *smooth!*

Moonlight and Razors

Clean shaving is important. Moonlight really puts a razor to the test. Every grad on the deb list knows this. And there's no point to shaving with a gadget that doesn't get you by cheek to cheek—or using misfit blades in your razor that usually hack, scrape and pull.

Today's Gillette Blade is a product of a great industrial romance. Gillette has invested more millions in precision equipment, spent more years in scientific research and made more blades than all other manufacturers combined.

Keenest Edges Ever Produced!

Gillette steel is finer than Damascus ever produced. It is electrically tempered to glass-cutting hardness. Rigid inspection of every blade assures absolute uniformity.

Don't let the low cost of Gillette Blades confuse you. Money can't buy *cleaner, smoother, closer* shaves or greater shaving comfort than these blades assure. Use them in your razor and you'll give *her face a thrill!*

Gillette
Blades
MORE SHAVING COMFORT FOR YOUR MONEY

A Gillette blade advertisement stressed the importance of a close shave if you had a big date. (Courtesy of Gillette Safety Razor Co.)

PARIS
GARTERS
NO METAL CAN TOUCH YOU

Well-dressed men used to wear garters to hold up their socks. These Paris Garters were a popular brand. (Courtesy A. Stein, & Co. manufacturers of Paris Garters, suspenders, belts and men's accessories)

169

Pleated, generously cut trousers of yesterday make to-day's Ivy League styles skimpy by comparison. (Courtesy Roger Kent)

Wide ties were the vogue, and diamond stickpins were big status symbols in the thirties.

Paisley suspenders added color to the gentleman's wardrobe and allowed his trousers to hang nicely.

in-hand or bow tie? In either case, it was wide, with enough material to display the fabric pattern. The noticeable tie is presently in favor again.

If he chose a straight tie, he'd need a stick-pin to hold it in place. The convincing status symbol was to have a big diamond glittering at the pin's end. Bow ties were either ready-tied and clipped under the collar, or had to be tied by the purist who disdained machine perfection. Some men never learned to make an acceptable bow.

Mr. Thirties shouldn't have forgotten his vest, as it was as much a part of the suit as the trousers. If he was a bit portly, the vest pulled into horizontal ripples across his front.

Our man-about-town might have chosen the smart pocket watch and chain with a key container on the end, to slip into the vest's watch pocket. With town clothes, Wall Street brokers favored this. Gold cigarette cases were just coming into fashion. All cigarettes were short—practically no millimeters! Later, when king sizes came, cigarette cases had to be made adjustable.

Suits of the thirties often came with vests.

Pictured is our nearly completed man. Note the massive shoulders and neat waist that appears corseted. He had a choice of single or double-breasted models. When the doubles went out of style, enterprising tailors made much business by altering them to single-breasted to save the garments.

Wall Streeters favored a pocket watch and chain, with a key container on the end. Gold cigarette cases were just coming into fashion.

If it was a cold day, Mr. Thirties needed an additional coat. Perhaps he wore a Chesterfield; possibly of herringbone weave with a velvet collar. He might prefer a Tyrolean-inspired coat of generous proportions. The Tyrol made important contributions to men's fashion.

Mufflers made great gift items when ideas ran out. They were worn by nearly all who lived where cold winds and snow swept around necks. Our man could don a Tyrolean style or the popular muffler woven from heavy wool in a black and red plaid with fringed ends. For dressy occasions, they were of white silk, either plain or with white-on-white patterns.

No self-respecting man would be caught without his hat, whether in his hand, on a rack, or on his head.

The thirties suit: note the wide shoulders and the narrow waist.

This well-dressed man is wearing a Chesterfield coat, with a velvet collar. (Courtesy Roger Kent)

Knapp-Felt Headwear said, "Nothing contributes more to a man's pleasure than the knowledge that he is properly dressed for the occasion." So, wherever Mr. Thirties went, he had a sizeable hat wardrobe to cover innumerable occasions and all seasons.

At the time of the "bank holiday" in the beginning of President Roosevelt's administration, the black derby and black Chesterfield coat was like a uniform most men in Detroit's financial district wore. Men loved caps better than most women loved them on their men. Young fellows would throw them on at a jaunty angle while the older

No self-respecting man would be caught without his hat.
(Courtesy Hat Corporation of America)

man set them primly straight. Stylewise, a hat was more becoming.

On a scorching summer day without air-conditioning, our man was cool as possible with a light Palm Beach suit and black and white sport oxfords. He didn't get many wearings between trips to the cleaners, but he looked snappy!

In the twenties and thirties another "jazzy" style was white flannels worn with boldly striped blazer jackets. These thrilled the girl friends at summer dances and very special dates.

Something distinctly "in" for our man's added pleasure and convenience was the Talon Slide Fastener. It slowly appeared on more items after its advent in the twenties

on snow boots. It was advertised for men's sweaters as an entirely superior departure from the former buttons. The copy said, "It's as supple as a row of soft, knitted stitches! Like the grand 'n' glorious freedom of a pullover . . . "

Let's leave Mr. Thirties in the ultra top of fashion, as "British as boiled beef," with morning clothes that were becoming increasingly important with stylish American men. They were used for Sunday afternoons and evenings or fashionable weddings. The coat was a one-button peak lapel cut-away. There was a waistcoat in the same unfinished worsted. Instead of a wing collar and Ascot, these were shown with turndown collar and four-in-hand tie.

Recently my husband needed a new pair of work

Palm Beach suits were popular for summer wear. (REG.
T. M. GOODALL SANFORD INCORPORATED, PALM
BEACH COMPANY, Exclusive Licensee)

Talon Slide Fasteners were a big improvement over buttons. (Courtesy Talon Division of Textron, Inc.)

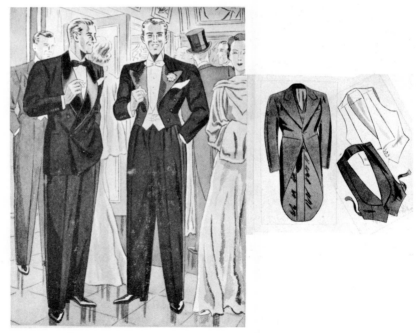

Some examples of formal wear of the thirties: the tuxedo,
the ultra-formal white tie and tails, morning clothes, and
waistcoats. (Courtesy Roger Kent)

A happy couple at a formal occasion, c. 1930.

HART SCHAFFNER & MARX

One of the longest known names in men's wear is Hart, Schaffner and Marx. The company was celebrating its golden anniversary in 1937, and here are two examples of its advertising for that year. At the left, a young Henry Fonda is shown in a triple-test worsted Savile Lounge Model double breasted; at the right, the gentleman is showing more concern for his suit than for his lady friend. (Courtesy Hart, Schaffner and Marx)

slacks. He foraged through many stacks of slacks as an indulgent salesman stood nearby with a patient smile creasing his face. He didn't assist my husband's frenzied search for a pair with pleats. He wouldn't give up and admit that they just don't make them like that anymore. You may not hanker to be a middle-aged Ivy-Leaguer as you stoop in the garden, but there's little choice unless you can wait for the trend to revert. Or—you might find a friendly, understanding tailor who comprehends how Mr. Thirties feels in the sixties.

15

Gladrags

Paris told women what to wear and they wore it! This French dictatorship lasted until the post-World War II period.

When the lady said, "I haven't a thing to wear," she didn't necessarily mean that she had no apparel in her closet. It might be that she hadn't anything her friends didn't see at least once before, or that her wardrobe dated way back to the year before. Perhaps a new trend had cancelled a closetful of good clothes. But whatever the situation, woman's natural love of raiment and accessories gives an army livelihood in more fields than merely sewing seams.

In 1926 the question arose as to what vanity was—it was the thought of one's self: for without vanity, femininity was lost. So vain she must be—or else be a mere haphazard person without chic, elegance, wit or the accessories of fashion.

Paris fashions of another era.

Had you thought of it that way?

There was a vocabulary for fashion used repetitiously, and although we know the apparent meanings today, thirty years ago a different atmosphere was created with class-conscientiousness about the well-dressed woman. Much of the reference was to high society or royalty, assuming that Jane Doe aspired to emulate those who were socially higher and more glamorous. Words seen often were correctness, chic, charm, smartness, discriminating, frocks, costumes.

Maybe you attended a wedding then with the lovely bride wearing this soft satin with side ripple drapery. Her headgear was not unlike a dust cap and the bouquet was draped limply over her arm. The bridesmaids' dresses were called simple frocks of net and taffeta. (We hasten to wonder what was complicated.) The maid of honor also rustled with a taffeta frock while the bride's mother got along with a simple gown of black and white striped taffeta. There's nothing like black for weddings!

The description for a pattern of the era gave this data for required goods: ladies' dress, one-piece straight skirt, 38 inch length, size 36 requires six and three-fourths yards of 38 inch material, three fourths yard 27 inch for collar and vest, and three yards of lace edging. Dress three yards wide, in sizes from thirty-four to forty-six bust. What would our size nines do? And at present material costs, we wouldn't make many of these creations.

Georgette was a favored material and blouses were called waists—some came with over-waists. A jumper was explained as a handy little accessory for changing the appearance of a frock. It took real know-how to sew the intricate drapery. You can plainly see that needle-pointed shoes aren't new.

In 1922 you could have strutted after buying one of the sumptuous coats pictured. Dolman sleeves made them easy to slip into and as if the fur trim wasn't enough embellishment, braid and embroidery were added. The model on the far right was so high style that one wearing could have finished it.

Bargain underwear of 1922 was advertised in colorfast sateen, impervious to soap, boiling, sun and water. Bloomers were $1.95 and princess slips $2.95. The latter had three-row hemstitch trims and luscious colors like honeydew, orchid and flesh.

These fashions are from 1915. These sweet young ladies would now be called teenagers. Note the fussiness with net, tucks, and gathers. (*World War I Magazine*)

Silk stockings were as much of a luxury for women in the twenties as silk shirts were for men. A hosiery ad glowingly announced that you could pay as little as $1.65, $1.85 or $1.95 for exquisite stockings. Thrift McCallums, a new group of lovely stockings, sold everywhere at prices so low that every woman could afford to wear them every day. These prices are probably the reason so many women wore lisle and cotton when you consider that $25 per week was a good salary. When hosiery sprung leaks and ladders, we mended them over and over.

Lane Bryant was a pioneer in recognizing that many women do not remain slim, and that finding clothing is a problem. So they specialized in clothes for the woman of "full figure."

Where did skirts go? Up to the limits of decency or down to trail the floor, and all degrees in between. If they were at ankle level during World War I, as seen in the bridal fashions, they climbed violently in the twenties. The flapper began gathering publicity with her bobbed hair, long strings of beads and beltlines falling off the hips. If she wore galoshes, the more buckles the better, for these were worn unbuckled and made a great slapping noise with each step. Modest "older" ladies wore boots with about three buckles and they were fastened.

These pictured dresses show a skirt length which has been repeated twice since. Short hair was prevalent so that skull-hugging hats were worn. Notice the lowness of waistlines.

While short skirts ruled, Phoenix Hosiery said in 1926, "Style decrees the revealed knee, so Phoenix covers it with lovely silk; to its very top, our special number 736 is all pure Japanese silk, long, brilliant and sturdy strands . . ."

The flapper era was not long in spite of the lasting fame her title carries. She passed away fairly quietly as another trend took over. In the end it was said that the flapper became delightfully dignified, her bobbed hair disappeared in that mysterious manner so baffling to *mere* men, and her facial expression became sphinx-like and sophisticated to match the new manner of costuming. Every detail of fashion tended toward subtle forms of coquetry undreamed of by the former flappers. No longer could her critics complain but they undoubtedly found new threads to pick as the sophisticated woman acquired new charm as you marveled at the disappearance of the one and evidence of the other.

Wedding fashions, c. 1915. (*World War I Magazine*)

High-fashion coats of 1922 vintage. (Courtesy Detroit News)

A Lane Bryant folder mailing piece for Fall and Winter, from the mid-twenties. (Courtesy Lane Bryant)

These dresses show a skirt length that has come back into fashion twice since these days.

matched rosee pearls for Christmas or birthday. It behooved you to have been a very good girl because the price tag in a 1927 Harper's Bazaar ad was $115,000 for these trinkets. Others were $125,000 to $200. Loose pearls cost a mere $20,000 to $10 per piece. The oddity of the copy writing was that the extremely high price came first, then the minimum—the opposite of today's psychology.

The uneven hemline was big in 1929. My baccalaureate dress of rose georgette, had a skirt at my knees in front and touched the floor in back. The variations were wide in the style and one had a single point that hung a foot longer in the front center.

The uneven hemline was big in 1929.

Have you ever wondered when the miracle zipper came along—the one we take for granted now? It was first showing on rain boots in 1926 in our town. An ad said, "So clever, these hookless fasteners that take the place of many, many buttons! One gentle pull closes or opens them."

Also in 1926 definite statements were made about hats. "The hat with a brim turned up in back has had its day and ceased to be. Brims now are turned down, cut off, or they do not exist at all." Woe be unto brims!

Linit advertising in 1926 said that the way to restore the original charm of artificial silk fabrics was to use their product. Rayon cloth was not enthusiastically received. The first material was always called rayon, not acetate or other nice names, and it was too shiny, sleazy and frayed easily. It was often used for linings and was plainly regarded as an imitation product that had to battle against the established silks. We little foresaw the day when wonderful materials of all textures and weights would envelop the clothing industry. I wonder what the silkworms thought of being inundated by man-made fabrics.

In case you had a well-heeled husband of generous spirit or a "sugar daddy" with more money and indulgence than caution, you might have received 77 perfectly

By the 1931–32 winter, our hair was emerging from hats and eyebrows could be seen. The newest fashions in millinery were harking back to 1880, so they said. Styles have always been throwbacks to inspirations of other days, for how many differences can there be for covering the body or keeping it warm? Hats were beginning to be set atop the head instead of enclosing the entire skull.

Formal afternoon attire underwent a change. You felt dressed up with clothing that could go through the dinner hour. Necks went high and skirts went low, some trailing the ground. Great attention was paid to varying slits in the back from neck to waist. Belts had gradually found the normal waistline.

By the winter of 1931-32, hair and eyebrows could again be seen.

Frills and flounces came back in the thirties.

With formal afternoon attire like this, you felt dressed up right through the dinner hour.

Appliquéd patterns appeared on underwear and lounging pajamas.

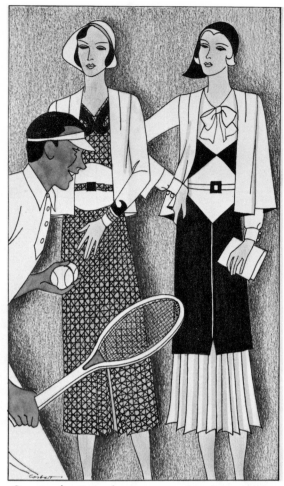

Sporty daytime dresses were ideal for tennis.

Frills and flounces, they said; so we frilled and flounced in profusion. Soft crepes and georgettes hung well for all of the ripples above and below the "new" natural waistline.

Elegant lounging pajamas, with legs so full that they masked as skirts, were recommended for leisure hours. Appliqué patterns were used for these as well as underwear. The "discriminating woman" was the one who chose these. Brassieres were not uplifting in 1932, and "step-ins" were the panties of popularity. Many underthings were made of honest-to-goodness silk!

Anyone for tennis? Distinguished, ten-heads-tall string bean ladies would be decked out in daytime dresses a little on the "sporty" side. Suntan was just creeping in as a new idea for fashion and started with a choice of suntan shades in hosiery. Previously sun was only for shining and burning—usually for men who had to work in it while the girls basked under sun parasols.

In the thirties, when our skirts weren't far above the ankles, tailored suits, many in menswear materials, were found in every wardrobe. Some men's tailors began to make women's suits, done impeccably in every detail. Glen plaids, all the way from boldly coarse to shadowy thin, were favored. The ghillie shoes were "in" with their long laces crisscrossed and tied on the ankles. Even the dog suggested the era, because Scotch terriers enjoyed phenomenal popularity after the country was aware that President Roosevelt's pet was a "Scottie" named Falla.

Between the extremes of long and short skirts was a period at "calf-mast," midway on the lower leg. Some of us loved it as the ideal compromise. It didn't look skimpy with unattractive knees outcropping, and it felt freer than the near-ankle sweep of material. Padded shoulders were definitely in and grew to football suit size on suits and coats. Even dresses and blouses had their inevitable pads.

In the mid-thirties a clever little lady, Gladys Parker, not only drew the popular Flapper Fanny cartoon, but designed unusual clothes with emphasis on slacks. She lived in slacks herself although many give the credit for getting women into trousers to Marlene Dietrich. Whoever gets

This thirties-era lady sports a tailored suit and a Scotty.

CAREFREE CHIC FOR SUNNY PLAYTIME

Slacks were all the fad in the middle thirties, but they weren't of today's skin-tight variety. (Sketch by author for the Detroit *Times*)

the credit, the ladies began to "wear the pants!" At first they were closely related to skirts and you couldn't tell the difference unless she stood with feet widely separated. This illustration, as late as 1940, demonstrates the leg width and draped fullness.

The middy-blouse slack suit emphasized that slacks meant just that—plenty of slack. There's little resemblance to stretch Capri pants of today, in fact, they looked baggy. Even I was lifting my eyebrows when my old-fashioned mother came out with seersucker slacks of generous cut for gardening and a neighbor snorted, "I suppose she'll be smoking cigarettes next!"

There was plenty of slack in the middy-blouse slack suit.

This *New York Times* headline heralded the advent of
silk substitutes. (Courtesy *The New York Times*)

Heels in the thirties could be high, but they were substantial at the bottom. (Courtesy *Harper's Bazaar*)

Meantime, what was happening to legs? When short
skirts ruled, Phoenix was a popular brand and the Onyx
Company produced "Pointex," with the reinforced heel,
which had been square, changing to a point that ran up
into the back seam. Other makers had a variety of points,
some using as many as three. The shine of stockings
gave way to a dull, matte finish called crepe. Many young
women wore hose wrong-side-out to get the less shiny
appearance. Elaborate clocked stockings had designs
either woven or even beaded on the outsides of legs to
add side interest.

In the late thirties the big news was nylon and you
were probably buying your first pair of nylons, not be-
lieving the advance advertising claims, or that coal had
something to do with the making of these gossamer stockings. Was it really true that these sheer delights were immortal, indestructible, non-running or snagging—and very
expensive? *Harper's Bazaar* answered these and more
questions by assuring milady that they would wear a
remarkably long time; that their smooth strands and ten-
sile strength would resist snags; but that if once threads
were pulled, runs could develop. As for cost, they quoted
a price range of $1.00 to $1.65, which was comparable to
silk stocking prices. Instead of the resistance or indiffer-
ence rayon encountered, women rushed to purchase
nylon.

We've had extremely pointed shoes for several years
and had to get used to them simply because there wasn't
much else available. It's refreshing to look backward to
the opposite in shoe styles (which ironically have begun
to creep into favor again while this is written). Flattery,
to make the foot look as short and tiny as possible, was the
keynote of designs. Heels could be high but they were
substantial at the bottom with slighter curves on the
shaft.

It's difficult to think of a classic style that's appeared
more regularly than the "spectator" in its varying forms.
They may change heel shapes from high to low, make
them in stacked wood or covered with leather, in oxfords or pumps; they may point or round the toe and use
black, brown, tan, blue or any color contrast with the
white; but they're unmistakably spectators.

These shoes were called sane. "They have sleek, simple
lines and look like shoes." (Courtesy *Harper's Bazaar*)

The "spectator" has always been popular. (Courtesy *Harper's Bazaar*)

This chic and popular model wore the large sculptured curls in a sleekly severe version of the up hairdo. (Courtesy *Harper's Bazaar*)

If you still clung to hair that went in its natural direction, you could wear the new hats; but it didn't work the other way around. There had to be mechanical engineering to make the dabs of hats stay where you put them. Most styles had round, elastic cords to stretch around the back of your head, while adjusting the front at the desired angle. Others used straps of the hat material, or else tiny combs were sewed under the sides to invisibly grip your hair.

These unusual shoes, designed by Perugia, are a reminder that even in our "archaic past," we had some far-out styles and designers. (Courtesy *Harper's Bazaar*)

To reverse the usual order, let's go from foot to head to see what was going on in the thirties-into-forties. In 1935 we were told to put up our hair and it was repeated in 1936 and 1937. Women were reluctant for several reasons: it was a violent change, it made long necks even longer, some ears weren't good for display, and many didn't know how to achieve a professional looking coiffeur. It also negated the lady's hat wardrobe. It was much easier to let your hair hang, although numbers compromised by putting up the sides and front while the back mane hung with curled ends.

The revolutionary hair change caused equally new things to happen in several branches of style. *Harper's Bazaar* had this to say; "Since hairdos have changed . . . necks look longer, therefore necklines and jewelry have changed. Hats have changed their position on the head. The silhouette has changed, therefore figures and foundations have changed. Because of all the purples and fuchsias, the colors of lipsticks have changed. Everything's changing . . . " and all because the fashion arbiters said, "Put your hair up."

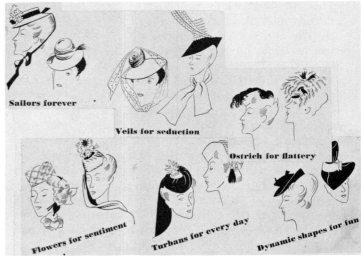

These sketches show some of the varieties of shapes in the little hats for "up-dos." They certainly were tiny when compared to the substantial head-covering crowns with honest brims and even linings. The new ones might have been doll's headgear. (Courtesy *Harper's Bazaar*)

Were you a turban-lover? Nothing was as flattering and at the same time covered a multitude of hair sins. We could buy already draped models or the wrap-it-yourself versions. The nicest to wrap were lengths of wool jersey or suede cloth with shirring across the center to help shape it to the head. There were cloth-covered sausage rolls that were inserted under the front to build height as you wound the scarf around. Demonstrators in department stores gave tips on turban-winding.

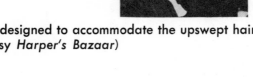

Hats were redesigned to accommodate the upswept hair-dos. (Courtesy *Harper's Bazaar*)

One utterly feminine compliment to faces of all shapes and ages was veiling. It was everywhere from fine silk film like bridal veiling, to coarse, staccato threads with fuzzy dots or woven squares for pattern. It could be a brief nose veil or cascade by the yard in a swirl around the hat or tie under the chin.

Madame Schiaparelli, the designer, introduced her "shocking pink," which caught on immediately. It was a fashion era when women complained less of the styles offered than in other periods we can recall—including the present. Women looked like women and were pretty instead of bizarre.

How could any mention of fashion ignore furs? Trimmings of fur on necks and sleeves or jacket and skirt bottoms came before furriers perfected the complete pelt coat. The most noticeable flaw with early fur coats was their lack of style. In the twenties we had the curly lamb (not like the later fine Persians), with fox collars. Mink was used too, but usually went in many directions—

Turbans, like this one, could cover up a multitude of hair sins. (Courtesy *Harper's Bazaar*)

You were considered feminine indeed if you owned a veil like this. (Courtesy *Harper's Bazaar*)

Rich, let out mink spelled elegance, as this model proves. (Courtesy *Harper's Bazaar*)

such as in horizontal bands or zigzagged here and there. Mink tails often fringed the coat bottom, but the true beauty of mink was hidden. Raccoon was used for men and women but it could scarcely win a beauty contest. Muskrat was serviceable, but not yet blended into pleasing color. My art teacher in the late twenties had a coat of leopard with a red fox collar, and a fingertip length coat fashioned entirely from little chipmunks. She was in extremely high style for those fur-bearing days!

In the thirties mink spelled elegance with its smokey dark color and detailing of neck and sleeves. Mink scarves were wonderful complements to suits. Three skins were the least you'd want; five were better, and if price was no object, you could be "dripping with mink."

There was a blazing rage for silver fox that you may remember. Twin fox scarves led the parade with jackets and sumptuous full-length capes following. By 1938 they were so prevalent, some considered them "common." Whereas minks, baum or stone martens were more proportioned to short or pudgy women, they nevertheless wore twin silver foxes in profusion.

Silver fox was all the rage in the late thirties. Above, full-length capes; below, a twin fox scarf. (Courtesy *Harper's Bazaar*)

This fur is an example of the let-out process: a long, unbroken line from shoulder to bottom. (Courtesy *Harper's Bazaar*)

Furriers began to do sewing tricks with certain pelts so that styling not before seen appeared with such skins as flat, workable caracul and broadtail. The let-out process of making a long, unbroken line from shoulder to bottom was used on many furs besides mink—even skunk. The mink-dye or blending of muskrat was popular and seal, real or otherwise, was prevalent. In many cases, only the furrier knew for sure when rabbit (coney), put on a disguise. Every part of mink pelts was used, including the gills and undersides. Beaver appeared as a sheared, velvety beauty. Perhaps you recall fitch, pony and monkey fur. It was after this era that furs had to show up with identifying words as to their origins because many women had little idea what animals lurked on their backs.

We've saved the supreme fur for last—the chinchilla, precious because of its rarity and costliness. So fine and soft that it ripples with a breath, and yet so perishable that care of it must be tender and painstaking. The little animal has an affinity for high mountains—the colder, the better the fur quality. The Ural Mountains of Russia harbor the best chinchillas and although many people have tried to raise them on farms, most met with disappointment and dead animals.

It would be unfair to overlook an important component of the style picture—the fashion illustrator. There have been far too many to mention all, but the dean of fashion artists was for years Carl Ericson. You may not have read the signature, Eric, but you've undoubtedly seen his work. All top fashion artists have the uncanny ability to create an aura of smart desirability around the clothes so that women clamor for the styles. Their taste in atmosphere must be unfailingly smart and the techniques distinctive. In the thirties two artists with recognizable styles as well as unusual names were Denevor Rhys and Malaga Grenet.

Opera star Lily Pons shows off her chinchilla. (Courtesy *Harper's Bazaar*)

Carl Ericson was considered the dean of the fashion illustrators in the thirties. This sketch appeared in *Harper's Bazaar)*

This is an example of the work of Malaga Grenet. (Courtesy *Harper's Bazaar)*

This lovely lady was drawn by Denevor Rhys. (Courtesy *Harper's Bazaar)*

Their ladies were dignified and aloof, without much eye visible in the sockets. These artists used simple, nearly flat tones on tall, ruler-thin figures.

Along came a lady with much more natural figure drawing and freer style—Ruth Grafstrom. Her sophisticated illustrations showed ladies with detached airs as they graced many pages in fashion magazines.

Have you wondered about or envied the sleekness of the flawless girls who model clothes for fine fashions? What are their schedules and lives in comparison to the average girl nextdoor? From the multitude who've graced magazines, clothed in creations from the great couturiers, we may remember a scant few.

Georgia Carroll was a popular fashion model in the late thirties. (Courtesy *Harper's Bazaar*)

For outstanding popularity and success, I'm sure none could surpass Georgia Carroll who went to New York in 1937. Miss Carroll thought of singing as a career, but when working in a Neiman-Marcus fashion show, the modeling profession picked her out. That was the beginning of a busy life for a girl not yet twenty. The work was exacting and entailed long hours of unflagging energy and freshness before the merciless lights and cameras. For this reason, models who hope to stay the limit in this work must have sleep instead of late hours and cocktail parties or anything that would deteriorate their looks. Simply, they must lead disciplined lives with meticulous care of health, face and figure to arrive and remain awhile in the shortlived career.

Whereas Miss Carroll was from Texas, another famous model, Elizabeth Gibbons, was from Montgomery, Alabama. *Harper's Bazaar* said of her, "She is a long, fluid Southern girl who loves luxury like a cat. She trails through the studios and agencies with Southern languor. But for all of that, she'll work until three in the morning

As can be seen, Ruth Grafstrom's work featured a freer style, and ladies with detached airs. (Courtesy of Ruth Grafstrom)

Elizabeth Gibbons was another popular model of the thirties. (Courtesy *Harper's Bazaar*)

for a good picture, and she's never been known to go dead on a photographer." Here they caught her in the middle of a healthy yawn.

Other famous models, Jinx Falkenberg and Anita Colby, went into other businesses and Elyse Knox married famous football star Tom Harmon. Many retired to marriage or various branches of entertainment.

After World War II, some violent fashion changes came. Paris had remained the absolute capital of the style world until America began to flex its creative muscles and weaned customers from their French couturiers. Italy came into the market with a flash and flare that brought serious flurries of attention. In 1927 *Harper's Bazaar* had a regular spread entitled, "Where to Shop in Paris," with small ads for many French clothing houses. Even New York stores, realizing the lure of France, assured their customers they'd receive "courtesy and personal attention, appreciated by the Paris shopper." Now this old order was changing.

No matter how men may pooh-pooh their wives' clothes and hats, fashion is here to stay in some form, whether it be as brief as a bikini or a head-to-toe swathing. No matter what place on earth is the favored fashion center, women will beat and scratch to get to its gates.

16

Powder Puff Kingdom

When vanity reared its head and I studied my face too long in the mirror, my mother would say, "Beauty is as beauty does." This philosophy would neither comfort the cosmetic manufacturers nor the ladies who have increasingly relied on beauty preparations to appear lovelier than Mother Nature made them. If not lovelier, at least, different. In the twenties we had a rhyme that went:

> Little dabs of powder, little grams of paint
> Make the ladies' freckles seem as if they ain't.

The girl with too many freckles found solace if she sent away for Stillman's Freckle Cream. (Courtesy the Stillman Company)

The author's portrait of herself, studying her face too long in the mirror.

Kind-hearted people told freckled girls they should treasure their spots as marks of beauty and distinction, but this was cold comfort to those who were generously freckled. The Stillman Company promised more than sympathy, and for only a half dollar!

In every age back to antiquity, beauty has been a prize too precious to estimate; but the standard beauty of one era would certainly look askance at the ideal of another. The lady of 1928 glowed with a milk-and-honey complexion that was never seared by the sun until well-done on both sides. Her nose, brow and chin were creamy, and if her cheeks didn't glow like roses, she could pinch them to bring up the blood circulation or practice the art of rouging. She knew nothing of complicated eye makeup to give herself intricate pools of allure. Eyes were "windows

to the soul," but windows without drapes. Mouths were not described as generous unless in a derogatory sense. Her hair would make a beauty operator's fingers itch to do something with it. But this young lady was attractive to us then.

Bobbing hair in the twenties created a furor. Women who had clung to long tresses, as if cutting it involved a moral issue, began to succumb. A fiftyish friend of our family came one day to show us her new bob. My mother was utterly disgusted. As a defense, the lady argued that her long hair "soured" in warm weather, and cutting it was the only cure. After she left mother retorted, "There's no fool like an old fool!"

Bobbed hair even caused a special shampoo to be created to light up the brief coiffure.

Artist's stylized portrayals of women in those days could make them look less than human. The fingers,

The ideal beauty, mid-twenties style. (Courtesy of Mrs. Frederic Leech)

An advertisement for a special shampoo for bobbed hairdos. (Courtesy J. W. Kobi Company)

As this advertisement shows, the "bobbed" hairdo created problems for the twenties girl. (Courtesy Wildroot Division, Colgate-Palmolive Company)

A 1926 direct-mail piece.

hands and necks grew startlingly long, and eyebrows were a thin pencil-line. On real women, brows that needed tweezing were comparable to a bleach that's grown out on either side of the part. Hairdos were plastered to the head, and mouths were precisely delicate in contour and size.

When nail polish first made its appearance, the vogue was to leave the tips and half-moons unpainted.

Fingernail buffers were used until sometime in the thirties after women were convinced it was much easier to paint on liquid that lasted and lasted; at least, until it chipped and peeled. A revolution was working at our fingertips after we'd been accustomed to cake or powder polishing agents that produced a delicate gloss when the chamois buffer was vigorously rubbed over the nails. Some buffers were very long, pointed at the ends, and with decorated handles and backs of real ivory or a synthetic called ivorene. A complete manicure included a white cream that was pushed under the nail tips to give them a ghastly whiteness.

Then as now, the reducing diet was popular.

Did you try to subsist on lamb chops and pineapple? Many misses did in the pursuit of the sylph figure. This fad diet was replaced by the Hollywood 18 Day Diet, guaranteed to make you a shadow of your former self if you didn't give up by the fifteenth day. You *had* to like grapefruit or you were defeated before beginning, for it was an ingredient of every meal. You needed 27 grapefruit, nearly 2 dozen eggs, 7 small steaks, 12 lamb chops, spinach, tomatoes, lettuce, olives, plain tea and black coffee to feast sumptuously. A few times you'd have the reward of a small fish fillet, bit of lobster or a meat salad when your gauntness became unbearable. I never lasted more than five days, so the weight loss was negligible.

When women were sure that nail lacquer wouldn't impair health or cause the nails to fall off, they began buying the new polish avidly. Colorless liquid was the first offering, then gradually the rainbow started—from pink to deep reds. Vogues changed several times in the manner of application, first the tips and half-moons were left unpainted. Then the moons disappeared and a fine line at the tip was rubbed off before the polish dried, to discourage damage while fingers were in use. It was years before pearlescence and unusual colors crept into the polish business. Each manufacturer's claim was that his product was longer-wearing and less likely to chip. Men never tired of saying about the red polish, "Your hands look as if they're dripping blood!"

Tangee created a sensation with orange lipstick. (Courtesy George W. Luft Company, Inc.)

A thirties-style finger buffer.

The first breakthrough in mouth make-up was Tangee's orange lipstick that magically changed color on the lips. Their ads said, "Are you tired of that painted look?" Another time-tested lipstick was Kissproof, which could be bought in dimestores in small sizes, along with their cake rouge.

Helena Rubinstein's "Cupidsbow" lipstick.

Helena Rubinstein, one of the greatest innovators in the cosmetic business, presented a most novel idea in lipstick. It was called "Cupidsbow," the self-shaping lipstick. She said of it; "A lipstick that forms a perfect cupid's bow as you apply it!"

In private life Helena Rubinstein was Princess Gourielli, and a great patroness of the arts, especially as an encourager of struggling young artists. She lived well into her nineties and was still inventing new ideas in her products to further women's beauty and youth.

No well-run boudoir was without talcum powder, but do you recall some of the brand names? Arden made a popular powder, also Mavis, and don't forget Princess Pat and her complete cosmetic line. At the Chicago World's Fair in 1933, you could enter the Princess Pat

The author painted this watercolor of Helena Rubinstein in the thirties, and it was autographed by her.

Salon as your tired old self and emerge as a fresh, raving beauty—without charge. Of course interest in you waned quickly if you didn't place an order for any or all of their products.

If you lived then you'll remember; but if not, you'll stop your back-combing and "teasing" long enough to admire hairdos we wore for two decades.

This dimpled young lady is receiving a fingerwave generously trimmed with "spit" curls. The latter were plastered to the skin with a heavy wave-set that dried very slowly.

Do you remember the origin of the allegedly "permanent" wave? Mr. Charles Nestle claimed he first did permanent waving in 1905. In 1926 the Nestle Circuline Wave stated that it lasted the life of the hair. The Nestle Lanoil Company, Ltd., ran a full page ad in 1926 to tell of their new X-ray invention for ascertaining from a strand of hair how best to insure safety and perfect results. They said, "Have your hair 'read' before you have it waved."

The close-clinging tightly curled hair styles were once very popular. (Courtesy Meyer Both Company)

Our hair didn't soar in any direction, but hugged close to "homepate." The curled ends were produced by various implements, but the bobby pin was king for years, starting as a device to hold the hair in place until there was greater use for them when pincurls started.

A metal curler similar to the holding bars girls now use was called the West Electric Curler. The name is a mystery since it had no connection with electricity. After the kinky waves were arranged, Rose Brilliantine was the favored sheen hair dressing in 1926.

Voluptuous sausage curls like these were achieved with the aid of metal rollers. (Courtesy Meyer Both Company)

To get the voluptuous sausage curls, metal rollers were used. If you were a nightly do-it-yourselfer, you had to learn to sleep on the hardware and like it.

This finger-wave style resembled the Marcel wave of the twenties—without the latter's inconvenience.

The popular finger wave resembled the Marcel wave of the twenties, but had none of the inevitable burned, crisped ridges from hot irons. The Marcel was born in Paris, but wherever it was accomplished, you'd be assailed by the smell of hot oil and hair—not pleasant. An ad said you could finger wave your own hair beautifully, but they couldn't convince me that I could get the uniform rows perfectly matched on the back of my head.

195

The wigs of the sixties are neither late nor new. In 1926 this was said about transformations, which were artificial hair pieces; 'The society matron must have several—the well-dressed and exceedingly smart women will surely have one."

After a complexity of curls in various directions, it was refreshing to have the sleek, single roll that started at one ear, passed unbroken around the back and ended at the other ear. The front treatment might be varied. Later, the feather cut enjoyed a vogue and was flattering to many heads. One revolution in hair shapes was experienced when Ginger Rogers wore a pageboy bob in a motion picture. The style swept the country for a considerable time in long and short versions.

In 1938 the "up" hairdo was gaining favor after an unsuccessful try some years earlier. (It proved that once in awhile women revolt or ignore the dictates of style arbiters.) On its second bid, it took to the heads in force. However, Clarita deForceville expounded violently in *Harper's Bazaar* about her aversion to it. She said, 'It is impossible to be charming when you feel you look like a summer squash. I have developed an inferiority complex since my hair is up, and I want to cry—just cry—silently and at length. What is this fashion that makes a folly of friendship and turns easy social conversation into a stilted, dismal despair?" Her opinion makes it sound upsetting indeed, like a traumatic experience.

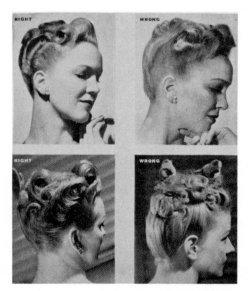

The do's and don'ts of the upswept hairdo. (Courtesy *Harper's Bazaar*)

There were beautifully good "upswepts," and pitifully bad, careless examples. Long wisps wandering on their own around the back of the neck were not pretty, nor were all sorts of miscellaneous holding devices. Whereas the hairdo could give a gangling look to the overly slender, long-necked girl, it was a godsend to us with plump

roundness and short necks. The style stayed for several years, but after long wearing of the coiffeur, the hair became listless and limp.

The trend changed, but a comparable look was achieved with a style that had to be cut—the ducktail. This was in the early fifties. It looked simple to care for, but what the beauty operator did easily could never be duplicated at home.

What about holding sprays? They've become necessities now, but they weren't always. In the twenties hairnets were big business. Dime, department and drugstores were obliged to carry big stocks of varying sizes, colors and styles of nets "made from human hair." By the thirties a spray was used and it was frankly called lacquer. This wasn't a joke because when the evilly perfumed cloud dried, your hair was like a board. Not a wisp strayed after it was trapped in the vice. You had to release the locks with a thorough shampoo.

Some things the young lady could do with her eyes.

Young ladies spend endless hours and dollars to make eyes alluring. What did we use in this area when we decided that something should be done about bald eyes? Deep red lipstick and no eye make-up gave faces an unbalanced look. In the twenties we had mascara but it was easy to have the lashes clump together. No matter what the advertisers' claims, it ran and smeared with the slight moisture around the area. Nothing looked ghastlier and everyone saw it but the wearer. "Beaded" eyelashes were a horrible fad consisting of a heavy coating the length of each lash—then to the tips was added a thick dab that formed the bead.

A beauty shoppe in the thirties could install eyelashes that you wouldn't believe possible. It was a tedious operation with misery and fear for recipient and operator. You reclined in a nearly flat position while the "expert" glued one artificial hair to each of your lashes. She had to be adept or you could end with an eyeful of adhesive. When the gluing ordeal was over, she trimmed the overly long new hairs to the desired length. Anything done this close to eyes is bound to make you squeamish!

If the eyelash installation sounds unbelievable, other

outrageous things were happening in the eternal quest for youth and beauty. Crude facial operations were performed to smooth wrinkled faces. The skin might look better at first, but paraffin was inserted inside to "plump out" the contours and it's understandable what could happen in tropical heat.

Face cream makers made elaborate claims. In 1926 one product proclaimed, "Use Produits Bertie once a day and there will *never* be a telltale wrinkle on your face, neck or throat."

A personal experience that started as an experiment for skin miracles turned into a bad joke for my husband. In 1936 I purchased a tube of beauty clay and applied a thick coat to face and neck in the late afternoon. To wait out the required treatment time, I napped on the davenport in the living room. When he came home, the room was nearly dark; and my ghastly, cracked-clay face glowed unearthly grey in the dim light. My breathing was shallow, almost imperceptible. He touched the clammy coldness of my face while his fright mounted to near-frenzy proportions. It hadn't occurred to me that he'd think it was anything but his foolish wife trying another beauty aid.

If you think that I was the difference between a vision and a sight, there were many examples of other women who went all-out to attain or regain beauty, to the tune of fancy salon prices. If these regimens didn't bring results, only one course remained—to give up.

Deodorants were advertised more discreetly in the twenties, as this Mum ad proves. (Courtesy Bristol-Myers Company)

Two beauty and charm problems were handled with the utmost delicacy in the twenties. It concerned the advertising copy for deodorants and depilatories. One advertiser was so roundabout in getting to the point that in an ad two columns wide and the length of a magazine page, you read to the fifth paragraph before they said

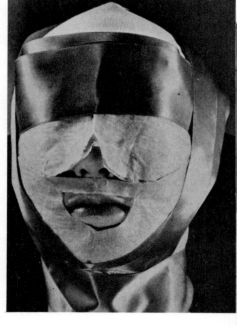

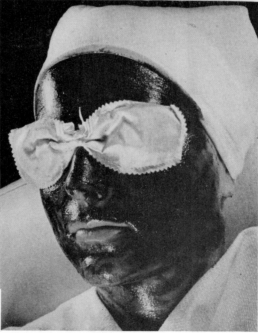

Two examples of women who tried to regain lost beauty at fancy prices. (Courtesy *Harper's Bazaar*)

No Hair Offends Where Neet Is Used

Neet dipilatory based its advertising on the premise that excess hair was· somehow offensive. (Courtesy Whitehall Laboratories)

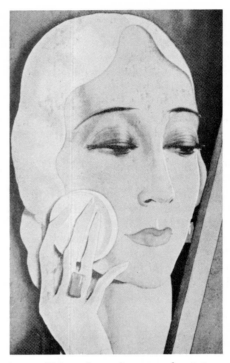

The powder puff has long been a feminine accessory. (Courtesy *Harper's Bazaar*)

that "it" is not a pretty word—perspiration—but that we had to recognize it. The first four paragraphs referred merely to "it."

The powder puff has been a feminine accessory back to the time when a piece of chamois skin was kept in the box of talcum. There were variations in the styles of puffs. Pictured is an exaggeratedly stylized drawing of a sophisticated lady patting her delicate skin with the flat puff. Her long, bony fingers indicate high style, not arthritis.

the thirties, compact manufacturers advanced to intricate compartmental cases for every beauty aid that could be used on-the-run. There was always the argument as to whether it was better or bad to touch up make-up at a restaurant table after dinner, or to suffer "eaten-off" lips and a shiny nose. Either way, it left little doubt as to the source of milady's beauty, whether a point of etiquette or vanity.

A lady applies her powder with the familiar downy puff. (Courtesy *Harper's Bazaar*)

A miniature compact. (Courtesy *Harper's Bazaar*)

A lady would flick the round, downy puff over her neck in a familiar gesture. To show the least shine or hint thereof was not permissible, so it was a constant battle with noses that were determined to healthily gleam.

We had compacts aplenty in the twenties, and many contained cake powder and a thin puff that soon showed soil. Deluxe models included a small cake of rouge. By

Miniature compacts were made containing only rouge. Some women applied the various shades of pink, rose or orange with deft touches that gave a hint of flattering glow. Others, alas, went at it with frightful vigor and finished with round, gaudy, clown-like patches whose edges ended abruptly. Almost white powder was plastered on like kalsomine and ended as soon as it reached the neck. These were the sins of unskilled make-up artists.

Yardley manufactured a popular brand of perfume.

What about the final, magnificent touch—the perfume? A Yardley advertisement put it elegantly into copy, "For glamor, a woman requires a certain setting; the sweep of a curved stairway, perhaps . . . a grand piano's stark magnificance . . . the star-hung backdrop of a terraced garden! Slippers, jewels, furs and gown that seem freshly created for her immediate mood . . . and above all—the pervading magic of a great perfume to blend all details into one brilliant flash of personality."

Each age of beauty will have its peculiar set of fancies and foibles, and there will always be the succeeding generation that will look back and utter, "How ghastly!"

17

Luxury Before Taxes

"High society is for those who have stopped working and no longer have anything important to do." Don't blame me for this pointed observation because President Woodrow Wilson said it in a 1915 Washington speech.

What has happened to so-called high society? Everything else changed, and there were contributing factors helping to erode society's original glitter. Not the least elements were the Depression, World War II and spiraling taxes. Social orders underwent revolution as founders of massive wealth aged and died. Some of the progeny had talent for running through fortunes by frenzied playboy and playgirl living which made spicy reading in society gossip columns. This gave the ordinary citizen an inkling as to how the "other half" lived. Not all fortunes were dissipated. Some pursestrings were tightly controlled, or ambitious successors swelled the wealth even larger. We're going to window-peek and crash a few parties to check on the heydays of the three decades.

In the twenties and thirties, one face of high society was its mansions, gala garden functions and chauffeur-driven limousines. Much of the entertaining was done in the homes and/or private clubs. There were set habitats where the leisured class spent its summers and winters. Until many were destroyed by fire, great homes were in Bar Harbor, Maine. There were several Eastern locales such as a private island, Cat Cay, where the carefully weeded-out, select set congregated.

A 1927 *Harper's Bazaar* said, "From December to the end of April, from all the capitals of the world, luxurious boats and trains carry their passengers to Cannes—the town renowned for its elegance and sport."

A 1926 article reported that the shooting season in Scotland brought the smart world to foregather in Scotland for the autumn shooting when life was a round of sports in an atmosphere of traditional charm.

It was not easy to crash the "400" of the Social Register, but some tried all of their active lives . . . to be invited just once to the right party where the *right* people were.

Money alone wasn't a ticket to the magical play kingdom, as witness one ambitious hostess who tried, but no one showed at her lavish party. It was as frustrating

High society, pre-income-tax style.

200

Two chauffeurs talk things over while awaiting their elegant employers. (From an advertisement in *Harper's Bazaar*, the Cadillac Division, General Motors Corp.)

as trying to crash Hollywood for those whose life ambition was to be on the inside looking out on the less-exalted world.

Mrs. Vanderbilt: note her ever-present beaded "sweat band." (Courtesy *Harper's Bazaar*)

As the thirties aged, some of the old social order wore out and subtly the new "Cafe Society" emerged. The "in" crowd preferred to do their cavorting in night clubs of their choosing—that again became a select group. Mrs. Vanderbilt with her ever-present beaded "sweat band"

was long the arbiter of the correct society, but she was getting very old. Her era was fading as the new breed danced past her.

Headlines told less and less of hundred-thousand-dollar debuts and weddings. Hotel or club coming-out parties became common on a shared-expense basis for the fathers.

Socialites seen and being seen at the Starlight Roof of the Waldorf Astoria. (Courtesy *Harper's Bazaar*)

One popular rendezvous for the smart set was the Waldorf's Starlight Roof which twinkled and tinkled with elite dancing feet. Other favorites were the Stork Club, El Morocco, La Martinique or The 21.

Tobacco heiress Doris Duke.

Brenda Frazier was the social sensation of 1938. (Courtesy *Harper's Bazaar*)

Becoming a debutante moved into big celebrity business with press agents. There were highly publicized "debs" but the all-time star of debbydom was Brenda Frazier. Many movie actresses would be ecstatically happy with the newspaper, magazine and gossip column linage that Brenda Frazier reaped in 1938.

No account of high society could fail to include the one who was called the richest girl in the world—Doris Duke. At thirteen she inherited a seventy million dollar tobacco fortune. The Depression did not mar her debut into society with all of the desired accouterments in 1930. Later Miss Duke became Doris Duke Cromwell.

"The poor little rich girl," Barbara Hutton, stayed in the glaring light of publicity much longer, if for no other reason than her multiple marriages. As the Woolworth heiress, she was referred to as the "dime store heiress," and after being a plump young lady, illness nearly took her life and left her wan and thin. This was at the time she gave birth to her only child, Lance Reventlow, whose father was a count. Miss Hutton epitomized the restless, endless search for happiness as she passed around on the "marriage-go-round," never grasping the elusive brass ring of love, no matter how lavish her gifts to husbands.

In 1937 Gloria "Mimi" Baker became the first nationally known glamor debutante, ranking number one. She was a style-setter and started the long bob for hair.

Beautiful twin sisters in high social circles were Lady Furness and Mrs. Reginald Vanderbilt, the mother of Gloria Vanderbilt. There was a drawn-out custody suit between Mrs. Vanderbilt and Gloria's aunt, Mrs. Harry Payne Whitney. The latter was given Gloria's custody, but the girl had to weather the publicity limelight and was truly a "poor little rich girl."

Gloria Vanderbilt at fifteen was not as yet a debutante, but she was on her way toward glamordom with her exotic beauty and definite personality. She made her biggest public splash when announcing her intention to marry Leopold Stokowski, the famous symphony conductor, who was more than double her age. Against everyone's warnings, she married him.

Since debutantes were news, they were given full publicity even to showing in a soap flakes advertisement the many busy hours an ordinary woman would have if she followed a debutante around the clock. Certainly the average girl could delight in the same product the personal maid of a debutante used!

If there were endless rounds of allegedly gay and assuredly expensive parties, then what did the devotees of this whirl do besides sipping champagne, dancing and chattering? The era was ripe for Elsa Maxwell, who was

"Mimi" Baker created a stir in 1937.

Mrs. Doris Duke Cromwell shown with her husband in her Hawaiian mansion. (Courtesy *Harper's Bazaar*)

Lady Furness and Mrs. Reginald Vanderbilt. (Courtesy *Harper's Bazaar*)

Woolworth heiress Barbara Hutton stayed in the lime-light partially because of her multiple marriages.

Gloria Vanderbilt at 15. (Courtesy *Harper's Bazaar*)

Cropping up in every issue of slick fashion and society magazines were the beauties of the upper brackets. Here in a shimmering gown of black pailettes is Whitney Bourne, a debutante selected by the famous illustrator Howard Chandler Christy as one of the country's ten most beautiful women.

not remotely glamorous, young, slender or beautiful. She was a chunk of a woman with a heavy-featured face, but she believed that parties should be something more than congregating a given number of people in a given location. She knew how to throw parties that gave the social butterflies something to flutter about even to the next day. Before her strange career ended, she played in several motion pictures and wrote of parties and society.

Elsa Maxwell. (Courtesy *Harper's Bazaar*)

Elsa Maxwell has the ear of the gentleman next to her. (Courtesy *Harper's Bazaar*)

This soapflake advertisement showed the ordinary woman what it would be like to spend 24 hours with Brenda Frazier. (Courtesy *Harper's Bazaar*)

In the late thirties a magazine page told debs what they did the year before as compared to what they must do now to be with the "in" crowd. To attest to the influence Brenda Frazier wielded on trends, she's mentioned more than once on the page. We learned that last year Brenda Frazier wore short white evening gloves, but this year Eleanor Frothingham wears short black *or* white evening gloves. It's quite a world-shaking news item when you stop to think of it. Miss Frazier was in the forefront of strapless evening gown devotees and was one of the few who looked right in them instead of a person half-missing. You were further told that you danced the Lambeth Walk last year and took rhumba lessons, but you must now dance in the Conga Chain and take Hula lessons. You'd followed the crowd, but now you were an individual. It's doubtful that any strayed into extremely individual channels on the pain of being considered an eccentric.

In New York City, Manhattan to be exact, the best address was Park Avenue where elder members of wealthy families built fabulous mansions. Unknown to the original owners, these too would pass as private dwelling sites. Taxes became overbearing, the valuable property was needed as progress pushed near and living habits of successive generations changed. It was much the same change experienced in suburbia all around America. Less and less of the famous old names were actively associated with great houses in town.

At Park Avenue and 57th Street was a hotel that not only dispensed the luxurious way of life, but influenced our language. It was clearly understood what "putting on the Ritz" meant. To describe an expensive or classy place, thing or person, we'd use the word ritzy. At the above address was the Ritz Tower which advertised itself as "fashionable, luxurious, comfortable . . . the finest residential location distinguished Park Avenue can offer."

Many emotions were touched and tears brushed away when the old Waldorf-Astoria Hotel was razed. But in the thirties the new Waldorf-Astoria proudly announced its opening and now it too has collected the patina of the years.

As we look back on this opulent social era, we who remember it can smile nostalgically and complain of the lack of color in present day society. If there was a definite doomsday for the grandeur that passed, the nearest date could be our entrance into World War II. It was incongruous that the mass of populace should roll up its sleeves for the war effort while the "play people" went on dancing among the potted palms and balloons. Victory was a mass effort and social lights found plenty of service jobs. They were proud of their new usefulness and it was no longer "smart" to live a butterfly life of all play and no work. Besides—what play life could there be if

The new Waldorf-Astoria advertised its opening. (Courtesy *Harper's Bazaar*)

the enemy took over our country? Debutantes served in hospitals, as car drivers, in office positions and in women's auxilliaries of various service branches. They learned to type, raise money in bond drives and generally to help the cause wherever possible.

When the war ended, these girls or the next upcoming crop of debutantes merely took time out from their colleges, painting and singing lessons, business, stage or Hollywood careers to be introduced to society. Class distinctions were not removed—just blurred.

18

The Royal Flush

When we were young we learned never to kill a toad because it might be a handsome prince hexed by an evil spell. We'd break up his romance with a beautiful princess in Never-Never Land on the other side of the mountain. Royalty furnished interesting reading for children. It didn't cease to have interest after the hexes were broken and as adults we avidly read of real, live royalty and their tribulations.

If you lived in the thirties and were old enough to know what was happening, you remember the greatest real-life fairy story of our time—the wooing and wedding of King Edward VIII of England and Wallis Warfield Simpson. Their love story fired the hearts of all romantic people around the civilized world, and gave newspapers and magazines much writing grist.

The Prince of Wales, later King Edward VIII, later still Duke of Windsor.

The crown and sceptre—symbol of the British monarchy. (Courtesy of Chesebrough-Ponds, Inc. Taken from a Pond's Creams Advertisement appearing in a 1937 *Ladies' Home Journal*)

Speculation ran high—would the love story be completed? Every element was a gargantuan obstacle; the nearly insurmountable odds were against their "living happily ever after." International gossips had a field day while wagering whether the King would abdicate, which he would surely have to do to marry this twice-divorced American commoner. Mrs. Simpson was from Baltimore and soon became known to America's public simply as "Wallie." If some members of the British Royal Family were tolerant of the romance, it was nullified by the disapproving finger of custom, tradition and the Archbishop of Canterbury.

The beloved young Prince of Wales became King Edward VIII upon the death of his father, King George V, in 1936. He was never crowned and reigned only 327 days before the abdication speech that sounded around the world via radio. After his long silence amid the rumors, he finally told everyone of his decision. It must have been gravely pondered while pressures came from every side—"do, don't, do, don't!"

Wallis Simpson met Edward, Prince of Wales, in 1934. In the spring of 1936, after he had become King in January, she joined him for an Adriatic cruise. This was oil enough to start tongues wagging, and the non-sanctioned romance began. Would love and the right to live his own life according to his own dictates prove stronger, or would duty to his station and country be the ruling power? The world learned the answer on the night of December 11, 1936, when the King uttered the famous words of the abdication speech in his clipped English: " . . . you must believe me when I tell you that I have found it impossible to carry the heavy burden of responsibility and to discharge my duties as King as I would wish to do, without the help and support of the woman I love." The last four words caught on and became a household phrase in America.

The day after abdication, his brother, the Duke of York, whom Edward named as his successor, became King George VI, and gave the former King the title of Duke of Windsor. The Duke married his future Duchess on June 3, 1937, but some Britishers winced at the thought of Edward's wife having a royal title. The couple stayed in France until the fall of 1939.

The Duke served as Governor of the Bahamas from 1940 to 1945, but it was small duty after renouncing the crown of the ruler of Great Britain and the British Dominions beyond the seas, as well as that of Emperor of India.

The Duke and Duchess of Windsor lean over the railing of the Governor's Mansion in Nassau. (Courtesy *Harper's Bazaar*)

The Duke and Duchess at ease, in Nassau. (Courtesy *Harper's Bazaar*)

The sleek, fashionable Duchess of Windsor was a top bracket subject for many illustrators and painters. Some emphasized the romantic angle by portraying both of them with heads together, or as a grand, beautiful lady in a painting commissioned by the Duke.

The Duchess was an influence on women's fashions, including hair styles. She's a person of great taste and smartness and the deposed couple were seen often at gay functions of the exclusive International Social Set.

Westminster Abbey. (Courtesy the Detroit *News*)

These photos show interiors of the house the Duke and Duchess occupied. Everywhere were royal reminders, such as banners in the hall, trophies on a staircase or a large tapestry crest above the Duke's bed. (Courtesy *Harper's Bazaar*)

Some scenes of the Duke and Duchess going about their daily routine. (Courtesy *Harper's Bazaar*)

An article in *Harper's Bazaar*, after an interview with the Duchess of Windsor, told of her life in Nassau and their official schedule as well as more personal aspects, now that they'd settled into a living pattern.

This socially-minded pair were much sought after by hostesses, whether well-established in the high strata of society or ambitiously climbing. Rarely was one Windsor photographed without the other nearby.

If the abdication in all of its aspects was a world-shaking event, disruptive to the natural flow of history, remember that this was at least the eighteenth one in recorded history. As an aftermath of World War I, there was a rash of abdications affecting many countries. None captured our fancies as did this one in Britain.

Young America fought a war to gain freedom from Britain's rule, but certainly in the twentieth century there's been more feeling of closeness and interest in England's affairs than in most other countries. Lack of a language barrier and a more allied way of life has probably contributed to this.

If the romance and subsequent abdication of King Edward VIII was avidly followed in America, so was the coronation ceremony of his brother, the formerly titled, H.R.H. Prince Albert Frederick, Duke of York. Even styles in women's wear were affected by the "Coronation Year." Royal indications showed in many ways, such as a blouse I bought with gold crowns for buttons.

For centuries Westminster Abbey has been the site of the crowning of British kings and queens. The coronation of King George VI was sent worldwide via radio, and was seen in all of its pomp and splendor by as many thousands as could crowd near in London.

This news picture, originally printed in full color, shows the newly crowned King and Queen Elizabeth in their royal robes and regalia. They also look very uncomfortable. (Courtesy Detroit News)

The Queen's two daughters, the Princesses Elizabeth and Margaret Rose, were eleven and six years old respectively at coronation time. (Courtesy Detroit News)

These are the crowns worn by Queen Elizabeth, Princess Elizabeth and Princess Margaret Rose for the ceremony. The largest one contains the famous Koh-i-nur (or Koh-inoor) diamond, one of Britain's best known crown jewels. (Courtesy Detroit News)

The new Queen Elizabeth in an attractive portrait, compared to the official one with coronation dress. She became the first Scotch Queen of Britain in centuries, on May 12, 1937. (Courtesy Detroit News)

These unsharp wirephotos were sent to America and printed the day after coronation. Consider how long it took for pictures of the crowning of King George V to appear in our papers! Still wearing the ceremonial robes, the new monarchs managed faint smiles, but Princess Elizabeth was the only one to broaden the expression. They greeted the throngs from a balcony of Buckingham Palace. (Courtesy Detroit News)

The Archbishop of Canterbury about to place the crown on the head of George VI, indicated by the arrow. (Courtesy Detroit *News*)

When George VI ascended to the throne, the Windsor Castle became home to him and his Queen. For the first time since his father's death, the royal standard of the House of Windsor was raised over the rather gloomy looking edifice. (Courtesy Detroit *News*)

Britain's Coronation

Ponds featured the coronation in their advertisements. (Courtesy Chesebrough-Ponds, Inc., taken from a Pond's Creams advertisement appearing in a 1937 *Ladies' Home Journal*)

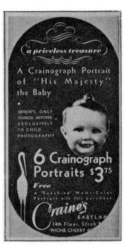

Even babies were crowned, as this portrait photographer's ad shows. (Courtesy the Detroit *News*)

Pond's Face Creams used titled ladies' portraits and testimonials for a long time in their advertising. The coronation brought them out en masse. They included Duchesses, Countesses, Viscountesses and Ladies with be-jewelled tiaras and pearls. The heading of the advertisement said that "Britain's Coronation awakens new interest in titled British beauties."

Advertisers of many products and services in America hopped on the royal wagon to stay abreast of the times. A beauty salon regarded its patrons as "queens," while a baby photographer referred to a baby boy picture as "his majesty."

There was a royal theater party during a visit of President and Madame Lebrun of France. There was a tongue-in-cheek attitude at the time about Chamberlain's attempt with Hitler to forestall war. It was predicted that it could be a fatal blow to the British Empire if his dangerous game failed. Now we can look back at history to see what really happened. How quickly a generation of people and circumstances can change! President Lebrun retired in 1940. This same year Neville Chamberlain left the Prime Ministry and died shortly thereafter. Hitler died in 1945. England was on the winning side after all, although after a great struggle.

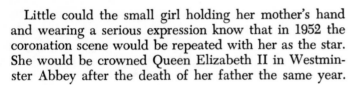

The future Queen Elizabeth II. (Courtesy *Harper's Bazaar*)

Beauty parlors jumped on the coronation bandwagon. (Courtesy the Detroit *News*)

Little could the small girl holding her mother's hand and wearing a serious expression know that in 1952 the coronation scene would be repeated with her as the star. She would be crowned Queen Elizabeth II in Westminster Abbey after the death of her father the same year.

Ahead lay the solemn duties and restrictions of a crowned head, but she has worn it well and displayed the discipline and attention to her country, befitting her station. "Long live the Queen!"

America has all but forgotten the romance of the now-aging Duke and Duchess of Windsor. Britain can no longer sing that the sun never sets on the British Empire —time marches on!

19

Sit This One Out

"I could have danced all night," was not a physical boast in any year between 1920 and 1950, because we had enough dance crazes to keep us hopping. With each new dance came righteous protests from elders who declared

Dancing, twenties' style.

that surely now young people were worse than preceding generations. If today's hipsters think they have an exclusive on dance floor oddities, they haven't investigated the heel-kicking and dervish-whirling of the historic age in which their parents and grandparents danced.

When entering the 1920's, we were still aware of ragtime, and those devoted to its ricky-ticky sound looked skeptically on the brash newcomer, jazz, that had worked up from the South. But then, jazz-lovers in turn had to adapt to the advent of "swing."

New York's Harlem, Where the Black Bottom, Truckin', and the Suzie-Q Were Bred, Breaks Out With Its Latest Improvised and Spontaneous Dance — *"Congeroo"*

An advertisement for the dances of Harlem. (Courtesy Detroit News)

In some instances it would be a long search to learn how, when and where the various dances originated. The craze taken up by duchesses and society dowagers might begin on the sidewalks of a city. Celebrities could give it a boost by performing the dance on a stage or in a movie. The music might be beaten out in a honky-tonk or wailed by the educated violins of a society orchestra.

In every case, there were the inevitable head shakings and tut-tuts of those who "sat them out," partly because they wouldn't learn the latest steps or their rheumatic legs couldn't limber to the exertion. Probably few parents performed the Varsity Drag with their college-aged children.

Clifton Webb expounded sadly on what had happened to that noble form, the ballroom dance. In roundabout language he properly clucked, "She has been stripped of all her grace and elegance and left standing stark and unsightly." He wasn't talking about a hapless female, but about the dance. "She has been torn limb from limb, until every vestige of beauty that she formerly possessed has been made unrecognizable." In a devious manner he eventually got around to blaming the juniors who were then known in society as the "young set." Mr. Webb could have easily been referring to goings-on at the neighborhood discothèque, about which today's elders may cluck.

The first famous proponents of a new dance craze that come to mind are Vernon and Irene Castle with their Castle Walk. It was rather tame by today's standards.

The biggest news of all crashed in with the Charleston. Frenzy hadn't known such heights. Dire warnings were given as to health hazards involved. Children went through the motions while at play, and not even grandma was unaware of the Charleston's impact. One thing about this dance is certain, it livened the 1920's and shall ever be remembered synonomously with the flapper's

Youngsters demonstrate a "new fangled" dance. (Janco Fotos)

Clifton Webb and Irene Castle demonstrate the Castle Walk. (Courtesy *Harper's Bazaar*)

reign. The Charleston got its name from the same-named city in South Carolina.

One mania that grew to large proportions on more than one continent was the Lambeth Walk. Starting as an imitation of the strutting people on the sidewalks in London's slum, Lambeth, it became famous as it climbed the social ladder from its beginnings by urchins on street

People from the Lambeth section of London demonstrate the Lambeth Walk. (Courtesy *Harper's Bazaar*)

These twenties-style swingers are doing the famous Charleston. (From *Collier's* Magazine)

corners until Anthony Eden was going through its paces at parties. The dance was introduced in a London show, "Me and My Girl," and it was first-rate as a social caste barrier-breaker. Its popularity jumped the Channel to fashionable Cannes, then somehow managed passage across the Atlantic and cut a swath at such sophisticated hostelries as the St. Regis.

Like the Charleston spawned in the South, another dance routine had a frenzied flurry—the Black Bottom. About a decade later, in 1937, a lively variation on the square dance, the Big Apple, was familiar to everyone—especially to those "jitter-buggers" who could endure the pace. All of these steps, like grandma's square dances, featured the separation of couples, unlike the proximities of our more conservative dances.

In spite of attempts to manufacture popularity for off-beat routines, the good old one-step, two-step and waltz still held forth in the lavish ballrooms. The most elegant date imaginable for a lucky small town girl was to have an evening in a big city dance palace. They were elaborate, with mirrors, rococo trimmings, statues, fountains, trick lights and balconies where soft drinks could be bought and sipped. For warm summer evenings, some had outside "gardens," with canvas tops in case of sudden showers.

Latin dancing has long been popular.

The big ballroom was once more popular than it is today.

Latin dances of many varieties have been like natives among us for years. We couldn't forget the smoothness of George Raft's dance through a Latin rhythm with Carole Lombard. We learned Rhumbas, Tangos, Congas, Cariocas and Mambas. Ah, the Continental!

The near demise of the big ballrooms was inevitable as times and tastes changed. But whether we're twisting, stamping, whirling, swaying or mopping the floor, then throwing our torsos out of joint, we'll find a place to do it and plenty of eager participants. We may not roll up the rug and dance as much in our homes to the music from the console radio, but the dance is here to stay.

20

But the Melody Lingers On

The phonograph was one of Thomas Edison's many inventions; this picture of him was therefore of great value in advertising the product. (Courtesy the Detroit News)

composers and conductors of classical and "pop" orchestras.

Mme. Ernestine Schumann-Heink. (Courtesy the Detroit News)

Even though their songs are ended, thanks to recordings, their melodies can linger on . . . to vary the lyrics of an old popular song. It's lamentable that the recordings of the twenties, thirties and even forties were not of the present-day quality, but we can be thankful to have some audible record of the great voices and instrumentalists that have been stilled forever. I never cease to thrill when hearing the actual voice of Enrico Caruso, even though it's a scratchy reproduction. Many artists are still living, but no longer perform what they're famous for. Let your memory wander, listen for the notes that you heard when you were younger. We will consider those of the concert stage and opera, as well as

The great lady of the opera, Mme. Ernestine Schumann-Heink, was a contemporary of the world's greatest pianist, Ignace Jan Paderewski. She was born in Prague one year after Paderewski came to the earth in Russian Poland. In the last decade of the nineteenth century they each visited America. It was not the last visit for either as their accomplishments were appreciated by Americans. Her contralto voice was successful in Wagnerian roles and his piano virtuosity held audiences enraptured.

Madame Schumann-Heink mothered a large family besides following her career that didn't end until shortly before her death in 1936. She appeared numbers of times on radio.

Ignace Paderewski. (Courtesy the Detroit *News*)

Paderewski was a great Polish patriot; he even became Prime Minister. He toured the United States as late as 1931, but was in Europe at the time of his death in 1941.

Sergei Rachmaninoff.

Another renowned pianist of the same era was Sergei Rachmaninoff, or Rachmaninov if you're Russian. I shall never forget the thrill of hearing him in what was advertised as his last American tour. He played his concert numbers and although the audience was appreciative, it wasn't satisfied. He hadn't played his most famous com-

position, Prelude in C Sharp Minor. Since the hall was so crowded that folding chairs circled the piano onstage, someone nearby with sufficient nerve approached the great, austere man and whispered the request. He struck the first thunderous note, then could go no farther until the frenzied crowd quieted. They stood and applauded for more than five minutes. A master cannot escape his creation.

Jean Sibelius. (Courtesy *Harper's Bazaar*)

A Finnish composer of the same era whose work found favor in America was Jean Sibelius. His most beloved and familiar work is "Finlandia."

It would be impossible to enumerate all of the composing talents who enriched America's music in our three decades. This group would certainly include George Gershwin who had so few years of life in which to produce a wealth of musical comedies, songs and his best known composition, "Rhapsody in Blue." In 1924 it was said that "George Gershwin, an extraordinarily gifted composer of popular music, wrote a 'Rhapsody in Blue' which is a concerto, the first ever written for solo instrument and jazz band." Also, "that as soon as jazz begins to be listened to and begins to be considered musically, we may look for greater melodic and harmonic interest. If the jazz orchestra ever becomes a concert body, the strings will have to be enlarged." We can now recall how strange it seemed later when such musicians as Duke Ellington and Benny Goodman pioneered with jazz concerts at Carnegie Hall.

A California baritone, Lawrence Tibbett, made his mark in the Metropolitan Opera, but started with "Aida" in 1923 at the Hollywood Bowl. His rich, powerful voice was popular through all of the three decades with which we're concerned. One of his most famous roles was in "Emperor Jones" first sung in 1933.

There was a great era for opera before divas became weight-watchers, or the singers craved more money and fame by going to Hollywood or the night club circuits. To be accepted at the Metropolitan was a lofty dream to realize for those hopeful of singing careers. Do you

Lawrence Tibbett. (Courtesy the Detroit News)

remember Amelita Galli-Curci, Alma Gluck or Marie Jeritza?

In 1926 the youngest lady to ever trill on the great opera stage was Marion Talley. She made her Metropolitan debut when nineteen, but after only four seasons suddenly left and appeared in movie musicals and on radio. She has not been heard in many years and the memory of her coloratura voice may be hazy to you.

Marion Talley.

You certainly recall some of the great male voices . . . John McCormack, John Charles Thomas, the Caruso-like Mario Lanza and James Melton. When Mr. Melton appeared in concert in Detroit, he attracted the largest crowd the huge Masonic auditorium had ever held for such an event. The management was so delighted that a panoramic photo was taken of the audience, including those crammed around the piano onstage, during intermission. Mr. Melton was also noted for his collection of antique automobiles.

Walter Damrosch.

In 1927 radio listeners were treated to the conductorial and lecturing style of Walter Damrosch, through the National Broadcasting Company's facilities. Children benefitted from his symphony appreciation hour which he long conducted as musical director for this network. Mr. Damrosch was also responsible for making the New York Symphony into a permanent organization. He had the ability with his talks about each passage of a composition, followed by the rendition of it, to help even the least informed person to listen and appreciate what he heard. "Peter and the Wolf" was one of his oft-repeated vehicles for explanation.

In a different key, some musicians had great popularity in radio, movies or other media, but no longer perform. In the twenties and thirties Ann Leaf was a star organist in radio. She had a daily program on the "mighty Wurlitzer" at noon. Any mention of organists would include Jesse Crawford and Ethel Smith. An adjunct of theater performances that always thrilled me was the organ interlude. The console would slowly rise from its pit, the spotlight would be turned on the organist, who was usually a balding man—then the magic tones would begin. From the right, left and everywhere came the

Ann Leaf at the Wurlitzer. (Courtesy of the Wurlitzer Company)

Harpo Marx.

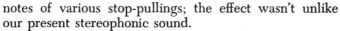

notes of various stop-pullings; the effect wasn't unlike our present stereophonic sound.

Alec Templeton brilliantly entertained as an amusing composer, pianist and wit. His blindness didn't keep him from success anymore than it has George Sheering.

When Harpo Marx, of the zany Marx brothers, sat down to play the harp, you little noticed the fuzzy wig, baggy comedy trousers or popped eyes. He played beautifully even on the stringed works inside a grand piano after pulling off the case piece by piece.

Paul Whiteman. (Courtesy Detroit News)

Alec Templeton. (Courtesy Harper's Bazaar)

The granddaddy of jazz orchestra leaders who gained the nickname, "Pops," was Paul Whiteman. The first phonograph record we bought for the crank-it-up Victrola was Paul Whiteman's "Three O'Clock in the Morning," in 1919. He also earned the title "King of Jazz" and it became the title also of a movie in which he starred in 1930. Many years later, he joined the ranks of disc jockeys.

An authentic pioneer in promoting and playing the real jazz early in this century, a man who developed great bands and individual musicians, was Ben Pollack. Although his family had other plans for him, he launched into his first big-time band job in 1922. A host of musicians came under his wing who later flew on their own, such as Benny Goodman, Glenn Miller, Charlie Spivak, Harry James, Freddie Slack and Jack Teagarden. Pollack has lived through such illustrious developments in jazz as this country will probably never know again. His influence on the musical scene cannot tarnish even though young people are now preoccupied with quite different musical forms.

220

Ben Pollack. (Courtesy of the Riverside, California, *Press-Enterprise*)

Ben Bernie. (Courtesy Detroit *News*)

"Yowsa, yowsa, yowsa, this is the old Maestro with the mosta of the besta for the leasta." Could this remind you of anyone other than Ben Bernie? They still play his theme music that always brings a yearning and tear for the dear, departed sounds of those days.

There were noted musicians who played the violin as it hadn't been played before—hot violin. Perhaps you remember Joe Venuti, "Stuff" Smith or Rubinoff and his Violin? Or there was Evelyn and her Magic Violin with Phil Spitalny's all-girl orchestra.

The piano had expert fingerers that you can't forget; Eddie Duchin, the smooth stylings of Joe Reichmann and Carmen Cavallero. With distinctively different approach was Frankie Carle, who will be long remembered for his "Sunrise Serenade." The upper ranges of the keyboard always bring to mind Jan August.

Oscar Levant caught on with radio audiences when his amazing storehouse of musical knowledge was displayed on "Information Please." He appeared as himself in numerous motion pictures as well as touring for piano concerts as a specialist with Gershwin compositions.

Some popular pianists had amusing names such as "Jelly Roll" Morton, "Kansas City" Frank Melrose, "Speckled Red" who was Rufus Perryman, also "Montana" Taylor. These men put a beat on many Brunswick Records in the forties.

One man was named after his instrument and will always be better remembered as "Ukulele Ike" than as Cliff Edwards. He made many records and appeared in motion pictures.

Larry Adler gained virtuoso rating on the harmonica, even though the instrument was scorned until its true beauty was exercised on something besides the "Irish Washerwoman." Then there was Borra Minnevitch and his Harmonica Rascals who not only brought wonderful sounds from all sizes of harmonicas, but put on an act while playing. Of course the smallest man played the largest harmonica.

Some of the ladies who left opera to make movies or to sing on the stage were Grace Moore, Gladys Swarthout and Helen Traubel. Miss Traubel was the biggest drawing personality on the Statler Hotel circuit. When she appeared in Detroit, we'd made reservations weeks in advance. The Terrace Room was so jammed there was scarcely walking room after tiny tables-for-two were added in every possible space. What did this crowd clamor the most to hear? Opera!

In these earlier days we sometimes heard a beloved Scottish burr from the throat of Sir Harry Lauder. Oh, to be "Roamin' in the Gloamin'."

A showman who carved indelible initials on our entertainment memories was Rudy Vallee, the "Vagabond Lover." He was the man who made the technique of crooning something besides singing a baby to sleep. His nasal "Hi-ho everybody," was a familiar trademark as his "Connecticut Yankees" played "My Time is Your Time." After his many years of playing a saxophone, the "Stein Song," leading his band and crooning through a megaphone, he proved to be an accomplished actor in character roles. In 1936 he received an honorary Master of Arts degree in Boston.

Bands may come and go, but few stay as has Guy Lombardo and his "Royal Canadians." Mr. Lombardo is also respected as a fine sportsman in boat racing circles.

A woman who made a definite niche in the all-time hall

Guy Lombardo.

of radio fame was always trying to get the moon to come over the mountain. If you guess it's anyone but Kate Smith, you're wrong.

Eddie Cantor discovered the beautiful boy-soprano voice of Bobbie Breen—also Deanna Durbin. The youthful freshness of each won approval of moviegoers immediately.

Mr. Cantor had an illustrious career from 1923 when he first got top billing on Broadway. Hollywood was to star him three years later. He was Eddie-of-the-banjo-eyes, and how they could roll as he went into perpetual motion while singing "If You Knew Suzie."

From these names and the music they represent, let your recollections come of the "Melodies That Linger on . . ."

21

We Used to Sing Sweet Adeline

Meade Schaeffer painting of a family orchestra. (Courtesy of the United States Brewer's Assoc., Inc.)

Something is missing in our ultra-modern homes—music. Don't misunderstand, we probably have *more* music per square minute in every twenty-four hours than ever before, but someone else is playing and singing it for us. We used to be do-it-yourselfers. No respectable living room was without a piano; daughter's and son's rooms were equipped with ukuleles and assorted horns. Probably the family music teacher was living within walking distance. We weren't persistently entertained so we amused ourselves in the evenings by producing music with varying degrees of proficiency. Playing a piano was basic accomplishment and could make an otherwise mousey girl the hub of social gatherings as the group sang around her whether she tinkled an old square, baby grand, upright or spinet piano. The sheet music business was booming and to have a large collection would compare to "platter" collecting today.

If there was enough varied talent in a family, an orchestra, though spotty, could set up for a home jam session.

When Adolphe Sax invented the horn named after him, he may not have anticipated the popularity his instrument was to enjoy with jazz devotees. He died in 1894, so never heard his creation lend its mellow tones to the Charleston.

It was quite another manifestation of home music-

Twenties' couple enjoy their friend's saxophone solo.

making when a formal party paused to sit in the drawing room for a selection by a consciously accomplished pianist. It was common for a lady who'd studied voice to render a number among the current solo favorites

Reluctantly, the boy is learning the piccolo. His mind is obviously on other things. (Illustrator: Vincent Civiletti)

("Danny Boy," "Chloe," or "Tosti's Goodbye"). She sometimes had a voice that could pierce steel plate on a battleship, but the listeners always politely applauded.

It was nearly mandatory for boys and girls to attack music in some form even though they couldn't hit a given note within a mile. Most girls learned to mechanically saw on a violin or plink a piano so their mothers could be proud at the periodic recitals. The boys agonized through music practice when the only music their ears wanted was, "Batter up!" on the vacant lot next door.

The ukulele enjoyed a reign of popularity. Note the sheet music containing little squares for proper uke fingering.

The ukulele had a phenomenal reign to the extent that all sheet music was imprinted with the little squares showing fingering for the "uke." The craze for the tinkling strings went beyond the familiar wooden models of Hawaii. They got crossed with the crisp-toned banjo and were called banjo-ukuleles. If you were "top drawer" you added a resonator across the open back to give the tone more body. Not many worked with the instrument enough to play full melodies, but settled instead for chords that sometimes matched the melody. Even though the ukulele wasn't seriously regarded by musicians, it traveled considerably—in a rumble seat, canoe, at the summer cottage or even as accompaniment to voices in programs.

Many years after most of these instruments had been donated to trash cans or gathered dust in attics, Arthur Godfrey became enamored with the ukulele, and because of his wide popularity on television and radio, many listeners were impelled to "take it up."

One musical mystery has never been solved. We know that alcohol brings out song in some people, but why "Sweet Adeline" was thusly maligned by over-mellow quartets, we'll never know. It became synonymous with drinking whether during prohibition or after repeal.

If you were caught in the lure of music, what did you sing? Many good old "pop" songs proved how really desirable they were by being revived, repopularized and updated to hit the current sound. Some lyrics had to be changed so the young crowd would understand them. For instance; would they know what the writer meant when he said, "You're just as hard to land as the Ile de France . . . ?" It might not rhyme, but they'd comprehend if the words were "Boeing 707."

Nothing rang a more sentimental tone in the thirties, and earlier, than that dear old "Sweetheart of Sigma Chi." She suffered parodies about being the "sweetheart of six other guys." "The Girl of my Dreams" was also beloved as were "Margie," "Dinah" and several other girls.

In the twenties more people began to learn tunes with the advent of radio. When a set first came into our house we heard "Oh Katharina," Irving Berlin's "Always" was big, and "The Prisoner's Song," "I'm Sitting on Top of the World" and "Sweet Child."

The Depression had affected most of us, so we were trying to sing ourselves into a roseate state with "Happy Days Are Here Again," "Keep Your Sunny Side Up" and "Painting the Clouds With Sunshine." It didn't end the Depression but we felt happier while suffering.

Love has always dominated our songs. It's so varied that it can make us long to find it, sing with delirious glee when we do, or slump into despair when it's lost. These phases of love are found in songs like these: "Some Day My Prince Will Come" (longing), "I'm Glad I Waited For You" (triumph), "A Cottage For Sale" (trouble in paradise).

As the Depression faded and prohibition was repealed, we made big sounds with "The Beer Barrel Polka," and Rudy Vallee's "Stein Song." When 3.2 beer gave away to stronger beverage, we had "Cocktails for Two," and a sad tale of a lonely guy who asked for, "One More for the Road." No one yet realized that the "one for the road" should be coffee.

We have no right to laugh at the unintelligible syllables of some present songs and singers. We should recall "Vo-do-de-oh-do" and "Boop-boop-pe-doop." Then there was "Hutsut Ralston on the River Rah" or "Furiagasaki, Want Some Seafood Mamma." "Mairzy Doats" had a wild popularity when the writer put down the words his child couldn't pronounce plainly.

In a Decca-Brunswick Record Catalog, listing all of their numbers from 1944 through 1946, we see familiar names of singing stars and song titles. Some are still going strong—but others are lost to the ages.

There were albums of big Broadway hit shows: *Carmen Jones, Bloomer Girl, One Touch of Venus, Carousel, A Connecticut Yankee, Up in Central Park* and *The Song of Norway.*

Among the most all-time popular singing sisters were the Andrews and Boswell girls. The Ink Spots and Mills Brothers have endured for years. There were famous mixed groups like the Merry Macs and Six Hits and a Miss. Names that shouldn't be forgotten are the Delta Rhythm Boys, The Jesters or The Song Spinners.

We were collecting and really listening to records again after a big lull in the business. It's logical why few wanted to crank up machines to play their wheezy old Victrolas after the advent of wonderful radio. Meantime, man's ability to preserve sound on wax was greatly improved, and so were the machines for spinning them.

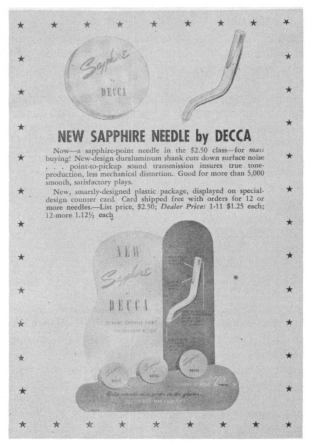

NEW SAPPHIRE NEEDLE by DECCA

Now—a sapphire-point needle in the $2.50 class—for *mass* buying! New-design duraluminum shank cuts down surface noise . . . point-to-pickup sound transmission insures true tone-production, less mechanical distortion. Good for more than 5,000 smooth, satisfactory plays.

New, smartly-designed plastic package, displayed on special-design counter card. Card shipped free with orders for 12 or more needles.—List price, $2.50; *Dealer Price:* 1-11 $1.25 each; 12-more 1.12½ each

These sapphire needles were ideal for playing your 78 r.p.m. records. (Courtesy of Decca Records)

Although juke boxes came on the scene in the twenties, this one is from the following decade, when they hit their stride, with cabinets of unusual design, gaudily colored panels and various jets of moving blinking lights. It cost a nickel to hear a record.

We began to tap toes to the insistent beat of boogie-woogie in the thirties and forties. Two masters of this form were recording—Meade "Lux" Lewis and Pete Johnson. If you preferred to rest your feet and listen to piano stylings, there was Carmen Cavallero, Art Tatum and Hazel Scott.

The much maligned harmonica stopped its reedy whine and showed what it could sound like in the capable mouths of Borrah Minnevitch and his Harmonica Rascals. Ethel Smith was making the organ sit up and talk,

Large consoles that worked electrically, with volume and tone controls, resided in more and more homes. We didn't have stereo and long-play 33 1/3's, but we didn't know the difference. Albums were equipped with several pages of records. They were described in catalogs as ten sides, twelve sides, or whatever number. Star performers from all entertainment fields were cutting records.

The amount of vocals by Kitty Carlisle might amaze you because she hasn't always been on a TV panel show. The lyric voice of Morton Downey was long popular. Some singers were usually associated with bands, such as Bob Eberly and Helen Forrest. Movie greats like Bing Crosby and Deanna Durbin were recording. Others were involved with so many kinds of entertaining, it was hard to classify them. Such were Dick Haymes, Eileen Farrell and Hildegarde. Mary Martin, with solid hit shows to her credit, came up often on wax, as did the original New York casts of the shows. A husband-wife team that enjoyed long renown was Frank Crummit and Julia Sanderson. You surely haven't forgotten Frances Langford's songs plus her unflagging interest in the soldier's welfare. She wrote a syndicated newspaper column called, "The Purple Heart Diary."

Some of the record albums featured in a thirties Montgomery Ward catalogue. (Courtesy Montgomery Ward)

while the jazzmen were congregating around Eddie Condon, Wingy Manone and Hot Lips Page.

You have a sketchy list of remembered stars, but what were the titles that might be coming from their throats or instruments? Of course, there were songs that never grow old— "The All-time Hit Parade." Bing Crosby with the Andrews Sisters were turning out hits like "Ac-Cent-Tchu-Ate the Positive" and "Along the Navajo Trail." "Besame Mucho" was selling well and it was common to hear someone whistling "Do Nothin' Till You Hear From Me."

"You Came to Me From Out of Nowhere," and so did the song, to be somewhere in our hearts. Dave Rose hit the loving ear when he wrote "Holiday for Strings," and violins had little time off from playing it.

When World War II broke around us, it changed the complexion of our music. One tune wasn't entirely identified with this war as "Over There" had been in the first one, but "Praise the Lord and Pass the Ammunition" came the closest. Some imports came across the oceans that we liked such as "Lili Marlene" and "Waltzing Mathilda," but meantime our writers were busy with themes for the girls the boys left behind, plus her hopes for the soldier's safety and a speedy end to fighting. This was reflected in such songs as: "When the Lights Go on Again All Over the World," "The Last Time I Saw Paris," "The White Cliffs of Dover" and "There'll Be a Hot Time in the Town of Berlin."

Songs could follow the boys from the draft board on: "You're in the Army Now," or a Navy man in "Bell-Bottom Trousers" who said, "I Got Ten Bucks and Twenty-Four Hour's Leave."

The girls were really praying for their fellows in "Dear God Watch Over Joe," "God Bless My Darlin' He's Somewhere" and "Say a Prayer for the Boys Over There." We heard about "Gertie from Bizerte" and sounded "Taps for the Japs," although most war songs centered in the European theater.

After the war was history and we were rebuilding our lives, television brought another change in musical habits. Movie sound systems had improved, high fidelity and frequency modulation (FM), was honey to our ears. What about our old love—radio? It had to function differently to remain an interesting and useful medium. Whereas record-playing was once for small, insignificant stations that had small power and no network affiliations, all of a sudden a new profession was born—disc jockeying. Even celebrities were spinning platters. Paul Whiteman and Ted Husing put in time at the well-paying turntable business that was giving records a new heyday. Instead of TV becoming an ogre for radio to fight, more radios for less money were sold than ever before. Every room in the house could jump to music, day and night from radio or hi-fi.

In all of this revolution what became of the orchestra that used to gather in the living room, or the homely, hit-of-the-party girl at the piano? The foregoing may explain why we don't gather around the piano as much as we did forty years ago. The radio, television and stereo would have to be turned off because they're drowning us out!

MUSIC — THE TIE THAT BINDS!
Self-played and Sung Music in the Home in which more than one musically-inclined member can participate, is one of Life's greatest joys and is a 'Tie That Binds' both family and friends together.

An advertisement depicting the joys of music in the home.

22

Before the "Boob Tube"

There was no competition among disc jockeys in 1901, but there was radio. If Mr. Marconi was here he could prove it because he made the first long distance radio transmission in that year. You thought radio was more recent? So did I, because it was 1921 when I was first confronted with radio paraphernalia while playing hide and seek in the home of a schoolmate. Her big brother was considered a bit "batty" because he spent much of the time in his cluttered bedroom where I'd chosen to hide. Later I asked my friend what the wires and unfamiliar gadgets were. I was none the wiser when she said, "He builds radios."

Radio microphone, vintage 1933. (Courtesy General Motors Magazine)

About 1925 my father told one night about a radio in a home where he'd worked that day. The lady of the house listened to music through earphones while doing her housework. This was the most wonderful miracle I'd ever heard of. Mother and I actually didn't see or listen to radio until some months later when father became acquainted with a radio owner who invited us to listen. That night their next door neighbors were having coal delivered and the noisy interference crackled against our unaccustomed eardrums. Otherwise, canary static whistled through the snatches of music, but we had touched that marvel—radio!

The first radio under our roof was owned by a couple who rented light housekeeping quarters upstairs. The thrill was overwhelming when they let us listen and showed how it operated. It wasn't as simple as now be-

cause you had to know digit combinations for three knobs to get a station. There were no networks and it was difficult to weed out a few strong stations such as KDKA in Pittsburgh. Most radio owners kept log books in which they recorded the three numbers for stations, the location and remarks about reception or related data. It made interesting Monday morning conversation, and caused boasting such as, "You'd never guess what I got last night! Of course, I have a more powerful set." And so the race was on to build ever bigger receivers, with more tubes until they were mazes of unsightly, uncovered parts that could scarcely be dusted or enhanced except by encasement. Dedicated radio "bugs" prided themselves on building their own, much as hi-fi buffs assemble components today. The size of one's radio was a status symbol in the 1920's.

An Atwater Kent ad in 1926 told of their radio speakers. "Tone, yes—and beauty too." Here was a desirable addition, "The Pooley radio cabinet is approved for Atwater Kent Radio because of the design and quality of Pooly cabinet work and because of tone qualities of the Pooley built-in floating horn." The RCA Company boasted, "This remarkable Radiola operates directly from your lighting socket."

Perhaps you'd forgotten how superior radios were in 1924. This was in an *Arts & Decoration* magazine advertisement; "Radio's greatest achievement—the remarkable Brunswick Radiola Super-Heterodyne. 1. Requires no outside antenna, no ground wires, you can move it from room to room. 2. Amazing selectivity permitting you to "cut out" what you don't want to hear and pick out instantly what you do. Consider what this means in big centers. Price range from $190–$650."

In 1929 we finally got a radio, although I was sure the day would never arrive because nearly everyone in the neighborhood already had them. But by waiting we got an acceptable piece of cabinetwork that looked well in the living room. Slowly the less cumbersome table models

A 1929 Atwater Kent table radio.

ground wire that could fasten to the bedsprings or some such. I used to fall asleep with an earphone nestled into my pillow. The worst feature of the crystal set was that the end of the "cat's whisker" wire frequently had to be relocated on the galena (a mineral, the chief source of lead), when reception faded.

Soon after the establishment of radio as a part of life came the radio stars. Until national broadcasting hookups were formed, the fame might be local, but it was satisfying when fan letters poured in. Writing requests for musical numbers was a popular pastime and one announcer boasted that his station had the phenomenal number (forty) of requests that day for "The Prisoner's Song."

One of the early and all-time great names in sports and newscasting was Graham McNamee. He became a member of everyone's household with his clear, smiling voice, vividly describing games and special events. Other men who distinguished themselves in the top echelon of sportcasting were Ted Husing and Bill Stern.

New professions were born with the advent of radio, not the least of which was announcing. To qualify these men had to have pleasant voices and the ability to accurately read many unfamiliar words, names of people and geographic places. Probably few escaped an occasional error, called a "blooper." Some announcers gained as much fame as the stars for whom they announced. Such were Jimmie Wallington and the well-articulated, satin-

and portables became popular. Atwater Kent produced a "Screen-Grid" compact model for $88, but the "Electro-Dynamic" speaker was $34. Big floor models were only slightly higher. These prices weren't modest in comparison to the small radios of today. Perhaps the speaker was separate because many people still clung to earphones even though long listening usually made the outer ears sore. A neat little crystal set, nickel-plated, and about the size of a thick slice of bread, could be purchased cheaply. I bought one in 1934. This was the simplest radio, with a

Graham McNamee, one of NBC's all-time great sportscasters, interviewing Babe Ruth during a game at Yankee Stadium. (NBC photo)

toned Milton J. Cross who was synonymous with operatic productions for years. Well known among announcers was the fascinating name, Alois Havrilla. A number prominent in radio survived the switch to television and are seen and heard today—such as Big Don Wilson and Harry Von Zell.

Reporting straight news or becoming a commentator about the news on radio became a populous business and some are with us yet. There was the late Floyd Gibbons, a dynamic war correspondent who lost an eye at the battle of Chateau-Thierry in World War I. He wore a white patch over the missing eye. An outspoken

Floyd Gibbons with "portable" equipment strapped to his chest in a briefcase while two men hold up necessary wire for broadcasting. (NBC photo)

A 1937 Majestic Radio.

and sometimes controversial commentator was Boak Carter. Do you remember H. V. Kaltenborn, the dynamic voice of Edwin C. Hill or the lilting name, Raymond Gram Swing?

It was becoming insufficient, as the new medium advanced, to merely manufacture radios that would receive programs. Vast advertising campaigns were launched to exploit not only cabinetry but colorful tone quality. The Majestic Company ran a series of ads showing each time a group of drab grey musicians against a big, colorful picture of the same musicians as they'd sound through a Majestic. The radio shown is their 1937 model. Our first console was a Majestic and it worked beautifully for over ten years without any repairs—not even for new tubes!

Competition mounted and many makes of radios were advertised . . . names that are nearly forgotten. Here are three 1934 buys.

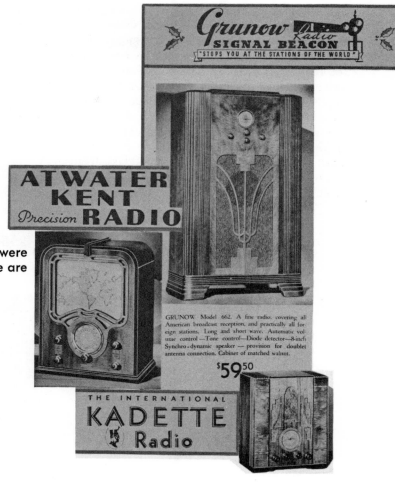

GRUNOW Model 662. A fine radio, covering all American broadcast reception, and practically all foreign stations. Long and short wave. Automatic volume control—Tone control—Diode detector—8-inch Synchro-dynamic speaker — provision for doublet antenna connection. Cabinet of matched walnut.

$59.50

A thirties magazine article showed to readers some of the techniques used by radio soundmen. (Courtesy Plymouth Motors Dealer Magazine)

It wasn't enough for people to talk, sing or play instruments, since everyone likes action, which in drama produces innumerable other sounds. Sound effects became big business. Many of these were not obtained by using the real thing. Iron washers were found to give a more authentic effect of clinkling coins than real money; tramping through thick underbrush was made by pressing down on a pile of broom corn; clocks had to strike on split-second cue and kisses of varying intensity were a "peck" on the back of the hand or pulling rubber suction cups apart and slipping cork across plate glass. Realism on the receiving end was all important, no matter how it was achieved.

A radio studio was a busy, if rather jumbled array when a drama was coming "live" to us. Actors in a group around the mikes held their scripts and jumped on cue to their lines. Sound men, musicians and technicians sprang into the right time slots like well-behaved gears in a complicated machine.

An opportunity long gone was the freedom for anyone to walk into the wonderful world of a radio station to audition if he thought he had talents the listening world should hear.

It would be impossible to name all of the programs and stars who entertained and informed us through the "air-lanes of radioland." These mentioned may rekindle your

A radio drama in progress. (Courtesy Plymouth Motors Dealer Magazine)

Amos and Andy. (NBC photo)

memories. After the *Two Black Crows*, probably no team in the thirties was better known and beloved than *Amos and Andy*, with all of the other characters they created.

Can you still hear the ring of Ed (Fire Chief) Wynn's comical voice?

Fred Allen and his wife, Portland Hoffa, brought a wealth of humor when the persimmon-faced comic gave us the friends in Allen's Alley; Senator Claghorn, Titus Moody, Mrs. Nussbaum and Humphrey Titter.

In 1933 one of the hottest comedy acts was Col. Lemuel Q. Stoopnagle and Budd. They reaped as many laughs as could be wished for, backed by an Andre Kostelanetz 25-piece orchestra and sponsored by Pontiac Motors.

Although unseen plays and serial dramas were perfected to a fine edge, and our imaginations filled in what we couldn't see, we identified voices and the people looked as we wished them to. Something could be said in favor of this. Daytimes, housewives' entertainment while working became "soap operas," so named because many serials were sponsored by washing products. These shows ran for years and provided steady work for actors. If a woman scheduled her daily chores, she could tell if

we could listen to *Gangbusters*, the *Green Hornet*, the *FBI in Peace and War*, *Famous Jury Trials* or run all over town mentally with *Casey, Crime Photographer*.

The Shadow knew what evil lurked in the minds of men. (The Detroit *News*)

There were spooky adventures in the *Hermit's Cave*. We were advised to turn out our lights, and leave them off while hearing the squeaky door of *Inner Sanctum*. Don't forget that *The Shadow* knew what evil lurked in the minds of men.

If you hankered for a regular play, you might join the crowd at *The Little Theater Off Times Square*. You'd be greeted by the First Nighter and probably entertained by Barbara Luddy and Les Tremayne—they were regulars.

Ed Wynn. (NBC photo)

she was on time by the program that was playing during any given job. Favorite medical dramas were, *Joyce Jordan—Girl M. D.*, *Young Doctor Malone* and *The Road of Life*.

Romance under varying or idealistic conditions found faithful listeners in such themes as a poor girl marrying a titled Englishman in *Our Gal Sunday;* or an older woman actually finding romance after thirty-five as did *Helen Trent*. One woman fought the problems of a second marriage in *The Second Mrs. Burton*, while another faced the challenges in *When a Girl Marries*. Writers appealed to the folksy and family instincts with *Ma Perkins, One Man's Family, David Harum* or *Pepper Young's Family*. *Life Can Be Beautiful* showed the generosity of Papa David, proprietor of the "Slightly-Read Bookstore," when he raised the waif, Chi-Chi. The trials, tribulations and jokes about the serial characters were legion because we suffered with them or hung from their cliffs until the next thrilling episode when we'd endure more problems with Pollyanna philosophy.

After dinner our radio fare varied. If crime chasing with the "good guys" catching the crooks was our meat,

Fred Allen and Portland Hoffa. (NBC photo)

Music lovers had food for their ears when "catching" *Fitch's Bandwagon* or "hopping" on the *Manhattan Merry-Go-Round* unless they preferred a ride with the *Camel Caravan.* Martin Block started the "original" *Make-Believe Ballroom* in New York. It caught on and for years, Al Jarvis played records in Los Angeles on a program of the same title. Mr. Chase did likewise in Detroit and there may have been others.

There were brainy shows that caused us to marvel at the intelligence of children—*The Quiz Kids,* or the storehouse of retained knowledge of the *Information Please* panel.

If you wanted your rafters to ring with laughter, comedy situations were furnished by *Vic and Sade, Clara, Lu and Em* or *The Goldbergs,* ably dominated by Molly Goldberg's warm personality. *Duffy's Tavern* brought happiness to many who wouldn't have taken a bite where the "elite meet to eat."

Tall tales were told by the incredible Baron Munchhausen, but no matter how you doubted him, it was hard to answer his "Vass you dere, Scharlie?"

The great wide West was kept in order by a valiant man who had an Indian friend, Tonto, and a great horse, Silver. "Gettum up Scout" was understood by everyone and the silver bullet meant the *Lone Ranger* had called. Some harrowing adventures unfolded under the searing sun in *Death Valley Days.*

Sponsors weren't giving away astronomical sums of money to listeners or studio audiences, but many people sat anxiously near their phones in case the *Tums Pot of Gold* rang their number. The odds were staggering.

One man whose speaking voice became familiar to millions, as he interestingly presented information, was John Nesbit on his *Passing Parade.*

Anyone who has cherished memories of the days be-

Some "mikes" we've known. (Photo from Plymouth Motors Dealer Magazine; sketch by author)

fore sound had pictures will likely say, "You forgot the *Cliquot Club Eskimos* and what about the *A & P Gypsies?*" I guess the Eskimos went north and the Gypsies are still roaming.

Many centuries ago, ancient philosophers and poets spoke of the "Music of the Spheres." Radio seems to have come the closest to achieving this dream of harnessing the ether in order to glean its ethereal music. Our twentieth century invention may sometimes transmit sounds less than musical, and certainly they're of this earth, but who could predict what may one day be heard through our speakers—since we've already had programs bounced back from satellites in outer space?

23

Salesmen in Your Living Room

If it was untold time before smoke signals were devised for communication, consider the struggles of those who finally produced television! If we could scarcely comprehend the miracle of radio when it first crackled into our consciousness through earphones, what greater amazement could we show when a picture was seen with sound? Incredible!

An NBC photograph showing the impact of television.

Television was a subject of conjecture long before it was a living room reality. Even after the public was aware that it was in the making, we were told it would not be christened until the screen pattern could be reduced from wide bars to fine lines. The flickering image couldn't fight its way through the screen. Nor could the picture be transported more than about fifty miles. It certainly didn't appear to be a big, bouncing baby, and only the wealthy or foolish would invest in an expensive set for the little it offered.

It would be exceedingly complicated to attempt a simple explanation of what went into television pioneering. Certainly no one person is responsible . . . not from the day in 1817 when Baron Jöns Jacob Berzelius discovered selenium, nor fifty-six years later when a telegrapher named May discovered that the mysterious element figured in better transmission of electricity when the sun

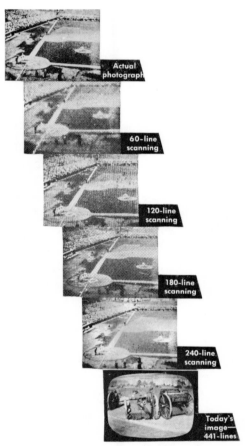

NBC photograph showing progress in the quality of the TV image.

shone on it. He'd stumbled onto the principle of the photoelectric cell. Through the latter nineteenth century many fragmentary, though all-important additions were made by many men.

Left: Iconoscope; right: Kinescope. (NBC photograph)

The 1920's saw steady advancements toward something resembling shadowy pictures and equipment was constantly being developed. In 1923 Vladimir K. Zworykin filed patent applications for the first camera tube, the "Iconoscope." Bell Telephone Laboratories in 1927 demonstrated television over a wire circuit between New York and Washington. Much was added again by Mr. Zworykin, of RCA, with his electronic-scanning device, a cathode ray tube called "Kinescope."

Considering when most of us got our first television sets, it's hard to realize that the first telecast drama was sent from WGY's Schenectady, New York, studios in 1928. Also, could you guess who might have been the first TV artist? It was Felix the Cat who patiently posed before engineers for their experiments.

You could have been stopped for a televised sidewalk interview as early as 1938—if you'd been in Rockefeller Plaza. The 1930's ushered in the use of the new wire line, coaxial cable, brought out by Bell Telephone Laboratories. This very important cable was stretched underground from the RCA Building to the Empire State Building as indicated on the chart. The reachable area is shown by the circled map.

The coaxial cable had a good bit of long distance stretching to do before television reception would become anything beyond a limited field. The prediction in 1939 was, "the possibility of a television network as extensive as present-day sound networks is remote. Transmitters in one hundred of America's largest cities could reach about half the nation's people."

In an American Motors history, it was stated that nine years later, 1948, television was still in its infancy awaiting cross-country coaxial cables. However, New York TV facilities were used to advertise the new Hudson Motor Car models for 1948.

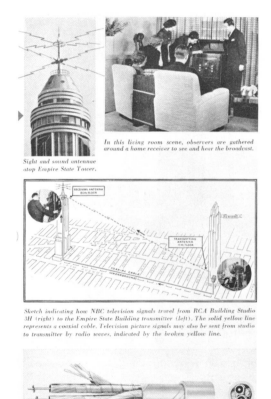

In this living room scene, observers are gathered around a home receiver to see and hear the broadcast.

Sight and sound antennae atop Empire State Tower.

Sketch indicating how NBC television signals travel from RCA Building Studio 3H (right) to the Empire State Building transmitter (left). The solid yellow line represents a coaxial cable. Television picture signals may also be sent from studio to transmitter by radio waves, indicated by the broken yellow line.

Photograph showing interior construction of coaxial cable used in television line transmission. Cross-section on right shows arrangement of essential parts. (Courtesy Bell Telephone Laboratories.)

This brochure describes the methods by which television is transmitted to people's livingrooms. (Courtesy NBC)

The television which is assuming shape in our laboratories will not, as many persons assume without warrant, replace sound broadcasting or make sound receiving sets obsolete. The present sound broadcasting services will proceed without interruption. Television must find new functions, new entertainment, and new programs.

There was much speculation about the effect TV would have on radio, movies, and the stage. It is interesting now to see with time's passage what has actually happened. An assurance of the status quo was expressed in this clipping.

In 1939, the year of the New York World's Fair, RCA was a pioneer with a few television programs which didn't account for full days of programming. It was an expensive, awesome toy, but the average person was not yet sure of its potential or future. There were probably not more than two hundred sets owned and they had to be clustered near the station to receive the meagre TV fare. The new art form wasn't attractive to big name perform-

Television was demonstrated at the 1939 World's Fair. (NBC photo)

TV was used to introduce the 1948 Hudson. (Courtesy American Motors)

ers of movies and radio because it didn't pay what they were earning elsewhere. Many regarded it as a clever gadget not to be taken seriously . . . at least not until someone else bought the TV sets which could cause other someones to pull good programming out of their collective hats. There were men of vision in this new medium; men who learned the complicated techniques of preparing television material. At first simple one-act plays, travelogues, newsreels, vaudeville and science demonstrations were used.

As we've now learned, the layman's view or opinion couldn't have been farther from what history records. Whereas not many could afford the luxury of TV at first, bars and cocktail lounges saw it as a great boost for business, and cheaper than steadily hiring live musicians. Paper signs went up across windows and buildings, coaxing you inside to *see television* . . . and you incidentally imbibed. As a customer entered a nearly dark TV lounge, he groped for a seat and whispered his order to a bartender or waitress who materialized out of the murk. To have spoken in a normal voice would have brought the wrath of the entire place upon the offender, and he couldn't see how vast the enemy was.

It was inevitable that the bar boom couldn't last as more people bought sets, prices leveled off and the mere novelty of "seeing" the picture, no matter what it was, would change. The customers of the baby TV industry became more selective and wished to turn the knobs themselves.

Screens were like picture post cards in comparison to present sizes and anyone who bought a combination with record player and radio would be in the market again as soon as screens enlarged.

Television was sold in combination with radio and phonograph in the early days.

Here, TV actress Elaine Kent shows the makeup changes from hard, contrasty color when cameras were less sensitive to Indian red lips and near orange complexions as techniques improved by 1939.

It wasn't long before other fields were affected or prodded into action when the baby began to toddle and America boasted more than 3000 sets. Cosmetic firms were quick to present a blackish red lipstick called Telecast Red. Then dark makeup needed for the cameras caught on with women in general.

You may not believe it, but fashion shows were the first sponsored programs. An article about the new medium boasted that you may *see* and *hear* at least one play a week, hockey and basketball games from Madison Square Garden, feature length films, the "March of Time" and—the familiar and perennial Lowell Thomas, a pioneer in TV after his many years on radio. You can see by the above that the late, late movie was already on its way.

There was talk about a possible network from Boston to Washington, D.C. It was known that the picture waves would have to be relayed from pylon to pylon to effect nationwide coverage, as radio networks had done. New or potential set owners were assured that they would operate on AC current as their radios did. Prices ranged from around $150 to about $400 by the time television was available in the Midwest.

When the first set came to our block in Detroit, we were thrilled to be invited to see it. As I recall, the program was *Kukla, Fran and Ollie*. Woe soon came to the only mother in the neighborhood who had viewing-aged children . . . particularly if they had lots of friends. Her livingroom became the mecca for all children within running distance as they sprawled on stomachs to stare at the built-in "baby-sitter."

At last—radio voices had a physique! The day of commercials being interrupted by programs was about to dawn, and the 1940's were to be known as the television decade.

Gertrude Lawrence in a scene from "Susan and God." (NBC photo)

Television produced family "togetherness" in a new way; all stared in the same direction.

24

Million Dollar Words

Have you cursed the radio or television announcer who shouted something over and over that you'd heard so often you dreamed about it? It may have been annoying the thousandth time around, but those words probably put a lot of money into someone's pocket. Manufacturers haven't only sold their products—they've done one of the greatest word-selling jobs. Words and phrases are repeated until they penetrate our inner consciousnesses. A picture, too, becomes readily identifiable with a product. Whether you buy it or not, you *know* about it. Some of these words and pictures didn't come easily or cheaply to the manufacturers because the best creative brains in advertising agencies labored with catch words that would sell, identify and suggest quality—but in brevity. Copy had to read fast and keep the seed of remembrance sprouting in the potential customer.

These words are effective because many ways of our lives have been affected by advertising whether or not we will admit or realize it. Like the quest for a better mousetrap, we've beaten a path to the better ad slogan or what it represents.

The familiar RCA trademark. (T.M. Reg. U.S. Pat. Off. by RCA)

"His Master's Voice" is one of the oldest illustrations-with-words. Dogs are here to stay and so is recorded sound. By putting the two together with the suggestion that the sound fidelity is so good the dog recognizes his

master's voice adds up to success in any century. Anyone who's ever seen his pet watch television knows the feeling the RCA Victor dog symbolizes.

The subtle approach was used by some manufacturers to the extent of not showing the product. "You just know she wears them," was enough to sell McCallum Silk Hosiery. The elegance of the lady's clothes and boudoir in 1920 to 1930, implied that this lady would only settle for the best in everything.

We were a generation of "Schoolgirl Complexions" brought about by reminders of the benefits of olive oil

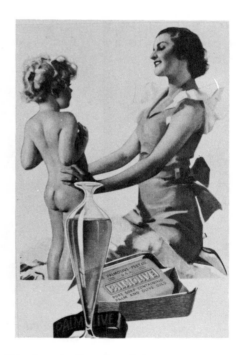

A Palmolive Soap ad stressed the importance of having a youthful complexion. (Courtesy Colgate-Palmolive Co.)

in our Palmolive Soap. It was one thing to clean the skin with soap and water, but to keep the schoolgirl glow had to become every woman's passion through clever advertising.

Way," to suggest the pleasant aroma of Chesterfield Cigarettes. Everyone of either sex knew which brand said, "They Satisfy."

The Old-Dutch cleanser girl. (Courtesy Purex Corp. Ltd.)

Pretty girls were used to advertise Coke. (Reproduced through the courtesy of The Coca-Cola Company)

There's one girl who needs no introduction because she's been relentlessly chasing out dirt so many years, she's the hardest-working member of our family. They may modernize the packaging, but the Old Dutch Cleanser girl will always be recognizable.

Cigarette advertising has undergone many changes from the time that "tailor-mades" were a new item. It was a long time before women were shown as smokers. They were present, but only said sweetly, "Blow Some My

Pretty girls have never appeared in more places at home and abroad than those who offered "The Pause That Refreshes." The Coca-Cola girl might be different individuals, but she was always recognizable by her fresh smile and inviting smoothness. She sold a lot of "Coke" before the advertising format changed.

Lucky Strike Cigarettes were great practitioners of the repetitive technique. They've had many slogans that were brought home effectively besides the constant one, "It's

In the twenties ladies weren't supposd to smoke in public. But Chesterfield hinted at the possibility that they might want to in this famous ad. (Courtesy Liggett & Myers Tobacco Co.)

The famous trademark of Philip Morris: Johnnie. (Used by permission of Philip Morris, Inc.)

proved the words had been heard. They changed this one to "Nature in the Raw is usually Wild!"

Have you done what one great slogan suggested? "Asked the Man Who Owns One?" Today it is more difficult to find a Packard owner to ask, but it was a million dollar slogan for many years.

Probably no voice was more familiar on our radios than little Johnnie when he "Called for Philip Morris."

A word, or letters and numerals, as names of miraculous new ingredients, have spelled magic to many products. There was a girl named Miriam, who had social troubles until she solved her dental film problems with the rhyming ingredient, "Irium." Poor Miriam finally had a telephone ring that was a busy thing after discovering Pepsodent Tooth Paste.

If beautiful full-color paintings made business for some companies, others found the cartoonist's format effective. They told a story to get reader interest, showing in the end how (trade name) had solved a problem or come to the rescue. Listerine made us halitosis-conscious with a cartoon strip about "Helen and Herbert."

In 1927 a Listerine advertisement in *Harper's Bazaar* used a then-popular appeal that would be laughed out of existence today. The social hauteur of the era plainly shows. It was part of a numbered series: "Case #244— Old New England family. Prominent social and financial connections. Brilliant student. Groton four years. Harvard 1919–1922. Won letter in two major sports. Substitute for No. 6 on crew. Socially inclined, but made no club. Humiliation fostered moody state of mind. After graduation, one year of big game hunting and exploration, Africa and Tibet. On return to U.S. offered position with well-known bank. Capable but made no friends. Resignation accepted after one year. Tried one thing after another. Perceptible discouragement for apparent

Toasted." One slogan explained the reason for toasting— "*Nature* in the *Raw* is seldom *Mild.*" There were many ways of illustrating this fact, in paintings done by top illustrators. Parodies on slogans by the wags of our time

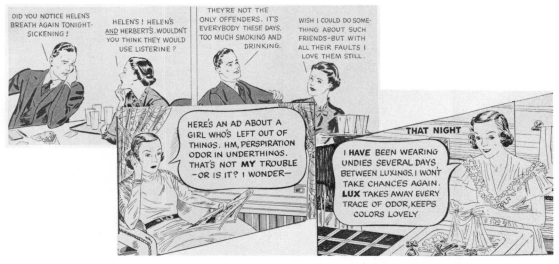

Cartoons were once used to sell deodorants and mouthwashes. (Courtesy of Warner-Lambert Pharmaceutical Company)

These jewelry ads were done by the author for the Meyer Jewelry Company, Detroit.

failure. Selling bonds (1925). Now (1927) Vice-President of growing Eastern bank. Happily married and residing in New York because . . .

"Nothing exceeds halitosis as a social offense.
"Nothing equals Listerine as a remedy."

Deliriously happy people were always smiling at watches as if to say, "Ha, ha, ha, see—it's half-past one by my beautiful (brand name) watch!" It was wonderful to be in a roseate condition every time we glanced at our diamond rings.

Advertising has done many things to and for us since the days when advertising consisted of solid blocks of old-style type, sometimes embellished with crude wood-carvings. Advertising slowly grew to the glittering force that we've known since engraving improved and myriad processes made color reproductions possible. But always the core of the selling business has been the clever idea that can make you run, not walk, to buy the X product instead of Y or Z. We know that some items are good "aged in wood," while others should be "spring fresh." Snob appeal made you aspire to keep up with the Joneses, and long, easy credit terms sometimes coaxed you to go over your financial heads.

Consider how different life would be if there were no signs, billboards, TV or radio commercials, not an advertisement in magazines or newspapers, or envelopes in your mailbox with advertising letterheads . . . heaven, you say? Perhaps; but an army of people would be unemployed. Let's admit that we're conditioned to advertising.

25

Who Said That?

"A woman is only a woman, but a good cigar is a smoke." Rudyard Kipling said this, but in 1920 Thomas R. Marshall came up with a smoking-connected remark that was due to go down in the annals of famous words oft repeated until they're pushed into the cliché class. Mr. Marshall said, "What this country needs is a good five cent cigar."

Have you wondered who said scores of other phrases and quips that color our everyday conversation? The origins of many sayings are remote—they somehow crept into usage but die hard. Some can be credited to definite groups, such as show business personalities, politicians, musicians and young people. It's amazing how many wards come from the jargon of drug addicts.

When we first heard many expressions they seemed disarmingly clever, but repetition has honed their edges smooth. Some speech is pure slang and may work its way into the dictionary, if used long and frequently enough. They pass on by word of mouth like seeds scattered by the wind, and mass communications spread them even faster.

Radio commercials have certainly added to the things we've found ourselves saying such as; "Don't be half-safe," from Arrid Deodorant, or Lucky Strike's well-established adage, "Future events cast their shadows before." Popular Amos and Andy, in our homes every night, could be counted on to have us talking their language. Everyone began to say, "Buzz me, Miss Blue." The fellow who was a model of efficiency frequently might have said Amos and Andy's "check and double-check."

A woman who advertised her allegedly ageless beauty sold cosmetics that could help you laugh at the years. On radio she raced through a short program which always ended when Edna Wallace Hopper shouted, "They're pushing me off the air!" Another often repeated Hopperism in newspapers and magazines was, "Would you believe I'm past 60?"

The amateur program was an important part of our weekly radio big shows. Major Bowes regularly intoned, " 'Round and around she goes and where she stops, nobody knows." He borrowed it from carnival jargon, and Ted Mack continued it when he took over the *Original Amateur Hour.*

Edna Wallace Hopper, 1926.

What Dorothy Dix or Beatrice Fairfax had done in print, Mr. John J. Anthony accomplished on radio as thousands descended on him to plead; "Mr. Anthony, I have a problem . . . " The wags were soon asking, "Mr. Anthony, *do* I have a problem?" Other words the public readily repeated were, "Got a deal"—said by Al when he had a new, hair-brained scheme for making a million dollars. He was Irma's boyfriend on the *My Friend Irma* comedy series that starred Marie Wilson.

Quiz shows with giveaway money brought in the crowds to try their luck. Professor Quiz characteristically

Dorothy Dix. (Courtesy of Pontiac Daily *Press*)

shouted, "Give that young lady (or man) ten silver dollars!" The stakes hadn't yet risen to astronomically sized prizes.

Radio newsmen had distinguishing words that became their trademarks and we repeated them. Gabriel Heatter had a greeting we still hear today, "There's good news tonight!" Or "Bad" as the case might be. "How-do-you-do, how *do* you *do*," may bring back the memory of the late Norman Brokenshire.

Who could forget the spine-tingling effect as a sinister voice chanted, "The Shadow knows," then a blood-curdling laugh rolled out of our loudspeakers. Was there a soul so unattuned to the times that he didn't occasionally mutter, " 'T'ain't funny, McGee?" Usually Molly McGee had a point well-taken when aiming this remark at her husband, Fibber. To have a Fibber McGee closet was understood by everyone.

Two rough-talking movie characters, Flagg and Quirt, did their stint to color our everyday lingo when they snarled at each other, "Sez who?" "Sez me!" They had us soon saying what's wrong with "The Cockeyed World?" when Victor McLaglen and Edmund Lowe made the picture by this name.

Mae West. (Loaned by Lorne Braddock)

An abundantly voluptuous femme fatale, Mae West, was never without her twangy invitation to "Come up and see me sometime."

Texas Guinan, a night club celebrity of considerable success, said things people repeated. Her remarks were salty if not Harvardesque when she bellowed, "C'mon, suckers, give the little girl a great big hand!"

We were richest in expressions that described how people and conditions were. These could have started anywhere. The words might have little related meaning to their normal definitions, but it didn't take a college degree to know how to apply them. These could be happy, grousing, complimentary or downright derogatory re-

Texas Guinan. (Courtesy Detroit *News*)

marks. You could carry whole conversations with slang. Life could be *duck soup* if you had *glad rags* when you went out to *cut a rug* with the *bee's knees* or *cat's pajamas*. You'd put on your *best bib 'n tucker, shake a leg,* for you were not only a *jelly bean* and *drugstore cowboy,* but a *good time Charlie* who didn't *ritz* his *tootsie wootsie* even if she said, "*So's your old man* or *oh applesauce!*" You thought she was the *cat's meow* even when she *D-double-dared* you to *fly along at 40 miles an hour* in the *flivver*. You *got the drift* so she *didn't have to snow again.* She giggled and said, "*Goody goody, more fun, more blood spilled, more people killed!*" This was a bit strong for your *Uncle Dudley,* but it didn't *cut any ice* with you. You wouldn't *strain at a gnat and swallow a camel,* for if you *couldn't be the bell cow, you'd fall in behind.* You weren't as *odd as Dick's hatband* when you asked her to *come up and see your etchings.* She said, "*Dunt esk,* or *horse feathers!*" Do you *recollect?*

Each generation has a language all its own—not better or worse, just different.

A Roosevelt campaign button from the 1940 campaign.

We owed memorable expressions to nimble politician's tongues which advised us to "Not change horses in midstream," while the other side asked, "Have you had enough?" "It's time for a change," and later enough replied, "I like Ike." A very quiet Calvin Coolidge declared, "I do not choose to run." Around Al Smith's unsuccessful Presidential try arose the words, "He'd rather be right than President."

Whether you were a "23 skidooer" or a "cool cat," it's made little difference except to point to the era in which you spoke.

26

Souls Sold for Cup Cakes

If you enjoy sitting in a deepfreeze, you wouldn't have objected to the chill attitude of fine arts painters a few years ago toward the blackguards who bartered their souls for gold—the gold mined from advertising illustration. Some of the painters preferred starvation to conspiring against the psyche. While the commercial crowd were well-fed, they could gaze into the gaunt countenances of the "real" artists who clung to Bohemia and their ethereal dreams.

A typical John Held, Jr. rendition of the flapper era. (Courtesy Mrs. John Held, Jr.)

As the field of advertising art opened ever wider, some great illustrators developed who became popular favorites—even of the laymen who "couldn't draw a straight line." To lesser artists these illustrators had as much celebrity rating as movie stars. The successful were imitated and aspired to by every art school student or practitioner at a drawing desk in engraving shops, stores and studios.

When the flapper was Charlestoning through her heyday in the twenties, she couldn't have had a more talented portrayer of her every move than John Held, Jr. While she was shown at her typical best, her "fella" was accurately etched too, from his center-parted hair to his balloon pants.

John Held, Jr. (Courtesy Mrs. Held)

John Held, Jr. wielded a "million dollar" pencil. He traveled and socialized with a clever crowd of intellectual, creative people and hosted many gay gatherings at his three homes, an apartment in New York, house at Palm Beach and spacious farm.

The flappers of America didn't have to rely entirely on Mr. Held to be vividly delineated. Ethel Hayes was do-

Ethel Hayes's famed "Flapper Fanny" feature. (By permission of the Pontiac *Daily Press*)

ing a creditable job with her "Flapper Fanny" newspaper feature. Miss Hayes was the highest paid newspaper woman artist in the country, and rightfully earned it by her skillful pen drawings in the flapper's heyday. Fanny didn't die when Ethel Hayes laid her pen aside because, oddly, two fashion designers took up the pen later to continue the cartoon spots, Gladys Parker and later Sylvia, yes—simply Sylvia.

Although during the three decades we're exploring, there were men who wondered why all women didn't

This frilly little lady was created by Nell Brinkley. (Courtesy Detroit *News*)

Rose O'Neill's illustrations demonstrated a sensitive pen point. (Rose O'Neill illustration for *Liberty* Magazine)

Maginel Wright Barney preferred a bold, simple line. (Maginel Wright Barney illustration for *The Woman's Home Companion*)

246

stay with their pots and pans, numbers of women gained recognition for their illustrative efforts in all mediums. There was Rose O'Neill who illustrated stories with a sensitive, fine pen point; she was best known for her "Kewpies." By contrast, Maginel Wright Barney made magazine cover designs or depicted parts of stories, usually those involved with children, using a bolder, simpler line than Miss O'Neill. Color was often a part of Mrs. Barney's pictures.

One of the all-time greatest pen and ink artists was Franklin Booth, known as "The painter with the pen." In the 1920's he could do with the delicate point what many artists needed a brush for—to create all of the detail and breadth of tone in the subject.

No account of earlier noteworthy illustrators could be guilty of forgetting Howard Chandler Christy. He had a fine eye for beautiful models, but also made notable paintings during World War I. By 1933 when this picture was taken, he was painting a series of lovely girls for a magazine. Mr. Christy was glorifying the American girl before Florenz Ziegfeld, and in a news article stated his choice of a half dozen women who exemplified to him beauty-with-brains. The most widely known were Amelia Earhart in aviation; Ruth Bryan Owen, the Minister to Denmark (the first woman in a major diplomatic post); Jane Cowl from the stage and Whitney Bourne, a leading debutante. The other two weren't publicly known.

This Franklin Booth illustration shows his ability to create with a pen point illustrations that many artists would have needed a brush to achieve. (Reprinted by permission of Art Instruction Schools, formerly Federal Schools, Inc.)

Howard Chandler Christy with one of his beautiful models. (Courtesy the Detroit News)

James Montgomery Flagg. (Courtesy of Chrysler Corp.)

Another man who used three names in his signature was James Montgomery Flagg. This top illustrator worked in all mediums and was the creator of a poster that has started many an uncertain young man off on military duty as he approached a recruiting center. Uncle Sam pointed a forefinger directly at him and said, "I WANT YOU!"

Mr. Flagg's work began to appear in publications in the nineteenth century, but he was with us until 1960—a long enough life to ensure him time for mountains of illustrations.

This James Montgomery Flagg illustration demonstrates his fluid ability with a pen. (Courtesy Metropolitan Life Insurance Co.)

Harrison Fisher was one of the instigators of using beautiful girl paintings for magazine covers. In April of 1930 he stated, "There is more character in womanly beauty. Women have grown more reasonable and less willful in recent years. There's new expression, a new figure and less of the old-time doll-face, insipid style of beauty in women today." What he's referring to we used to call "candy box" beauty. Pictured is the Fisher technique as applied to faces and diagrammatic idea about subtle changes after women became more active, athletic and interested in a wider life. However, as a sidelight in an interview, Mr. Fisher said that he was tired of drawing beautiful American girls and would like to put cows on magazine covers for a change.

Famous columnist O. O. McIntyre delighted in the company of artists and publicized America's celebrity painters. In one column he said, "That block of West 67th St., running directly off Central Park West is where art flourishes with a big A. They are not the long-haired dreamers gnawing crusts in garrets but the short-haired producers who stir out of sleep for cold showers and work ten hours a day in tapestry-hung salons . . . and otherwise live in a world of superlatives. In such settings will be found Harrison Fisher, a study in grey from hair to spats, and Russell Patterson, the sartorial Greek god of the artist's quarter. James Montgomery Flagg lives there, as does Henry Raleigh . . . "

Henry Raleigh's work had underlying bones of fine lines with variously colored inks to give texture and interest. As happened to many of Mr. Raleigh's contemporaries, styles and times changed and he was swept over by the new breed who made the work of many passé. It's a sad fact of the business.

Some writers, artists and critics believed the best known American illustrator through the twenties and thirties was McClelland Barclay. His reputation was international and demand for his services overwhelming. He also painted beautiful women, the most famous of which was the "Fisher Body Girl." The shadow in Mr. Barclay's otherwise ideal life was that he married his models. This seems like a practical arrangement but for one flaw—they became obsolete. His first wife grew plump when he was painting "meatless" wonders of the '20's. But wife No. 1, who had helped him from obscurity upward, didn't feign jealousy of his painted girls because she assumed they were from his imagination. And coincidentally they were—until a girl in her late teens ascended to the swank Barclay penthouse, looking identical to those in his paintings. Her friends in Virginia noticed the resemblance, so she wished to see the artist who had "created" her. This was the entrance of wife No. 2 and the exit of wife No. 1. As this marriage seemed ideal, again the trend in beauty changed, and away went

Harrison Fisher (at left) with some of his drawing secrets. (Courtesy the Detroit News)

Henry Raleigh's depiction of a languidly beautiful woman
in 1933. (Courtesy of Sheila Raleigh Winsten)

No. 2 "through no fault of hers." He got a current model
but claimed no matrimonial intentions because models
became obsolete too fast. When World War II came,
McClelland Barclay became a Navy painter and was un-
fortunately on a vessel that was sunk by enemy fire.

During these years a young illustrator appeared who
was to hit the peak of fame in magazines—John LaGatta.
He had an amazing talent for painting the aloofness and
languor of beautifully relaxed women. It isn't easy to
paint a lady's bare back well, but this was one of Mr.
LaGatta's accomplishments. There was sophisticated
elegance in his settings and the women had fluid, almost
feline grace.

When trends changed, these top moneymaking illustrators probably couldn't believe this fame wouldn't last,
or that the techniques that had been their trademarks
would be inundated by the surge of fresh recruits pouring from the art schools, anxious to shoot new-blooded
ideas into the way illustration should look.

You were smiled at by luscious girls for years, whether
in America or abroad. They coaxed you to refresh yourself with Coca-Cola, become beautiful with Palmolive
Soap, Camay Soap, enjoy Maxwell House Coffee, drive
a Packard or ride on Goodyear Tires. But did you know
that hundreds, maybe thousands of these girls came from
the able brush of Haddon Sundblom? In 1930 he was
a smooth-faced young man of Chicago; his work was
also smooth, sure and definitely commercial, as attested
to by the Art Director's Club of New York gold medal
award for his exceptional advertising art.

McCLELLAND BARCLAY

McClelland Barclay, right, and one of his drawings.

Illustrator John LaGatta was expert at depicting women's bared backs, as in this scene. (Courtesy John LaGatta)

Haddon Sundblom (insert) and one of his advertisements. (Reproduced through the courtesy of the Coca-Cola Company)

George Petty was famous for exaggerating the proportions of his models, as in this Jantzen swimwear ad. (Reproduced by permission of Jantzen, Inc., Portland, Oregon)

Maude Tousey Fangel, at left, specialized in drawing children. (Courtesy American Artists Rep., Inc.)

Surefire interest could be generated every time a "Petty Girl" appeared on a page . . . or anywhere else she might show up. This busty, leggy girl, proportioned as few are, got the gentleman's attention even though his wife might have been more jealous than enthusiastic about the work of George Petty—that is if she didn't know that many of the paintings were modeled after his daughter. She always wore a beguiling smile (but who wouldn't with such a figure!) and a famous father to paint it with perhaps just the right exaggerations.

Maude Tousey Fangel caught the beautiful girls (and boys) before they had had a chance to grow up. She probably painted, or drew with pastel crayons, more babies than any artist of her day. She called them all "my babies," even though her own baby grew up and Mrs. Fangel had to hunt elsewhere for models because her paintings were not of imaginary little ones. She was as sunny in disposition as the light was bright in her babies' eyes, and she had a way with her tiny sitters.

In spite of the disdain that some painters had for commercial artists, newspapers were ecstatic in their praise of the Detroit Institute of Arts when it gave "new evidence of its freedom from prejudice. Directors of the Institute have hung in their galleries for the first time in such an institution in America, originals of some of the nation's best advertising art. The prejudice against advertising art, as art, has no justification. Why, for instance, a drawing by Rockwell Kent sold to a private gallery as art, while a drawing of blast furnaces by night for a rolling mills and by the same artist, is not art."

Another writer said, "The advertising artist may well be called the poet laureate of modern trade and commerce. Oddly enough, though these men carry off the most handsome rewards given to the modern artist, their names are seldom known by the layman. Few people have a real conception of just how commercial art is produced. Frequently an artist must work against the most rigid time limitations in cooperation with others in the advertising business." How true!

Besides the realistically presented illustrations, there were masses of great cartoons produced in the three decades. Only a few of the greats can here be included, but in the strip cartoon classification with a continuing cast, who could have rated higher and longer than George McManus with his "Bringing up Father," more commonly called "Maggie and Jiggs"? Mr. McManus struck a chord that resounded in nearly everyone. He made us conscious of corned beef and cabbage and rolling pins—the social-climbing wife and the glamorous, luxury-loving daughter. When Mr. McManus died, other artists carried on and have kept very close to his creations.

Fontaine Fox had great success and facility with "The Toonerville Trolley." An item about Mr. Fox and his work states, "It looks easy, yes—because the pen of Fontaine Fox so completely hides the time and thought that go into his works. And that is the genius of his art."

A unique addition to the store of laugh lore were the zany inventions of a man named Rube Goldberg. He's put his special stamp on our language because people know the meaning when something's called a "Goldberg invention." He was also an amusing author who wrote an article about his starting tribulations as a young man wanting to be an artist, under the title, "It Happened to a Rube." Come to think of it . . . were his inventions so zany after all?

It would be difficult if not impossible to recall all of the beloved strips, who created them, or to count the hours of pleasure they afforded us. They came to be

George McManus with his comic creations, Jiggs and Maggie. (Written and illustrated by George McManus for *American Magazine*)

253

Fontaine Fox with the Toonerville Trolley. (Courtesy Gruen Industries, Inc.)

The portrait of cartoonist Rube Goldberg is by the author. The cartoon is Mr. Goldberg's, of course. (Cartoon reproduced through courtesy of Rube Goldberg)

Left to right: Little Orphan Annie, Blondie, and Dick Tracy. (Courtesy of *Harper's Bazaar*, from an article, "The Funnies," by George Dangerfield)

more than just comics, as some found their ways into motion pictures or the characters started fads, influenced our habits and inspired items we wore or used. Can you imagine not knowing what a Dagwood sandwich is—or realizing the value of spinach-eating or the love of tripe? Some of the make-believe people aged while others stayed forever young.

We sometimes wonder what happened to the glamorous art business and the practitioners in it, that newspapers and magazines used to find them newsworthy subjects. It used to be fascinating to read about the beginning struggles of would-be artists and the lavish doings of those whom success had rewarded. Illustrators were interviewed on beauty in general, women in particular and were quoted in testimonials. In many areas today, artists for large companies are considered as "the help." The degree of change in illustration today probably is no more violent than in any other field—maybe it just seems that way to someone who's closely watched the metamorphosis.

Trends may come and go, but Norman Rockwell still paints on, as popular as ever with a public that enjoys his insight, wit and ability to get to the heart of a people who largely prefer to recognize and understand what they see of the painted American scene.

27

Art is Long... And Suffering

What went on behind shuttered windows in artist's studios? It couldn't be good—when girls disrobed and posed for male artists! Many laymen would have been delighted to peek. Artists were good copy for news reporters, just as were movie celebrities, telling tidbits about their lives, successes, parties and escapades. Few average citizens mingled with bona fide artists in day-to-day proximity.

Contrast this with our present condition. Behind every tree or under thousands of umbrellas you'll find "artists," painting their hearts out. If a housewife puts brush to canvas, she's an instant artist and can find outlets for exhibiting. This isn't to be construed as criticism because it's a fine hobby. It's great relaxation, self-expression and therapy. But coupled with the competition prolific hobbyists create for full-time artists, there's a league of freaks who are making a travesty of art. It's mongrelized out of countenance in the name of "emotional sensation," or any abba-dabba-woo-woo the alleged artist wishes to concoct. Some ride the modern bandwagon as fakers with glib explanations that confound the layman who'd like to know the language. It's difficult to establish any kind of standard of ability and/or attainment. Perhaps this isn't an aim in art during the present bond-breakings, but it would be nice to know who's real and who's faking!

As far back as 1265, Thomas Aquinas said, "Art is simply a right method of doing things. The test of the artist does not lie in the will with which he goes to work, but in the excellence of the work he produces." Fine, but who can say what excellence is?

The following century, in 1320, Dante believed, "Art imitates nature as well as it can, as a pupil follows his master; thus it is a sort of grandchild of God." Have you seen much in a modern art show that you could easily relate to God? If we wish to lay aside the eternal arguments about what art is or should be; "Can you recognize what it represents, explain it if it isn't representational—or mutter about what the crazy artist had in mind," we can settle it quickly by what Arsene Houssaye said in the nineteenth century: "When art is understood by everybody it will cease to be art."

One of the controversial modern giants of our time is Pablo Picasso. He's called the founder and leading practitioner of what is known as "Cubist" painting—a geometric system that makes no pretense of nature copying. Picasso has gone through many periods and styles. His earlier works had a faithful feeling for ancient classicism. Slowly he evolved to a psychical nature, getting at the picturization of emotions rather than an external copying of nature. This is where he departed from the audience that will only applaud a brown tree trunk with green leaves above.

In the mid-twenties Jean Cocteau said that "a bad painter covers the curtain of a theater. He raises it on nothing. A true painter, in proportion to which he covers his canvas, raises it on a theater where the eye and mind penetrate. The theater of Picasso is not a popular theater. One day or another, the most tightly shut theaters must open their doors. I do not imagine that this theater can even half open its doors."

Therefore, forty years ago a well-known writer such as Cocteau recognized that Picasso's art wasn't readily digestible, but in spite of it, students avidly adore the master's every stroke; collectors and devotees, who follow the leaders, pay handsome sums to possess even a scrawl by Picasso. As a living master Picasso has enjoyed the fruit of success that's usually reserved traditionally in a fame-after-death reward.

At the far other extreme there were such painters in the Hudson River School, for instance, who faithfully stroked in every leaf and twig on heroic trees, caught the mists and sun rays and generally neglected not one pebble on the ground. They lovingly preserved nature for all to understand. If the people of an era were unabashed by sentiment and pretty scenic vistas—this was for them.

We will only see a few examples of the arts that may

"Kindred Spirits," by Asher B. Durand. (Art and Architecture Division, the New York Public Library. Astor, Lenox, and Tilden Foundations)

bring a memory of art experience to you. These were the sights and sounds, the latter being the furor created when modernism—which had started long before—began to accost the American "man in the street." He is still much incensed.

The cover of a 1927 *Mentor* Magazine (pictured) depicts the concept of an artist with which we've all been familiar. It's a wood engraving by Howard McCormick —an art form that requires more patience than many artists now possess. This refined publication dealt with art, travel, history, literature and science.

Howard Pyle represented a gentler day in the art realm. He died before 1920 but his loving students certainly streamed into our era saturated with the inspiration and integrity that Mr. Pyle implanted. One of his appreciative students, N. C. Wyeth, told of his fond recollections of Mr. Pyle. "Breaking the tense silence he would talk in a soft, hushed voice of art, its relation to life, his aspirations, his aspirations for us (his students).

Howard Pyle poses on balcony. (Courtesy *The Mentor Magazine*)

Only too soon he would say good night and leave us in the darkness, and as we felt for our hats and coats, each one knew that every jaw was set to do better in life and work and in some measure to express our deep gratitude to the one who had inspired us." This referred to "jam sessions" the class had with Howard Pyle in the twilight after a hard day's study and painting.

1927 *Mentor* Magazine cover by Howard McCormick. (Courtesy *The Mentor* Magazine)

An August Saint-Gaudens sculpture of Lincoln. (*The Mentor* Magazine)

Mentor Magazine told of another man of dedicated devotion, Augustus Saint-Gaudens, the sculptor who made heroic figures and bas reliefs that inhabit many American cities. Like Mr. Pyle, Saint-Gaudens was forever helping struggling young artists who would be sculptors, and the more his health failed, the more involved he became in commissions and good works for his fellowmen.

Maxfield Parrish built a reputation to be esteemed, not only as a painter-illustrator, but as another who was devoted to ideals, earnest work and application. One of his works was so popular that two hundred thousand copies were sold to hang in homes. He's particularly famous for creating "Maxfield Parrish" blue, a luminous, elusive hue achieved by transparent glazes. Like many artists of distinguished achievement, he felt that his ability wasn't equal to expressing his ideas. In the deep New England winters he was snowbound, but reveled in this privacy for work as others value money.

Many would-be artists gave up the struggle early when disappointments or criticism crushed their spirits. Their setbacks were pygmies in comparison to the heartrending experience of an already established painter of reputation, Frank Brangwyn. He was one of London's most illustrious decorative artists until his death in 1956. Lord Iveagh commissioned Mr. Brangwyn to paint sixteen panels to decorate the House of Lords. After seven years of painstaking work, his intricate scenes depicting the people and atmosphere of various parts of the British Empire were flatly rejected as being unsuitable for their surroundings, when presented in 1932. It is a colossal understatement to say that this was a tragedy for the artist. Nevertheless, he was knighted in 1941, and Americans can see panels by Sir Frank Brangwyn in Rockefeller Center in New York.

A Maxfield Parrish painting of a New England scene. (*The American* Magazine)

Panels from a Frank Brangwyn mural. (Courtesy the Detroit *News*)

Some More of Diego Rivera's Frescoes at the Art Institute That Have Aroused Criticism

THIS fresco is representative of one of the city's large pharmaceutical plants. This is one of the few smaller panels in Rivera's work and shows that Detroit is known also for some industries other than the automotive.

IN ONE of his large frescoes Rivera has painted likenesses of Edsel Ford and Dr. William R. Valentiner, director of the institute. Dr. Valentiner is shown holding a tablet on which is written: "These frescoes, painted between July 25, 1932, and March 13, 1933, while Dr. William R. Valentiner was director of the Art Institute are the gift to the City of Detroit of Mr. Edsel B. Ford, president of the Art Comission." The spelling of commission is as it is written on the tablet.

RIVERA in this fresco shows the assembly line at the Ford Motor Co. River Rouge plant. In the foreground workmen are seen lowering a V-type-eight motor into a chassis while visitors to the plant look on.

Some examples of the frescoes of Diego Rivera. (Courtesy Detroit *News*)

The problem of the $100,000 mural panels by Brangwyn nearly found a parallel in the same era in Detroit, where Diego Rivera was commissioned to paint frescoes on the walls of the city's Art Institute. A storm of protest followed the unveiling, and it made much fodder for conversation and newspaper writers. One writer said, "Old Man Rivera, he don't say nothin', he just keep rollin' in his $20,000." If this amount seems small compared to Mr. Brangwyn's, less work was involved and it was during the Depression. One newsman commented, "It is charged that Mr. Rivera has failed to paint the spiritual aspiration of Detroit, and we wish to add furthermore, that he has proved himself utterly unable to divine the true inwardness of a people that turns on its radio at seven in the evening to listen to Amos 'n Andy."

Mr. Rivera ran into difficulties in other areas, such as New York, where his supposed political injections came under fire, causing his work to be destroyed. He had come under the influence of Russians and was believed to be an admirer of Communism. There were Detroiters who read into their frescoes dire Red symbolisms.

If these criticisms of ambitious murals sound ruthless, bear in mind that the final word in most instances of judgments came from committees of laymen, no little more qualified than you or I to say, "I know what I like and this I don't like!" But they held the purse strings and made the decisions.

It was a cliché for a man to say to a girl, "Come up and see my etchings," but in many cases, a man might actually have had a collection of this popular art form. Few practice this painstaking art today.

Rivera shown at work. (Courtesy Detroit *News*)

In 1931 the Depression was being reflected in the work of artists. An art critic in Detroit said, "Many Michigan artists see a sad, sick world. Assuming that art of a country represents the degree and taste of its civilization, just where would the man from Mars think Michigan to be?" He concluded that "civilization is in a state of bewilderment and high nervous tension and that art is being used by the bulk of its practitioners as a means of escape from reality . . ."

This etching is by Sears Gallagher. (Courtesy *The Woman's Home Companion*)

The critic's view of an exhibition provoked this evaluation, "Jumbled planes, muddled colors, staggered outlines seem to predominate." We called it "The Mud Cult of the Ugly."

If modern art confounded the ordinary man in the street, a writer had this to say, "All around us, in art galleries, museums, libraries, there are strange hieroglyphics, some charming, some enraging, known as modern art."

It has been a longtime sport to lampoon modern artists and their works. One way to accomplish this would be to submit paintings framed for hanging in exhibitions. After they won prizes, they would be revealed as the work of a child, or a chimpanzee. Or they might simply be the old board an artist tried his paints on. A California minister, who was disgruntled at rejection of his wife's paintings, decided to get even. He took the name of Paul Jordanowich, "founder and supreme master of the Disembrationist School of Paint." There was laughter, anger and chagrin among Bostonians who'd gaped and admired the great "Russian's" conception of Aspiration, Exaltation, Adoration and Illumination, when they learned that a minister had done it for a joke.

In 1934 a Philadelphia art club pondered the question, "Art, sane or insane?" Homer Saint-Gaudens, son of the famous sculptor, quoted his father as having said, "Artists have the same brains as other people, but they are over at one side of the head, sticking out like a bump."

This hasn't been a one-sided argument over the years, with only the conservatives doing the talking. In 1932 a Chicago group of artists rose up as one and declared, "The art institutes, private and endowed galleries of the nation are giving art a knockout blow. To have a picture accepted for these institutionalized institutions, one must meet requirements that stifle the creative ability." The gallery these rebels intended to start was for the underdog, the unrecognized and the non-conformist. In some instances it may have been also for non-artists.

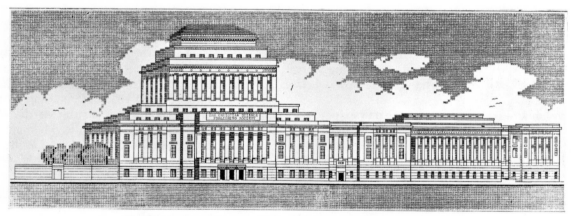

Roy Streeter re-created the Christian Science Publishing Society Building of Boston in this remarkable work of art that was done entirely with the typewriter. (Courtesy *The Christian Science Monitor*)

261

All articles weren't about painters and sculptors. Some remarkable art work has been done on a typewriter by a patient and clever typist, Roy Streeter, who re-created the Christian Science Publishing Society Building of Boston. It was the result of seventy hours of careful work on four sheets of paper.

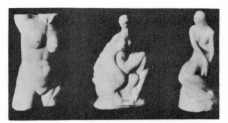

Some prizewinners in the Procter & Gamble soap carving contest. (Courtesy of the Procter & Gamble Co.)

This head of Mark Twain was done with a typewriter. (Loaned by Lorne Braddock, the artist)

It must have been even more difficult to type a portrait. The head of Mark Twain was the painstaking work of Lorne Braddock, an artist who usually worked in easier mediums.

One champion and friend of artists was newspaper columnist O. O. McIntyre. He often wrote of them and during the Depression he said, "Artists have had little sympathy during the withering bleakness of the passing trio of years. Never in history have they been forced to endure such leanness. Hundreds swept into boomtime opulence have had to return to the Village garrets. Such topnotchers today are finding it difficult to maintain the moderately priced studios."

Every form of art wasn't necessarily nurtured in art schools and academies. Procter and Gamble gave many

thousands of dollars in prizes for sculptures carved from Ivory Soap. This contest started in 1923 as a promotion to sell soap, but it brought forth a wealth of young talent. My high school art class worked for the competition in 1925, but although I carved a rabbit that looked amazingly like a mouse, no one in our class could compete with the exquisite entries.

These soap carvings by Lester Gaba were used in an Ivory Snow advertising campaign. (Courtesy the Procter & Gamble Co.)

A series of ads for Ivory Snow used the clever soap carvings of Lester Gaba. At the height of his renown, he'd be seen in night clubs accompanied by a beautifully gowned, life-sized mannequin. The store window dummy would be seated beside him, he'd order her a drink and in every way act as if she were real. Artists played colorful pranks then.

One of the greatest sculptors of our time, Carl Milles, from Sweden, lived until 1955. He became a naturalized American and was a resident master at the Cranbrook Academy of Art in Bloomfield Hills, Michigan, where I studied briefly. He was "modern" alongside the conservative realists, although he'd be "academic" by today's modernists.

The figures pictured are a portion of a beautiful fountain on the campus of Cranbrook. His work is also in Chicago, St. Paul, St. Louis, Wilmington, Harrisburg and New York City. One of his best known fountains is in his native Stockholm. As great as were the attainments of this quiet, gentle man, he once contemplated suicide

How the Sculptor, Carl Milles, Fashions Monumental Art Works That Bring Fame

In background, assistant patting plastic material onto figure getting it ready for sculptor. In foreground, roughly modeled figure ready for work of sculptor.

Removing plaster cast spoils the clay models, but makes possible a permanent mold.

The sculptor Carl Milles at work. (Courtesy Detroit News)

Carl Milles's work on display at the Cranbrook Academy of Art at Bloomfield Hills, Michigan. (Courtesy *Harper's Bazaar*)

when faced with discouragement as a young Paris student.

A surrealist painter who gained worldwide fame is Salvadore Dali. Born in Spain, as was Picasso, he came to the United States to live in 1940. His first major American exhibit was in 1934 in New York. His influence on art was great, even reaching to advertising illustration. In Paris Dali came upon surrealism in 1928 when this idea was new. It is like a psychoanalysis in art, a probing, on canvas, of the subconscious mind. Imagine that you put into a painting what you think you saw in last night's dream. You too might be a surrealist!

Mr. Dali painted ideas for a "dream house" from his fertile imagination. No matter what the combination of elements in his creations, each part is recognizable because, first of all, he's an accomplished draughtsman.

We've reached no conclusions about art or whether artists are sane. One writer took pokes at modern art magazines by having a young lady speak as she thumbed through an art publication. "Oh, here is the new art magazine. Let us look at it and then hide it before Father comes in. Poor Father! He knows so little about art, and he thinks his ribald comments are funny. See this charming picture of a child. Isn't it naive? The head is out of proportion to the body—Father would say the child is hydrocephalous, but he doesn't understand that the artist deliberately created the disproportion to define his purpose, which was . . . well, it doesn't say what it was, but evidently he had a purpose. Poor Father! He's still living in the days of Velasquez and Rubens."

We haven't attempted to strike a stand for or against any opinion of artists or critics. As in most arguments, something can be said for academic *and* modern art. When life or thought stands still it stagnates or dies, but uncontrolled new forces and ideas can go so far afield that they cease even to be symbols. If art is all sensation or emotion with no intelligent backbone, then it is of no more value for humanity than an opium smoker's imaginings—or today's "acid-head" on a "trip." If an artist merely sets out to copy everything he sees, then he's competing with a camera lens which can do a far better job.

Honesty and sincerity of purpose should be the virtues of any artist, for without these—plus curiosity, love of life, color and nature—he can slip into the class of freak fakes. Art deserves more than that.

A Dali rendition of a dream house. (Courtesy *Harper's Bazaar*)

28

The Great White Way

"All the world's a stage." (Courtesy Detroit News)

"All the world's a stage, and all the men and women merely players: they have their exits and their entrances, and one man in his time plays many parts . . . "—Shakespeare said it in *As You Like It*.

The motion picture is a precocious infant upstart when you consider the history of the theater. In the fifth and sixth centuries B.C. it was a building for dramatic or spectacular productions in ancient Attica.

The first regular American theater dates back to 1766, so our stage presentations have a fairly historic background. It was located in Philadelphia rather than New York, where a permanent theater wasn't erected until the following year. Ever so gradually physical improvements came into theaters, the more recent having to do with lighting effects, richer costumes and more elaborate settings. Theaters-in-the-round and little theater organizations have done recent renovating to stimulate new interest in live plays and musicals. Most of the theaters are run by individuals or corporations as commercial businesses. The Theater Guild of New York takes in its money on a subscription basis so that it has some idea where it stands financially.

In the three decades we've seen many plays and comic operas that were written in the nineteenth century. Good writing wears well. How many times have you heard and seen the well-seasoned works of Gilbert and Sullivan? We performed "The Mikado," "The Geisha," "H.M.S. Pinafore" and "The Pirates of Penzance" in the twenties with the high school glee club. These operettas were still being done by professional stage companies although Gilbert and Sullivan wrote them from 1878 through the 1880's. Ibsen plays as well known as "The Doll's House" were staged in London in 1889. Four decades later it was showing in America. How familiar are some of Oscar Wilde's titles, such as "Lady Windemere's Fan." Yet it first came to light in 1894.

One of the most brilliant playwrights of our time was George Bernard Shaw. Americans are most familiar with his "Pygmalion," lately further popularized as the musical "My Fair Lady." What else can be invented for this story other than making the leading characters into "hippies?"

Americans are certainly cognizant of the Sir James Barrie charmer, "Peter Pan," first known in 1904. In the early American theater, we were almost entirely dependent on England and Ireland for dramatic material, even for players to speak the lines. Whereas there was a scant group of 500 regular actors for the American stage in 1870, today there are over 10,000 professionals. No wonder it's difficult to break into a stage career!

Who were and are the illustrious greats of Broadway—our "Great White Way?" One of the earliest in our period was John Drew who lived until 1927. His father had the same name and was classed as an Irish-American actor. Mr. Drew was the Barrymores' uncle, so the latter were cushioned by theatrical tradition. After a run of juvenile parts in New York, he specialized in Shakespearean plays and was president of The Players, which was originated by Edwin Booth. This Mr. Booth was the brother of the infamous John Wilkes Booth.

Five years after John Drew, Otis Skinner appeared and stayed on to the creditable age of eighty-four. Many actors of the legitimate theater have been blessed with longevity. It's assumed the atmosphere is healthful or the struggle keeps them alert. In 1928 Mr. Skinner won an Academy of Arts and Letters medal for his stage diction. When he was seventy-four, he was accomplished as Shylock in "A Merchant of Venice." I remember him for the lead in a filming of "Kismet."

Four illustrious stage personalities were born in the 1860's and lived into our period. Henry Miller was a theatrical manager as well as actor. He played opposite Ruth Chatterton in "Daddy Long Legs." And he also starred with the famous Minnie Maddern Fiske, who was born five years after Mr. Miller.

Mrs. Leslie Carter went from Kentucky to study drama from the great David Belasco. In the twenties she appeared with John Drew in "The Circle," and was tempted to make some motion pictures.

Minnie Maddern Fiske got an early start on the stage because she received tutoring from her mother and put this education to work when she was only four. Mrs. Fiske lived until 1932 when she was nearing seventy.

David Warfield also prospered in the healthful atmosphere of greasepaint for many of his eighty-five years. He perfected both Irish and Jewish dialects and gave over one thousand performances of "The Music Master." He also had parts in Shakespearean plays and "The Return of Peter Grimm," which Lionel Barrymore enacted in pictures.

Julia Marlowe was another octogenarian. Although born in England, she received dramatic training in New York. Her preference was for Shakespeare also, but she entirely retired from the stage in 1924.

Maude Adams lived a year more into her eighties than her contemporary, Julia Marlowe. After playing Juliet opposite William Faversham's Romeo, and scoring a success as Peter Pan, in 1937 she took up a career teaching drama at Stephens College, which she continued until her death.

George M. Cohan came into this world the same year as Lionel Barrymore, but with a different variety of talents. He was not only a performer, but an American playwright, producer and composer. He is probably best remembered for his famous songs: the World War I hit, "Over There" and the immortal "Give My Regards to Broadway." He was truly a "Yankee-Doodle-Dandy."

The 1880's produced some infants who later distinguished themselves behind the footlights. An outstanding lady of the theater was Jane Cowl who lived until 1950. Like many others, she started with the David Belasco Company and made her debut in a play with the provocative title, "Is Matrimony a Failure?" Miss Cowl was not only a great actress, but co-authored a number of plays. The best known was "Lilac Time," which many of us saw on film with Colleen Moore starring.

Two years before the turn of the century, an actress was born who chalked up as distinguished a roster of successful roles as any lady on stage. Katherine Cornell

Jane Cowl. (Courtesy *Harper's Bazaar*)

Katherine Cornell. (Courtesy of Joan B. Leech, daughter of Neysa McMein)

was best known for her characterization of Elizabeth Barrett in "The Barretts of Wimpole Street," but she was well-received in Shaw's "St. Joan," "Candida," "The Green Hat," and "Alien Corn." The famous portraitist and cover illustrator Neysa McMein made a pastel likeness of Miss Cornell. The actress's husband was the theatrical producer and director Guthrie McClintic, who directed her in many productions.

The year after Miss Cornell's birth, Eva LeGallienne and Noel Coward came along. Miss LeGallienne was the daughter of the famous English writer and journalist Richard LeGallienne. She was well-educated in Paris and received numerous honorary degrees in American colleges. She was starred in a long line of successful plays as well as being one of the founders of the New York American Repertory Theater in 1946.

Noel Coward's versatility is difficult to categorize. As a playwright, actor, director and composer, this English-born genius has enriched our enjoyment for many years. His "Bitter Sweet" was a favored production here. It contained music Americans whistled and sang.

The Barrymore family. (Courtesy Detroit News)

No recollection of stage greats could overlook the "Royal Family," the Barrymores, Ethel, John and Lionel. They were the niece and nephews of John Drew. Ironically, although Ethel was the eldest, she outlived her brothers by staying on until she was eighty, surpassing John's hectic life by twenty years. One of her well known roles was in "The Corn is Green." She was in numerous motion pictures, sometimes with her brothers.

For those who only remember John Barrymore as a handsome film star—"the profile"—you might be surprised to learn that he earned acclaim for a long season in "Hamlet" in England with a company he organized in 1925. There were so many stage and film roles that they couldn't be named, but "The Royal Family" dealt with his own family.

Lionel was the beloved, crotchety fellow who developed a delivery much imitated by impersonators. In his latter years he was so crippled by arthritis that it was necessary for him to use a wheelchair. In spite of the infirmity, he outlived John by twelve years.

Ruth Chatterton. (Ruth Harriet Louise photo)

Many of us recall Ruth Chatterton in the movie "Dodsworth." She was one of the New York stage stars who moved to Hollywood with the advent of sound. Her career was distinguished by many roles in both mediums, plus ability as an authoress. In 1951 she appeared in "Idiot's Delight" as her farewell to Broadway. Of four novels she penned, her first *Homeward Borne*, was a 1950 best seller. As if these activities weren't enough, she also wrote songs and piloted planes.

We've enjoyed several husband–wife teams on stage— many have been married for years. Two fine examples are Alfred Lunt and Lynn Fontanne. Miss Fontanne was another English performer who divided her time between London and New York, after her start in Drury Lane Theater. With her husband she played many Theater Guild productions. It's heartwarming to see a married couple that gains fame and stays married. The American Alfred Lunt played mainly in Theater Guild plays with his wife. I first saw them in "Idiot's Delight" on the road, and they were delightful.

Alfred Lunt and Lynne Fontanne.

Helen Hayes.

Tallulah Bankhead. (Courtesy *Harper's Bazaar*)

You must remember other couples such as Frederick March and his wife, Florence Eldridge, Charles Laughton and Elsa Lanchester.

Helen Hayes, also known as Mrs. Charles MacArthur, has had a renowned stage and screen career. She won an Academy Award in 1932 for "The Arrowsmith" and later scored as Queen Victoria in "Victoria Regina" on the New York stage.

Tallulah Bankhead was a colorful addition to the theater. Her electric and unpredictable personality has been much publicized. She was born as an Alabama belle and her father was once Speaker of the House.

When the first World War was devastating to the European theater, the American theater movement was steadily progressing, to a degree that made New York the dramatic center when the War was over. Much talent was encouraged and developed in writing and acting by such outstanding "little" theaters as the Provincetown Players. They recognized the abilities of Eugene O'Neill, who won the Pulitzer Prize twice.

Although motion pictures caused a temporary decline in legitimate theaters in the early thirties, there was renewed activity at the end of that decade with Pulitzer Award winning offerings, nearly all of which eventually found their ways to the screen. Who could forget "You Can't Take It With You," or "Death of a Salesman"?

There are extravaganzas defying description or background scenes of great beauty from all parts of the world that could only be shown on film, but these couldn't be a whit more exciting than the magic moment when the house lights dim, the footlights brighten and the curtain begins to rise on a stage with real live actors!

29

Heigh-Ho, Come to the Fair

Have you ever wanted to do something so much that you could "taste it"? Perhaps this amount of desire is only concentrated in the hearts of youths, but it's the degree with which I wanted to attend the 1933 "A Century of Progress" World's Fair in Chicago. It would have seemed just as likely to wish for a trip into space, mainly because there was no money in the Depression for tripping—even to the nearest town. But miracles *do* happen, and in this case a part-time job was the miracle that provided enough for a bus ticket to Chicago.

Some of you were there and probably remember Sally Rand and her famous fan dance—the stellar attraction on the midway. And you certainly rode the Amos and Andy tram, high in the sky between metal towers where you got a thrilling view of the fair, the skyline of Chicago and Lake Michigan.

The buildings, examples of early modern architecture, were garish in color; but to a young person on her first trip away from home alone they were wonderfully exciting. Harry Horlick's A&P Gypsies could be heard over the crowds and other sounds of the midway.

It was a "must" to go to the Art Museum on Michigan

Avenue to see the original "Whistler's Mother." No beautiful young lady could have attracted the crowds that this plain, little old lady sitting in her chair did. I had never before been in the presence of such a famous work and it inspired awe.

There was an Oriental torture ship docked at lake's edge, which drew many who enjoyed savoring the fate of those hapless devils who had been punished on it.

A row of houses of the future pointed to many trends that have come to pass in home designing, even though they were exceedingly extreme for 1933. An all-glass house was not unlike the concept of the Capitol Record Building in Hollywood, California. A home in the hills above Universal City, California, also follows the idea by being a "pedestal" structure with rooms around a central core. All rooms can look out on the view in every direction.

Chicago's Adler Planetarium.

The world's most famous mother. (*Mentor Magazine*)

Adler's Planetarium was included as a part of the fair, to lure people to their realistic star show. Here's a bird's-eye view of the Century of Progress site. The two tramway towers dominated. In the left foreground is the Adler Planetarium; across the street to the right is the Chicago Natural History Museum, which was built by the philanthropic merchant Marshall Field. Behind the museum lies Soldier Field, looking a bit like the Roman Coliseum. Fortunately, the fair visitors could easily enjoy all of these permanent Chicago attractions.

This G.M. tram-styled truck was used for guests to the 1933 Chicago World's fair. (Courtesy General Motors Corp.)

General Motors had not only one of the outstanding exhibit buildings, but also built sixty tram-styled trucks for guests whose feet needed to be rescued.

Officials predicted that 25,000 cars would be driven to Chicago each day, making an anticipated total of four million vehicles to be parked somewhere for the 1933 fair season. They promised ample parking space on the outskirts with transit service to the fairgrounds.

No exhibit buildings could have had more renowned names connected with their preparation than those of General Motors. Albert Kahn, the famous industrial architect, planned structures to house a replica of a GM assembly production line. Frescoes, appropriate to the subject, were painted by Mexico's muralist, Diego Rivera. A heroic figure of the skilled automotive worker was sculptured by the great Swedish sculptor, Carl Milles.

This folder told all about Cleveland's Great Lakes Exposition, 1936.

A person doesn't have to wait many years between fairs and expositions, if this is his idea of the best in vacation fare. Some of these mammoth displays might require considerable travel, although our own country has its share. In 1936 Cleveland came forth with the Great Lakes Exposition. Advertised were the astounding miracles of science, art, industry and commerce.

A fair of world dimensions could not have chosen a more readily recognizable trademark symbol than the 1939 New York World's Fair with its Trylon and Perisphere.

Inside the Perisphere was an exciting show called "Democracity," which was a city of the future, planned according to an idealistic arrangement. You may recall climbing to the walkway just above the bottom of the globe, and awaiting your turn to step onto a turntable walk around the darkened interior. It was inky black until the show began—then you were slowly conscious of a faint light that subtly grew brighter until dawn broke. The sun shone brightly to reveal the city as you moved around the scene. Then afternoon and sunset—twilight and the twinkling stars—completed a day in Democracity.

The United States Building, 1939 World's Fair. (Chester Janczarek Photo)

gleamed white and stately with only a lining of dubonnet color behind the columns. We just missed seeing the King and Queen of England pass through the entry under the giant golden eagle, during their Canadian and American visit.

The Russian Building at the 1939 New York World's Fair. Ironically, the American flag seems to be flying in the Russian's face! (Chester Janczarek photo)

The heroically large Russian worker holding a red star dominated the Russian Building and was the tallest structure aside from the Perisphere.

In spite of criticisms that are always forthcoming about a project as large as this fair, the buildings were generally superior in taste, materials and color to the Chicago fair. In spite of all that was done to cheapen the Trylon and Perisphere, they remained the fair's best. From gleaming white in the sunshine, they glowed blue at night and seemed to be floating in space. Murals on some exterior walls were overdone or so symbolic that the average visitor couldn't interpret them, but colors were not garish and many white statues abounded.

We photographed points that caught our eyes in this photographer's paradise. The United States Building

The National Cash Register Company building, 1939 World's Fair. (Chester Janczarek photo)

We entered a cage that lifted us high above the grounds for a panoramic view that included the unique National Cash Register Company building. Daily, the fair's attendance was "rung up" at the top of the revolving replica of the company's machine. You may judge its size by the people crossing the lagoon bridge.

From the sublimity of heroic statues and buildings, visitors were amazed to come upon a fully grown wheat field, complete with a fashionable scarecrowess, dressed by Hattie Carnegie. Few scarecrows can make this claim to smartness.

The foreign countries' buildings had unusual architecture and effects. Italy's contribution boasted of a waterfall that cascaded down the step-like front to wispily tumble across immense windows, then end in a large pool.

Water was again featured at the Libby Owens Ford Glass Company building. Fountains played upward, close

An heroic statue, 1939 World's Fair. (Chester Janczarek photo)

A waterfall at the Libby Owens Ford Glass Company Building, 1939 World's Fair. (Chester Janczarek photo)

A scarecrow and a wheatfield, 1939 World's Fair. (Chester Janczarek photo)

Europa is being transported by Zeus, disguised as a bull, to Crete, 1939 World's Fair. (Chester Janczarek photo)

The Italian building, 1939 World's Fair. (Chester Janczarek photo)

The Polish building, 1939 World's Fair. (Chester Janczarek photo)

to the concave curve of the front wall, and nearly to the structure's top. A projection of glass encased the streams near the entry, but a sudden breeze could drench you by carrying fine spray.

Europa, the beautiful Phoenician princess, was shown being transported by Zeus to Crete. The God was disguised as a bull according to Greek mythology. Dolphins happily leaped around them.

The Polish Building was distinguishable at a distance by its glistening gold tower of openwork design. One aspect of all sections that we appreciated was that in spite of the large daily attendance, the streets were never oppressively crowded. Walkways had an abundance of benches alongside, and even young feet were bound to give out.

The famous illustrator, Albert Dorne, painted a happy group representing three generations, enjoying the myriad sights of the New York fair. There were carts and rickshaw carriers for hire, but not for those on a limited budget.

At night the fair took on a mysteriously spectacular appearance, especially around the Lagoon of the Nations

At the Lagoon of Nations, tremendous fountains played over jets. (Courtesy of Mrs. Albert Dorne)

where a display of tremendous fountains with changing colors played over jets. These watchers were bewitched,

Albert Dorne's rendition of a happy group enjoying the 1939 World's Fair. (Courtesy of Mrs. Albert Dorne)

not only at ground level, but in the swank French Pavilion. Coffee was a half dollar per cup which spelled "swank" to the working classes in 1939.

The Billy Rose Aquacade was the outstanding attraction on the midway. Rose was a mighty impresario for his small stature; and on this occasion, he outdid himself. Eleanor Holm, the swimming star, not only starred in the Aquacade, but became Mrs. Billy Rose. Seeing the show was like trying to watch all rings in a circus simultaneously.

Also in 1939 was the San Francisco Bay Exposition.

Many people couldn't travel from coast-to-coast for the New York event, but could and did attend the exposition. It was officially called the Golden Gate Exposition and was held on a manufactured site in the harbor called Treasure Island. This show ran 254 days and was seen by nearly ten and a half million people. The island was to be a city park thereafter.

World's Fairs are great, but after seeing two my thirst was slaked for all time. One could locate now in the next block and I'd skirt around it.

Some scenes from the Golden Gate International Exposition, held in San Francisco in 1939.

30

Yesterday's Madonnas

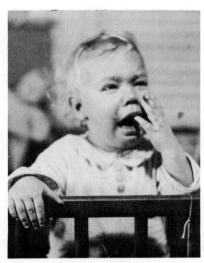

This infant (the author's daughter) obviously wants her mother. (Chester Janczarek photo)

kitchen looked like a scientific laboratory. She swept with a broom until a vacuum cleaner or carpet sweeper finally replaced it. Everything was stirred or whipped manually. Baby care was bound to be more primitive too. My

Your world crashed around you as pain wracked your body; friends deserted you and took your most precious possessions. Life was never at a lower ebb—and who did you turn to with trust? In this black hour you ran to your mother because you were only two years old.

"Mother" is a noun always near the top in lists of the ten most beautiful words in the English language. It's never archaic, needs no synonyms or varients, even though some vary it with mom, mummsy, mama, or momma. Of course some oldtimers used the ugly substitutes ma and maw. But the original word, mother, sounds just right as it is.

Mother has changed the cut of her clothes, her multiple activities, political status and influence on society, but to her children she was and is (or should be) the hub of the universe. Her work has violently changed. In my youth mother didn't live in a push-button home where the

The author with her mother.

mother bathed me in a galvanized metal "foot tub" instead of a deluxe bathinette. I was dressed in clothes she'd sewn or friends made as gifts. The dresses were twice as long as a baby and had rows of tucks and lace insertions.

A happy family scene from the twenties. (*Woman's Home Companion,* 1926)

In spite of the mountainous work and myriad other demands on mothers, they somehow had time for us. There wasn't a gadget that held nursing bottles to our mouths so she could be elsewhere. She usually breast-fed us and held us cozily close while we were rocked to sleep. Mother made rag dolls because we didn't have the kind that cried, wet their diapers and felt like real skin.

When mother had to run errands, we went along in a big wicker buggy, and other women peered in and said, "What a beautiful baby!" (Even if we were the ugliest they'd ever seen). My mother was never more incensed than the time two women passed as she wheeled me in my chariot. One was overheard to say to the other, "My gawd, did you see the mouth on that kid?"

Baby-sitting hadn't become big business and it was amazing when a neighbor gave me a dollar for this service when I was twelve. It got to be past my bedtime, so

I was asleep on the davenport when she returned. I'd never heard of being paid for sleeping.

We didn't have a library of gayly illustrated books. There was a well-thumbed Mother Goose and tattered cloth books about Peter Rabbit and the Three Little Kittens.

Child psychologists hadn't yet forced their theories of child-rearing on the country's mothers. It wasn't bad to be rocked, cuddled and generally fussed over by a mother who didn't know any better. Mother sang "Rock-a-bye Baby" when we were tucked into bed.

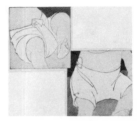

In 1926 women were shown the wisdom of changing from three-cornered diapers to the rectangular fold to give baby more leg freedom. (Courtesy William Carter Co.)

When we were older, mother allowed us to wear half-socks, but by the end of August, they were changed to long lisle stockings. The half-socks were held up neatly with an elastic band that was a separate accessory concealed under the fold-over cuff that might have had a dainty design on it. Only the kneecap was bare. It was a sad day when mother said I could no longer wear half-socks—"it wasn't ladylike after I was twelve." The occasion was tearful but we didn't argue, and wouldn't have won anyhow with our unindulgent mothers.

The bare kneecap was once seen only on little girls. (*Pictorial Review*)

These are 1926 mail order patterns. (*Woman's Home Companion*)

Since mothers sewed most of the children's clothes, and there were few who didn't number sewing among their womanly accomplishments, the magazines ran pictures of dresses and rompers for small fry. The patterns could be ordered by mail.

High chairs were less modern and didn't fold down into play chairs. The one pictured was styled much like grandfather's old Windsor chair. Mother could wash out the spilled milk with a strong laundry soap.

A Maud Tousey Fangel illustration done for the Quaker Oats Company. (Courtesy The Quaker Oats Co.)

A high chair, twenties style.

Maud Tousey Fangel was the outstanding baby and child artist for many years. My mother clipped and saved her favorite illustration by Mrs. Fangel. It appeared in a Quaker Puffed Rice advertisement in the twenties.

Mother was never too busy to play with us. She squatted on a child-sized chair to share a "meal" we had fixed, and she was always invited to tea parties. She pushed the swing so we could sail higher and played catch with the big rubber ball. Mother taught us songs and poems, even when she was doing the washing. We were made to feel important, loved and necessary around the house.

Mother made us mind her rules because she believed a badly behaved child was a reflection on the mother. Her rules were firm, simple and basic. We knew where we stood—not because she screamed at us, but because she showed us why we should or shouldn't do certain things. If we disobeyed, a spanking was quite likely—or even worse, a session of sitting quietly in a chair to "think things over." I have no recollection that these punishments caused shock, trauma, hate of parents or a desire to lash back at society. We probably felt more secure because of the framework of rules about respect for another's property, respect for our elders and knowledge of the wrongness of stealing, lying or breaking promises. We usually did as she asked, and even though we wanted to go our own ways, we knew mother had the right to govern our actions. Once a neighbor woman spanked me and I was furious. She didn't have the rights my mother had for punishment!

Photographer Chester Janczarek captures a happy moment from childhood.

From whatever position a child looked at the world, mother was a big part of it and her influence aided us all through life. The older we got, the more the rightness of her course seems.

It's small wonder that a Mother's Day was created to honor her. It's always the second Sunday in May and was an idea of Miss Anna Jarvis of Philadelphia. In 1914 Congress empowered the President to issue a proclamation of Mother's Day and President Wilson inaugurated this observance.

This clipping proves that the generation gap is not a modern phenomenon.

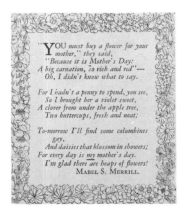

A poem in honor of Mother by Mabel S. Merrill, 1926 *Woman's Home Companion.*

The clipping shown is a sad commentary on the changing social order as the reins of parents loosened and children took over their destinies at a frighteningly early age.

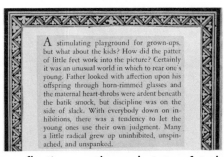

A clipping reflecting on the sad state of today's child-rearing.

A boy whose dad was locked up for opposing the war grew to manhood with the filial urge to annoy his government. He soon specialized in the Eighteenth Amendment and spent the 'twenties proving that prohibition did not prohibit. It was a successful piece of work but there was no future in it.

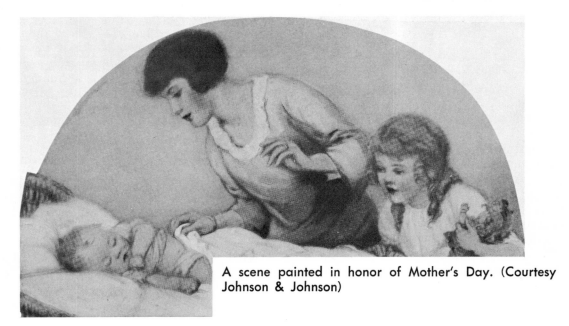

A scene painted in honor of Mother's Day. (Courtesy Johnson & Johnson)

31

Readin' Writin' and 'Rithmetic

We had every reason for a protest demonstration in school. They didn't let us whisper during class. Rioting was considered when we had to eliminate our chewing gum—a strike was imminent against the ban on LSD (*Late Some Days*). But we had divided leadership and weak agitators—we were dumb dupes.

Teachers actually spanked us, stood us in corners, kept us after school and wrote warning notes to parents. Conditions were bad. In high school a reprimand was given first, then a traumatic experience in the principal's office if the first collective bargaining didn't work. There was one member even expelled from the union—Union School No. 9, that is. This discriminatory act robbed him of his seniority. They said his offense was heinous when he joined a cell known as a fraternity. The student body would have struck until he was reinstated, but as mentioned, we were unorganized pawns of the system.

When we went to school in the twenties, boys wore "knicker" suits, neckties and cloth caps. The girls had hats too, and children this young carried books for homework. Two boys in the background have squatted to watch spinning tops.

In 1923 "knicker" dresses were the rage, and continued for several years. Bloomers matched the dress and the farther they showed below the dress, the higher the style. Some had cloth bands that buttoned on the sides with as many as four buttons. This was ultra!

Screw curls were the envy of straight-haired girls. I wore them until I was thirteen. Mother rolled the hair on rags every night, then brushed the curls into shape each morning. It was expected that the boy sitting behind a girl thusly curled would dip them into his ink-well.

You didn't get through the first eight grades without an accident on the playgrounds at recess time. You could be pulled from swings; heels jammed under teeter-tawter ends; hands lost their grips when the giant stride whirled high; boys tried to see how fast the merry-go-

A schooldays scene from the twenties. Note the knickers on the boys. (*Pictorial Review*)

round could be pushed. There were all sorts of cuts, bruises and abrasions in between.

Nearly every grade had a "Tom-girl" and "Peck's bad boy," but rooms were generally well-disciplined. We expected it and I can't remember an instance of a teacher

This may bring memories of school rooms in the lower grades. Teachers were seldom young in schools I attended. (Janco Fotos)

"Knicker" dresses were all the rage in 1923. (Courtesy Detroit *News*)

The author, age ten, displays her screw curls—the envy of straight-haired girls.

This girl is enjoying her recess on a swing. (1930 lithography brochure)

Boys used to amuse themselves with old automobile tires. (Janco Fotos)

being shot, knifed or fired for it. Parents must have felt that Johnnie had it coming to him. There were penal jobs for offenders—such as cleaning felt erasers and blackboards, or writing "I won't whisper during class" a hundred times or so on the board. Good kids usually got such choice jobs as running errands for the teacher. Report cards had an item called deportment. This is when your behavior "got on the blotter."

Some school subject names have disappeared. Suddenly what we called geography became social studies. We had civics, hygiene and physiology. We earned Palmer Method buttons and certificates for proficiency in the push-and-pull and circular exercises in penmanship. Spelling bees were popular.

There were projects devised by teachers to promote interest in subjects beyond the textbooks. In the fourth grade we brought earth-filled tin cans to class and planted peas or beans in them. After a waiting period, one seed was unearthed to show how it sprouted. We could learn what went on underground. By the eighth grade our teacher tried to instill an interest in newspaper reading beyond the "funnies." We got extra credits for submitting clippings about current events—items on political or scientific subjects. One girl couldn't comprehend why her clipping of a notorious divorce case wasn't acceptable.

After you read your books, added your sums, spelled Mississippi and learned where Constantinople was, what did you do in leisure time? Girls usually set dining tables, dried dishes and ran errands while boys mowed lawns, had paper routes or got into mischief.

Swinging has never ceased to be popular, although not nearly as many are hung from high limbs on big trees as of old. City apartment dwellers have to settle for something less.

An old automobile tire was good amusement when hung by a rope or used for the riskier sport of crawling into the center to be rolled down the street. The landing could be mighty abrupt.

How long has it been since you heard the clop clop of stilts on a sidewalk? If you could manage to stay up longer on higher stilts than the neighborhood kids, you earned a respect and distinction. The "in" thing was for boys to wear buttons of all sorts on little caps that might be cut from father's old felt hats. They could be political campaign buttons or pins with advertising messages. Patched pants and well-seasoned gym shoes were the mode.

To recall how differently we talked and wrote: a 1926 ad for shirts and suits said, "Dress your boy in "he-boy" styles. Don't set him apart from other lads by dressing him in sissy clothes . . . he wants to be manly." How would he measure up with today's young fellows?

No girl was without a jumping rope, which was most often a piece of her mother's clothesline. Boys may have played leapfrog but their neckties were in place and they looked suspiciously neat.

Breathes there one of you with soul so dead that you haven't wished you could have said, "I'll meet you at the

This boy is trying hard to keep his balance while on stilts, but his dog isn't helping him any. Note, too, the buttons on his hat, which was probably cut from an old felt hat of his father's. (Courtesy National Biscuit Co.)

swimmin' hole?" Country boys were more fortunate in this ecstatic sport. Where could anyone find a place nowadays for the boys to swim in the altogether? Girls, the decency league or police would surely nix it.

Recreation wasn't limited to outdoor rough and tumble. You might have been pushed into music and the dance. All scrubbed, combed and dressed to the teeth, you showed your advancement at a ball for small ladies and gentlemen. You can bet the girls enjoyed this the most.

Somehow you bumped, bruised, laughed, cried, played

Girls always enjoyed a fast game of jumprope. (Janco Fotos)

and studied your way through eight grades and four years of high school. This was the division of grades before junior high became a separate entity with its own buildings and graduation. Kindergarten was optional in those days and once only was the hallowed cap and gown worn —at high school graduation. A generation ago many closed their books after six or eight grades, especially in rural areas which boasted only the wooden, one-room schoolhouse. The term "drop-out" was unknown but many parents needed the extra hands to help the family income. College educations were scarce and high school diplomas were treasured attainments.

Smartly dressed young ladies of the twenties were extremely fortunate. They could take their liberal arts courses and bicycle from class to class. Note the hats, shoes, silk hose and intricately styled dresses. They undoubtedly had little thought of careers following college, but it was nice to have culture they could acquire in a

Twenties co-eds used bikes to get around campus.

girl's institution of higher learning. Some preferred co-educational schools in the hope of meeting future husbands. It was amusing when one of my friends frankly admitted that this was her reason for college; then she came home to marry the non-college boy nextdoor.

In the late thirties and early forties our colleges and universities began to pop at the seams with the same growing pains as the cities. By the time soldiers got out of uniforms and took advantage of the GI Education Bill, college populations were unprecedented. It was suggested that girls shouldn't enroll in the busiest schools unless they seriously planned to work in professions that required degrees.

Goldfish swallowing was popular with college boys of the thirties: The youth's father seems not to believe his eyes.

reation. Occasionally fraternities were reprimanded for overly rough hazing practices in which some pledges were injured.

It seems innocuous now alongside of the dope experimenters, sex freedomists, agitators and "ism" followers who recklessly "blow their minds," jade their senses and seem to rejoice in undermining the homes and country that has sired them. After they've run their courses to the vague social order they envision beyond the abhorred "establishment," their children will probably shower them with similar accusations for the world they find themselves in.

Two campus queens display collegiate fashions of the thirties. (Courtesy *Harper's Bazaar*)

The little red schoolhouse of another day.

The prewar 1930's coeds looked vastly different from the bicyclists of the twenties. Bobby sox and saddle oxfords were so popular that other styles looked freakishly nonconforming. Skirts covered the knees and clothing was neat, tailored and often plaid or tweed. Girls looked good then with freshly scrubbed faces and inconspicuous makeup to enhance rather than to command attention.

An antic that created a furor a little less than thirty years ago was live goldfish swallowing by college boys. It was impressive to be the champion in the squeamish prank. One boy supposedly died in the pursuance of this lark, and his father demanded a thorough investigation. Later, panty raids in girl's dormitories afforded light rec-

If schools are today overcrowded and understaffed in inadequate buildings, it is not a new condition. This was a familiar complaint twenty and thirty years ago. Authorities said then that more than 2.5 million American children of school age were not going to school because there were no buildings for them. Another 2.5 million went to schools that were not adequately equipped. And still others would go only a few months because there was not money enough to keep the schools running a full term. Does this sound familiar?

An article stated: "The trouble is that children and money don't always grow in the same places. It is the plain duty of the more fortunate to help to educate the children of the poorer areas." Here's the way it led to our present Federal aid: "The whole town must help its poorest districts, the county must help its poorest towns, the state its poorest counties and the nation its poorest states." They knew they needed and wanted help but they were skittish about Federal hands on local affairs. They said, "Federal aid for schools must never lead to Federal use of the influence of education to break down the very ideas on which a free nation is built."

Criticisms of schools and teaching isn't new either. The late columnist and commentator, Dorothy Thompson, had something to say about the method of educating our youth. She asked, " . . . is it not too mechanical and utilitarian? Our children, it seems to me, learn the history of events, but are woefully unversed in the history of thought. Many of our history professors now teach our youth to interpret history from the standpoint of the characters or material condition of men who set the events in motion." She tells of articles about the Constitution written by Hamilton, Madison and John Jay, called *The Federalist*, a treatise on government. She deplores our graduates by saying, "It is perfectly amazing to me that an American boy or girl can graduate today [1930's] from an American university without ever having had to thoroughly study and pass an examination on these American documents, which are on a plane with Plato's 'Republic' or Aristotle's 'Politics.' In the latter treatise on government, Aristotle dealt with problems that are acutely actual at this moment . . . with a passage describing the reasons why democracies degenerate into tyrannies."

Shades of ancient Greece and Rome. It sometimes causes one to wonder if we're on the waning side of a cycle, as history is measured. My daughter graduated from high school within the last five years, yet with little knowledge of our country and its illustrious past having been taught beyond the fact that George Washington was the "Father of our country" . . . that is, unless she was the nation's worst student.

32

Love, Honor, And...?

Weddings have changed less through the years than almost anything you can recall except getting hungry, dying and paying bills. We looked different in our wedding finery but grooms were just as nervous in the twenties through the forties, mothers of the brides shed the same quantity of tears and vows were the same except that "obey" gently changed to "cherish." Emancipated womankind didn't like the chattel implication of obeying a "lord and master."

There are still big weddings and small, elaborate and simple church weddings and civil ceremonies before justices. There are indoor and outdoor ceremonies and vows are spoken in atmospheres quite foreign to tradition. Some couples, because of odd necessity, or others with a desire for the bizarre, get extra publicity now as then. Weddings may be run through a "marriage mill" without beauty of ceremony or memories.

Let's assume that you weren't wed in a balloon, submarine or Mammoth Cave. You had a lovely ceremony that's still a vivid memory, disregarding the usual slip-ups and unexpected incidents. You did a variety of traditional things, but do you know why? It's bound in superstitions, amulets and customs from many countries all the way back to antiquity. It's adhered to unquestioningly and probably won't soon disappear in spite of the space age.

If you wore a bridal veil, it signified youth and virginity. White is obviously a sign of purity. Ancient Romans carried herbs and it was the Saracens who started us on orange blossoms because they symbolized fertility. Spring and June are a lovely choice of times for marriages because roses bloom then in many areas. The early English loved roses.

We call it the engagement ring, but it's been called the betrothal or pledge ring and dates back farther than the wedding band. The Egyptians felt that a circle was emblematic of eternity, but have you wondered about the choice of diamonds as favored gems? They're very hardy stones and even the Italians of the Middle Ages recognized this. They suggest enduring love. You wear these rings where you do because it was considered the most direct line to the heart.

The bride is "given" by her father because if you'd have lived in earlier times, he'd have been giving up one of his possessions or chattels. Now, in this century, his accompanying his daughter to the altar should suggest approval of the union.

Grooms used to capture their brides in ancient times and keep them in hiding at first. The term "honeymoon" dates back to the Teutons. They drank a honey concoction until the moon waned—hence, the word.

We trace the rice-and-old-shoes tradition to the Orient. Rice wished you an abundance of food and a shoe thrown on the roof meant a honeymoon was taking place inside. A shoe was exchanged by Hebrews as a good faith gesture when property changed hands.

Men were coaxed into marriage, starting in the Middle Ages, by the lure of a dowry. This has deteriorated to the symbol of the bride's trousseau. You wore something blue as another sign of purity and fidelity.

The wedding shower started a long time ago when a girl wished to marry a poor boy who couldn't afford to set her up in housekeeping. Friends provided the wherewithal for the couple. In more recent days, sometimes the friends are left the poorer after attending a full round of showers before the main event.

Church bells really pealed loudly in England to provide what we call "wedding bells." According to old custom, you should travel to the church in a horse-drawn vehicle. Now it would be hazardous and downright illegal on the freeways.

Have you considered planting a tree after the ceremony so it could grow with your years together? Be sure first that the apartment owner approves because he could inherit a forest if many newlyweds moved into his building. Many young couples don't live in their first apartment long enough to see a new twig grow!

Winding staircases and weddings went together. Sometimes the bride came down the steps with a solemn ex-

Placing the ring on the bride's finger is still the basic part of the wedding ceremony.

Tossing of the bridal bouquet. Which bridesmaid will be the lucky one? (Courtesy of the Colgate-Palmolive Co.)

pression befitting Joan of Arc going to the stake, but it was an excellent place from which to throw the bridal bouquet for the bridesmaids to scramble for below.

Maybe you didn't have a big, formal wedding in what we call the "Depth of the Depression." Have you any idea how $25,000 would have been broken down in terms of a wedding deluxe in 1936? The veil alone was $3000, flowers cost $1500, photos $1000, and $600 was spent just for shoes! This figure didn't include $5000 for the bride's trousseau. At this rate it shouldn't have been difficult to run through the money at a time when most of us

In 1926 we were assured that the dinner roll was quite correct for the formal wedding breakfast. This event was being "done up" in lavish and approved fashion. (Courtesy the Fleischmann Yeast Division of Standard Brands, Inc.)

hoped the next month's rent was available. It was casually suggested that, "Of course, $25,000 weddings do not happen every day." This lucky bride went to her honeymoon in a little Paris original for a mere $550. Lucky were the guests who swarmed into town and were put up by the bride's parents at an exclusive hotel while the same opulent providers "paid the piper" to the tune of a fourteen-piece orchestra for the reception. Money wasn't scarce everywhere during the Depression.

We were told that even in a deluxe wedding, people of good taste never spent money for ostentation. Further, at our exclamation of "extravagance!" we were reminded that in a difficult financial period, this wedding gave employment to an army of caterers, carpenters, engravers, decorators, florists, seamstresses, waiters and clerks. Maybe there was good intent after all!

The inconsistent oddity is that with all of the expenditures for the bride, the groom got the formal cutaway attire with accessories for the slight sum of $75. His bachelor dinner, including food, liquor, tips, flowers and allowance for breakage, averaged under $10 per person. This was a knock-down celebration so breakage was expected.

In the thirties I was often at showers where the bride's gifts were spread on the big dining room table for inspection. One clawed her mind to make all of the appropriate and expected ohs and ahs at the collection of "loot."

The beautiful bride was finally on her way out. They've always been lovely with a glow from the occasion that is

In quite a different atmosphere—probably the bride's parents' home—everything was smaller, more intimate, but nonetheless something that the sweet new Mrs. would long remember. (Courtesy Wallace Silver Plate)

seldom seen thereafter. This happy girl of forty years ago smiles confidently at her guests and displays the regalia that made her the loveliest bride. By now she's a grandmother—or even a great-grandmother. Who can tell the children about the time when granny was a blushing bride?

The beautiful bride on her way out.

33

Birth Miracle of the Century

What period of history would you like to have been born into if you had a choice? How about the three decades we're reviewing? There were exciting and unusual happenings in these years, and one auspicious event was the birth of the Dionne quintuplets in Callender, Ontario, Canada.

According to scientific estimates at the time, quintuplets only occurred once in approximately 500,000,000 births. Other sets have been born, but the uniqueness in 1934 was that they lived! This "blessed event" fired the interest, curiosity and sentiment of civilized humanity. It created a furor.

The five little girls became movie stars. The motion picture contract was signed in 1936 on their second birthday. It provided them with $250,000 in cash.

It was not difficult for these attractive children to earn money from all sorts of product testimonials. Here they're happy over Dr. Dafoe's selection of Colgate Toothpaste for their tiny teeth.

Artists saw the children in different ways; one emphasized their luxuriant eyelashes, whereas another gave them admirable complexions to advertise the virtues of a beauty soap.

In the summer of 1936 it was estimated that at least

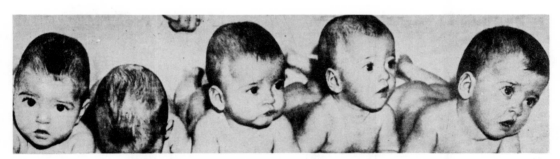

The Dionne quints as infants. (Courtesy Detroit *News*)

If all five girls had weighed-in equally, each would have bounced the scales to two pounds with a fraction left over, because their total weight was less than fourteen pounds. It's miraculous that such tiny wisps of life could survive the rigors of entry into this world.

Much credit and fame came to the local physician of Callender who delivered and cared for Marie, Emilie, Annette, Yvonne and Cecile. He was Dr. A. R. Dafoe. The babies were housed in a nursery building named after the doctor. The Ontario government and Canadian Red Cross Society acted as guardians, and erected the hospital for the famed children.

450,000 people visited the Dafoe Nursery to watch the girls from an observation gallery where they could see without being seen. Eyes and attentions were always trained in their direction, and cameras forever clicked, as here, while the children played.

Some said that the village of Callender became like an amusement park as the influx of people grew. Mr. Dionne purportedly sold charms that were supposed to work the multiple magic for other couples, since it was apparent that he took full credit for the miracle. There were bound to be jokes of an indelicate nature, as well as those who always hang around the fringes of an event for the coins

Dr. A. R. Dafoe, who delivered the quints, poses with them. (Courtesy of the Colgate-Palmolive Co.)

The five little girls, who became movie stars. (Courtesy Detroit News)

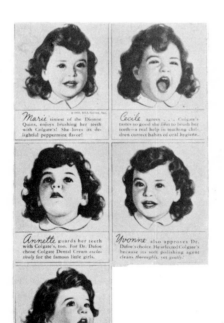

Artist's rendition of two of the quints. (Courtesy Colgate-Palmolive Co.)

The quints were used in ads. (Courtesy Colgate-Palmolive Co.)

The girls at play, Summer of 1936. (Courtesy Detriot News)

Artist Bradshaw Crandell speculated as to how the quints would look when they were twenty. (Courtesy of Mrs. Myra Clarke Crandell)

they can collect. Some were obviously jealous and covetous of the fortune that had been gathered for the quintuplets after reasoning that they'd struggled harder to support the same number of children—born, in the ordinary manner, one at a time.

A famous illustrator depicted how he envisioned the girls would look when they were twenty years old. Bradshaw Crandell, renowned cover artist, adhered to their complexion and hair coloring, but beyond that he was speculative. Other illustrators contributed to this series but went as far afield as to show his ladies of twenty blue-eyed and blond; certainly the quints were not.

Mr. Crandell imagined the girls would be similar to each other in tastes and temperaments; others thought they would be individualistic. One would be athletic, another the clinging vine; Cecile as a gay, naughty girl; Emilie, who hated the glare of fame, wanted to study for the highest degree. Marie would be coquettish, endowed with singing talent and a love of public clamor.

This illustrates how wrong predictions can be; and how easy it is, even for quintuplets, to gain obscurity. Today they are mature women in their thirties—and there are only four. No one has heard of them in years. I asked a young lady of twenty-three if she's heard of the Dionne quintuplets and she rewarded me with a blank stare.

By the time they were six, their earnings amounted to $750,000, which grew to one million dollars four years later when the Crown relinquished guardianship, except over the money until they were of age. Meantime, they joined their family, which had grown since their birth. There was a sizeable family before they were born.

In November, 1953, Marie entered a Quebec convent, "Servants of the Blessed Sacrament," a contemplative order. However, she did not take the final vows that would have kept her from thereafter going out in the world. She left the convent less than a year after entering.

The saddest note was the death of Emilie from epilepsy, just before Marie's emergence from the convent. The girls are completely assimilated into the world, unknown to most of our young people.

If the Dionne quintuplets tired of public adulation and clamor, their wishes for obscurity have been granted.

34

Durable Celebrities

Do you intend to admit you don't remember George Young? He was famous in the middle twenties for doing something that had never been done before. His $25,000 prize was a lot of money then, and is still an acceptable sum today. Since your memory is sketchy about this man, we'll explain that Mr. Young was the first person to swim from Catalina Island to California, landing near San Pedro. The feat nearly equalled the English Channel crossing.

The foregoing emphasizes the difficulty of achieving enduring fame. Today it's much more difficult to be a national hero, make a million dollars or leave a distinguished record for succeeding generations to remember. So much happens so fast that we're caught in a grey, massive blur. Many new ideas are developed by teams so that no one person's name stands out. Our advancing technology doesn't allow for long-remembered stars. Our children only briefly wear the wide-eyed expression of curiosity before taking the "I couldn't care less" attitude. Few records in any field have remained unbroken until now.

In the first half of this century we were able to breathe the same air as inventive genius Thomas Alva Edison, who singly gave the world a wealth of inventions that affect the lives of millions of people throughout the world.

We take the light bulb for granted; we criticize movie stories and stars. But without Edison, there wouldn't have been motion pictures (unless another Edison was in hiding as a reserve in case the first one failed). Many improvements in telegraph, including automatic telegraphy, were born because of this man. The phonograph, mimeograph and the carbon transmitter—which made Bell's telephone practical—were all Edison's. At one time, he had forty-five inventions in the works simultaneously. Yet, he'd be in trouble today with school authorities because he was "addled" at school. Ultimately Tom's mother taught him at home, and he sold newspapers to finance his experiments. According to present standards, he

Thomas A. Edison. (Courtesy Detroit News)

wouldn't be allowed to enter a university, so he wouldn't have degree credentials that would allow him to work in modern laboratories.

A great man among us who lived until 1943 was George Washington Carver. After birth into a life of slavery, this gentle and learned man became what has been called the "first and greatest chemurgist." He did with the soybean

George Washington Carver. (Automotive House Organ)

own an automobile changed the face of America when the Model T's dotted the countryside by millions.

Helen Keller. (Courtesy *Harper's Bazaar*)

The greatest triumph over handicap was accomplished when Helen Keller broke the walls of her dark, silent prison to reach out and "speak" to a world she could never see or hear. She might never have emerged had there not been a wonderful, patient teacher, Miss Ann Sullivan.

what had never been done before, developing an impressive list of products made from this bean. Dr. Carver was also in the forefront of experimentation with the peanut's potential as an industrial material. He has been honored here and abroad for his addition to science. We used to joke about being able to eat our car's steering wheel, which was a soybean derivative.

Henry Ford. (Courtesy Detroit News)

An industrial giant of our time was Henry Ford. As in Edison's case, Ford didn't complete his formal education—he left school at sixteen. After Ford became fascinated by the future possibilities of the horseless carriage, his direction was straight ahead to produce one of the greatest fortunes, industrial empires and revolutionary concepts for manufacture. He was responsible for the conveyor belt assembly line system, and the five dollar minimum daily wage that in 1914 was unprecedented big money for the ordinary working man. His aversion to involvement with partners or stockholders was unique. He was the sole head of a billion dollar enterprise after buying out his original backers, James Couzens, Horace Dodge, John Dodge and John Gray. Henry Ford's idea that a cheap car could be mass-produced so the working man could

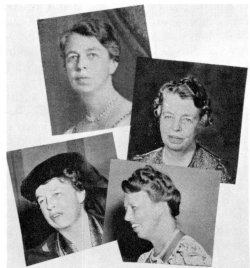

Four views of Eleanor Roosevelt. (Courtesy *Harper's Bazaar*)

Eleanor Roosevelt was an eminent lady who put her indelible stamp on the thirties and forties, not only as the First Lady, but by extra activities. She wrote several books and a newspaper column, was active in the United Nations and a tireless worker for educational, social and political causes.

If you were an avid newspaper reader, you probably recall such names as O. O. "Odd" McIntyre, Arthur Brisbane and Mark Hellinger—all of whom might have been as regularly imbibed as your morning coffee. While browsing over your paper, you couldn't have been unaware of a name that brought scandal unto itself—Samuel

O. O. ("Odd") McIntyre

Insull, who after building a fantastic "house of cards" empire, lost $750,000,000 of investor's money. When he was brought back for a fraud and embezzlement trial after fleeing the country he was acquitted. His stigmatized freedom must have been cold comfort, but he had been instrumental in spreading a utility network whereby many areas could plug into the system so that cost to the consumer was greatly lessened.

How many years the familiar voice of Lowell Thomas has greeted us via radio! Can you think of anyone who has logged more miles into the remote places of the globe? He has written books about areas no other Americans have seen. Lowell Thomas stood on the ground of Shangri-La and talked to the Dalai Lama. His Cinerama travels are so vividly shown and narrated that we can feel as if we've been on these enchanting trips—without the discomforts. He's been a teacher, editor, writer, commentator, lecturer and traveler, which should constitute a full and active life. It must be agreeable because time has dealt gently with his appearance.

A beautiful, illustrious woman we shouldn't forget is Clare Boothe Luce. She has combined enough different works for a half dozen careers, proving the adage; "If you want something done, ask a busy person to do it as the others have no time." She had time to write three stage hits, "The Women," "Kiss the Boys Good-bye" and

Lowell Thomas with 1934 Hudson. (Courtesy American Motors)

Claire Booth Luce. (Courtesy *Harper's Bazaar*)

Jack Earle, who was 8'7", being checked into Detroit's Hotel Statler by credit manager B. J. Collins.

"Margin for Error." She had time to do war corresponding during World War II, to be in the House of Representatives and serve as U.S. Ambassador to Italy. In 1929 she divorced George Brokaw but after several years, married *Time, Life* and *Fortune* publisher Henry Luce. Meantime, she raised a daughter, ran three homes and still had time for the demanding social obligations of a prominent and lovely lady. Do you think that keeping one house is a big job?

While reminiscing about those BIG years, we can't omit a BIG man, Jack Earle. He rose eight feet and seven inches from the floor, making him the world's tallest man although in my childhood there was one of similar height, Harold Wadlow. The life of such a giant may be in jeopardy because Mr. Wadlow died from the infection that followed a skin irritation from his huge, made-to-order shoe. After a start in movies, Jack Earle spent most of his life in the largest circus, Ringling Brothers and Barnum and Bailey. For a time he was a wine salesman. It's needless to mention the day-to-day problems of a giant in a pygmy-sized setting.

There is one man we shouldn't forget because of his bringing to millions of readers incredible but authentic facts he dug from the world's storehouse of oddities. This was Robert L. Ripley. He traveled extensively to learn of unusual or unbelievable things and events, and he was never caught in an untrue statement. The title of his feature became a household expression, "Believe It Or Not."

We've mentioned a pitiful few individuals in the mass march of those who in varying ways were above the crowd of ordinary people. With the hordes who've swarmed over this earth, it's commendable to be noticed in the forward push—and more remarkable to be historically remembered. Of course, some gained attention from less than admirable works. May this scanty list jog your memory about some that "You Forgot to Remember" (apologies to Irving Berlin).

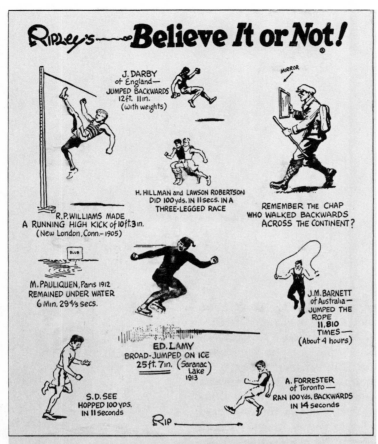

THIS IS THE FIRST BELIEVE IT OR NOT DRAWING BY ROBERT RIPLEY, PUBLISHED IN THE NEW YORK GLOBE, DECEMBER 19, 1918.

IT IS REPRINTED TO MARK THE 50th ANNIVERSARY OF THE WORLD SYNDICATED FEATURE IN 1968.

The first *Believe It or Not*. The insert is of Robert Ripley. (Courtesy of *Ripley's Believe it or Not*)

35

Habit Became Custom

You've been in the center of a bloodless revolution whether you realize it or not. You've changed habits, manners and customs, even though you're as stubborn as a mule. It was so gradual that no one could say "that" stopped yesterday and "this" started today.

Ladies used to carry sun parasols in white, silk-gloved hands and leave calling cards at friend's doors when afternoon visits weren't consummated. Maybe the only card you find now in your door is from the Acme Vacuum Cleaner Repair Service. These proper ladies might have carried drawstring bags that contained a fancy linen handkerchief, some face powder in a box and a coin purse.

Today's woman may carry a bag as big as a suitcase, bulging with a packet of facial tissues, bunch of keys, package of cigarettes, matches or lighter, an assortment of cosmetics for a whole new face, hair accessories and a wallet. There might be a tin of aspirin, pep pills and stack of credit cards. Her purse is a home away from home.

Why did the genteel practice of making afternoon visits pass away? It's hardly practical when numerous women are away at work, and others resent not being forewarned by phone. In the twenties, many didn't have phones and housewives were happy to receive visitors or expected them—afternoon tea was popular. Job printers have really lost the calling card business.

Dozens of social changes have occurred because of inventions; for example, housework-lightening devices that advertisers have mass-sold to homemakers. Articles once only imagined are now necessities. For all of the jobs and duties eliminated, new ones have been created. For instance, the iceman has been replaced by the TV repairman.

Our mother's or grandmother's "big" Sunday was to have friends and family gather at the old homestead. It was usual to find croquet wickets set in the lawn. Today a sporting goods merchant would starve while waiting for croquet-set customers instead of golfers.

In the good old days Sunday afternoons were spent at croquet.

Probably no indoor pastime went over bigger than the auction bridge party. It appealed to old and young, all the way from two playing honeymoon bridge to parties of five hundred tables or more.

School girls taught each other the game learned from mothers who belonged to bridge clubs. These gatherings undoubtedly helped the delicatessen and canned goods business when the "girls" played dangerously close to dinnertime.

Arguments would frequently develop at bridge parties.

The joke about a mate being shot for trumping an ace may have been funny, but it has been known to happen. For less serious players, bridge served a variety of purposes: it was a meeting ground for the latest gossip; an easy way to occupy guests and dispel social obligations; a chance to try fancy recipes seen in magazines; a good

The auction bridge party appealed to young and old alike.

method for organizations to collect money for causes by charging admission to play at large parties. I had a collection of bridge party "loot" although I'll admit that most were consolation prizes.

In the twenties, what were the joys of the dining room table the mothers or "grannies" set? It's certain that little of the food came from magic mixes, cans or other than natural sources. It was made from "scratch"! The chicken may have been killed and dressed in the backyard; vegetables were picked from the garden; bread and pastries were baked earlier, from separate ingredients. The pickles and preserves usually were homemade too. The dining room was often as large as the living or "sitting" room and contained a sideboard—the forerunner of buffets. There were fancy, hand-painted dishes in curved, glass-fronted china cabinets. The dishes were seldom used except for special occasions, but scarcely ever were "special" enough. The sparkling white damask tablecloth was a tedious ironing job, but it kept the housewife's spare time occupied.

The ironing story changed too. I remember grandmother's wood-burning kitchen range not only as a cooking surface that was fed from a woodbox that always needed refilling, but as a place to heat the heavy irons. Some were molded from one piece of iron so that handles were nearly as hot as the business end. There were vastly better irons with detachable top sections with

The family gathered around the dining room table for Sunday dinner. (Courtesy of H. J. Heinz Company)

This pen sketch by the author shows the evolution of the iron.

A pencil drawing by Kyo Takahasi for the Magazine Publisher's Association's "Freedom of Choice" campaign. (Courtesy J. Walter Thompson Co.)

wooden, curved handles and a metal sheath that fitted over the hot iron. Several bottom parts would be heating simultaneously on the stove. One of the kindest acts performed for womankind was the invention of the electric iron. The early ones were heavy compared to present-day models. We little dreamed of the day of the small travel iron to tuck in suitcases.

If ironing was a hard reality of keeping house, it was preceded by an equally arduous task—the Monday washing. Gleaming washer-dryer combinations didn't set attractively in the kitchen or utility room. The center of the steamy, strong soap-scented operation might be the basement, laundry room or the backyard on warm summer days. The process started Sunday night for many zealous women who sorted the soiled clothes, and put them to soak in a copper boiler. Early Monday morning the "cooking" began. Cakes of soap were shaved or shredded through the heating clothes.

When the load came to a boil or had simmered awhile, the "moment of truth" arrived. Getting the wash out of the boiler into the tub was heavy and hazardous, to say the least. Even if you'd advanced to the 1920–1930 washing machine, it hadn't eliminated the loading process. Many women clung to the belief that the machine alone wouldn't get things really clean. The race wasn't yet running about which washing solution was best for whiter whites or brighter brights. The first breakthrough was when soap powders appeared—before detergents were made for home use.

Piled in an old wicker basket, the wash is being hung out to dry on an old-fashioned clothes line.

store's floor to demonstrate their unbreakability. Many women learned differently at home.

Not having a washing machine, this housewife resorted to the scrub board.

The author did this illustration for the Michigan Consolidated Gas Co.

Prior to a washing machine in every house, the scrub board was indispensable. They came in various sizes and the big ones were heavy, with water-soaked wooden frames around the ribbed, roughened metal scrub surface. It was revolutionary when someone produced the glass wash board. Salesmen could throw them on the

After the washing had graduated to heaps of wet cloth in a big wicker basket, the little woman's back and arm muscles got a workout on the trip to the clothesline in the backyard. Rivalries developed on the street as to who would hang sheets on the line earliest. It was also a chatting break with the neighbors.

In the days before cake mixes, baking was a lot of work. This lady of 1926 is kneading dough. (*Woman's Home Companion*)

If cooking from scratch was an expected accomplishment of every girl approaching housekeeping age, canning and preserving were also necessary. Before most girls took outside jobs and quick-freezing had not yet been invented, the canning art was all-consuming when it was the season for markets to be heaped with bushel baskets of fruits and vegetables. Or, you might have enough homegrown garden and tree produce to "put up." There used to be a tinge of scorn for the woman who entirely used commercially canned goods. When homes were shown to friends, a woman's proud moment was to display her well-stocked fruit cellar with neat rows of Mason jars, labeled with contents and canning date.

What went on in the kitchen the other days of the regular week? If a housewife ran a "tight ship," each day had a major project, the same as restaurants have a specific day for bean soup. If Monday was traditionally washday, Tuesday was for ironing; then came days for housecleaning, shopping and baking. Now we pop the contents of a box into an electric mixer and within minutes we can eat cakes, breads, muffins and cookies. We used to stand endlessly over a board kneading bread dough and keeping the temperature warm enough so the loaves would properly rise before the long, slow baking. If cake was in the oven, children were warned to walk lightly, lest the center of the cake fall. Mother always selected a broom straw as the perfect cake-tester.

Some early telephones . . .

Now! Preserving Time is Here.

This 1928 direct mail folder reminded the housewife that it was time to get out the Mason Jars.

The telephone has existed so many years it's intermittently cursed, blessed and taken for granted. We soon forget how it has changed before our eyes. A friendly act used to be the offer of your phone to a neighbor who didn't have one. This old wall model stayed on into the twenties and even thirties, especially in rural areas, before it became a prized antique piece. Many were the jokes about the shenanigans on populous party lines where it was like broadcasting your business to those who had nothing better to do than listen in. They could gather gossip and be entertained.

It was a sad day when the "hello" girls gave way to dial phones. We could always blame them for wrong numbers, laugh about the way they said numbers, especially nines—"nigh-on." Whether they were sweet or brusque, they added the personal touch to your telephone.

The styles of dial phones continued to change. Remember the first lightweight instruments with the bell box on the wall? It was an improvement when the entire mechanism was incorporated into a neat box so the

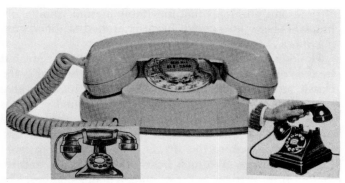

and some more recent models. (Courtesy American Telephone and Telegraph Co.)

phone didn't skitter around the table as you attempted to dial.

At the Chicago World's Fair in 1933, telephones were demonstrated that had remarkable and revolutionary sound capabilities, but I've never seen them since—anymore than many experimental automobiles are seen on the road. No doubt, one of these days we'll say when Aunt Mary calls, "You're looking well," because we'll see as well as hear her.

teacher wore a gold watch on her shirtwaist and occasionally reeled it out on a delicate gold chain and read the hour after flipping open a lid that protected the face. Slowly we began to wear time on our wrists. The popular 1920's models were often in white gold covered with engraved designs on the edges. A sapphire was in the stem end and a black grosgrain ribbon was the usual wristband on these big watches. They got smaller and smaller until it was difficult to read the time. They were increasingly encrusted with diamonds until they served more as jewelry than accurate timekeepers. The majority of boys and girls owned their first wristwatches at graduation from high school.

It's a long way from sharpened quills for writing to the variations of pens we've had. During schooldays in the twenties we had a fad of metal penpoints with attached, fluffy feathers, but they became frayed and we tired of them. Glass blowers were popular entertainment for schools, and they made glass pens that weren't wild successes as writing instruments. A girl wasn't of the "in" crowd unless she had a sterling silver pencil and/or pen to dangle from her neck on a ribbon or chain. The workings inside pens and methods of filling have undergone changes, but the biggest revolution was the ballpoint pen. Little did we dream in the thirties, when Reynolds presented the ballpoint principle, that they'd someday be popular giveaway items for advertising purposes.

The famous Ingersoll pocket watch. It only cost a dollar.

Eyeglasses of the thirties. (Courtesy Meyer Jewelry Co., Detroit, Mich.)

The dollar pocket watch was the brunt of jokes, but the Ingersoll went merrily on ticking. It kept time faithfully without a fancy case, engraved or otherwise embellished. It performed a function without upsetting the budget. Vests concealed pocket watches attached to gold chains that were good for swinging when nervous, fumbling with when making weighty decisions, unless you preferred to jingle coins in the side pocket of your trousers. Charms such as elk's teeth or a rabbit's foot might dangle from a watch chain for good luck or to show lodge membership.

Women's timepieces changed too. My first grade

Eyeglasses had an evolution after the small-lensed, metal-rimmed styles we see in historic pictures. Ben Franklin wore the lately revived half-lens variety, convenient for those who only need reading lenses. In the thirties metal rims were eliminated in favor of rimless spectacles. Advertisements gave us the idea that these

303

scarcely showed. Larger-than-life sized color photos of actors and actresses in optometrist's windows proved that we could be as attractive as they, wearing rimless glasses. We could see better and tickle our vanity at the same time.

Lens shapes were varied to adapt to all facial types. There was one glaring trouble with the rimless style—breakage. A careless person could always break them from the connections to nosepiece and bows. The lens grinders were never busier. Later, to combat fragility, a narrow metal strip ran across the lens's tops on the backside for extra bracing. Bows were once connected in dead center on the sides until someone discovered that side vision was improved by raising them to the tops.

After a decade of trying to look spectacleless, the vogue changed to emphasizing the frames with width, color and jewels. In the society realm, nothing surpassed the matron's ornately framed, long-handled lorgnette. Glittering with diamonds, it was impressive at the theater or opera.

A charming custom that passed away and is nearly forgotten was the old May Day celebration. No, it wasn't a Communist parade. When I was young, it was fun and complimentary to anonymously leave flowers at the doors of people we liked. The bouquet was picked from the garden—not a florist's shop—and arranged in a vase or basket. We placed the offering near their doors, rang the bell, then disappeared before the favored person could see who'd come.

Other holidays had significances that died natural deaths or were outlawed. How long has it been since you played a rascally trick on April Fool's Day, or had a really creative prank pulled on you? Maybe yesteryear's pace left more time for such invention, or we thought differently. One favorite gag was to make an attractive parcel, or take an old purse; a strong, long thread was attached that could be inconspicuously strung along the ground to the fooler's lookout. The box or bag was placed near a walk so passersby wouldn't miss it. When he stooped to pick up his lucky "find," we'd pull slowly so the object moved from the finder. He'd look around in astonishment to see if anyone was watching. Again he'd start to pick up the quiet object, but it would move before he could grasp it. We'd jump into sight and shout, "April Fool!"

Did you have a stock of fireworks on the Fourth of July? They were legally sold anywhere in my home state until the late twenties. The misuse and carelessness of the increasing young population brought on the destruction of this freedom. Mother couldn't afford an expensive amount of fireworks for me, and she supervised the buying and kept an eye on the firing too, so there was never a burn or accident. Since my supply was limited, I rationed the destruction of them and made a few firecrackers, torpedoes, red devils, serpents and sparklers last through the day and into evening.

Elimination of fireworks for public use is one loss I won't mourn. Each year on July 5th, newspapers told of gruesome accidents that inevitably injured young celebrants. There are enough hazards around without buying more.

Hallowe'en had hijinks too, which have been defeated by the "trick-and-treaters." The wagon on the roof is the classic story that has come through the years, but there was other mischief born in the goblin's minds. Sheets and old clothes and a dimestore mask, or stocking pulled over the head, was the extent of masquerading or costuming. We took to the streets, and with soap in hand "fixed" windows. We took frost-bitten cabbages and tomatoes from gardens to throw on neighbor's porches. The mushy vegetables made a splashy mess for the unfortunate lady-of-the-house to clean up. The least harmful sport was doorbell ringing, to keep people bobbing out to see an empty porch. These pranks were certainly mischievous, but could hardly put us in the delinquent classification. We only did it one night out of 365!

The maid performed many services, and wore a different uniform for different tasks.

Have you been asked lately about your servant problem? Here is an area of violent change, due to several causes. Men and women seldom look upon domestic service as they once did—a lifetime calling. The inconsiderateness of many employers gave workers a feeling of menialness or stigma to those who were not trained for other work, but had to earn a living. As the labor union movement grew, much more money could be earned in shops and factories. The domestic work force was drawn away. It was once possible in an average-sized house to have a full-time housekeeper "live-in." Now to compete, the salary would be prohibitive for many people who must rely on babysitters and a cleaning woman once or twice per week.

Emily Post was the arbiter of good taste. (Courtesy of The Emily Post Institute, Inc. 1930)

The wealthy always have and probably always will have staffs of servants, because mansions couldn't be run without them. But in the thirties Emily Post, the arbiter of manners, whote an article about the etiquette a bride needed to know when she hired her first general maid. This was in a publication for average income readers—not the wealthy, so you can see that help in the home was commonplace.

How casual our manners have now become! Emily Post stated, "When you interview an applicant, it is a fixed rule of propriety that in your house she should stand. If you go to an office, it is proper to invite her to be seated while you talk." The applicants had to show references attesting to their honesty, sobriety, capability and good disposition. Mrs. Post went into detail about the proper morning and afternoon uniforms to be furnished by the employer for the maid.

She spoke of the ideal adjustment between the lady and those she employed as the heart of the whole domestic problem. She said, "We all have certain neighbors whose houses suggest the smoothness, the tranquility, and the beauty of a sun-dappled mountain brook. Others live in a storm center of perpetual upheaval."*

In a 1927 *Harper's Bazaar* it wasn't unexpected to find an article concerning servants and domestic help problems. "They say that in New York there is only one old lady left who ventures to have a footman wait for her at the door with a rug draped over his arm. A footman in claret livery, with buckskin trousers and boots—one of those amazing and amusing parodies of a man that seems an anachronism in this titanic age of overseas aviators and youth striving upward as never before."

If the foregoing seems comic, read further; "Servants, we have learned, are human beings, like the rest of us . . . if there are stupid servants, there are likewise stupid masters and mistresses."

"A lady I know was bitterly complaining that she had returned to her apartment and discovered her cook bathing in her tub. [I wonder if this haughty woman expected to find a ring of cooking fat around the tub.] I asked her where the cook usually bathed. She said she hadn't the least idea. When she finally looked into the matter, she was startled to see that there was a common bathroom for ten servants—a room as dark and dingy as it is possible for any room to be." Is it any wonder that the servants fled to the comforts of factories?

The writer further stated, "I have yet to meet a servant who does not respond to warm, human treatment. Even taxi-drivers, who are public servants, which is worse than being a private servant, are responsive to politeness and consideration. A valet is quick to discover whether his master is a gentleman or not; and a lady's maid is frequently much more of a thoroughbred than her mistress. It would be interesting to probe into the minds of our serving class and find out exactly how we stand with them."

Isn't this unbelievable as an attitude and display of class consciousness that was common only a few years ago? The accident of birth was a sharp definer—even to the amazingly profound discovery that servants were human beings!

Many manners and customs have suffered, relaxed or disappeared altogether. Rigid rules swayed and bent in the breeziness and familiarity of today's behavior. Chaperons have joined the ranks of museum pieces. Frankness, directness and permissiveness have replaced many an enforced propriety of forty years ago. "Hiya" has become a standard greeting and many of us are uneasy in the presence of anyone for whom our best manners must show. It's no wonder that we're now feeling the effects of the generation gap that's slowly, ever so gradually been nurtured for forty years. Maybe our behavior is better or worse, but to the person in whom a standard of manners has been inbred, we must seem immeasurably crude.

* Reprinted by permission of the Emily Post Institute and Elizabeth Post.

36

Gone Forever?

I'll wager a celluloid collar that you haven't smoked a Melachrino Cigarette lately—mainly because they're gone. A distinguished Portuguese nobleman endorsed them, but they've vanished in spite of him. Numerous other items are gone too—maybe forever. They could be sights we don't see, places we can't go or articles we'll no longer use. How many can you recall? Some may escape your memory, or possibly you hadn't even missed them.

Portrait of a Proud Champ Who Conquered the Falls

M. Jean LUSSIER

The Bob Curran column, "Curran's Corner," July 5, 1968, which appeared in the Buffalo *Evening News.*

It's a considerable time since you heard of a person preparing to take a plunge over Niagara Falls in a barrel —not just any old barrel, but a specially rigged and strong contraption that would withstand the pounding when it landed with its cargo in the angry rapids below. Many considered this to be a trick spectacular enough to assure fame and fortune if accomplished. And if this wasn't hair-raising for the public, some stayed in sight for a show by walking across the area on a rope. As early as 1876 a woman aerialist succeeded, not only in being able to tell of the feat, but she did it with baskets strapped

Jean Lussier, as he looks today. (Courtesy of M. Lussier)

to her feet! If the name Jean Lussier rings no memory bells, perhaps you weren't among the 150,000 persons who crowded the edges of Niagara Falls to watch this man go over the Falls forty years ago. Every Fourth of July is the anniversary of the day, the great day when Jean Lussier confidently stepped into a 1037 pound rubber ball, plunged over the mighty waters and ten minutes later emerged smiling and unhurt. He's not only the only living man to accomplish the feat without injury, but probably did so with the best rig. It was built in Akron, Ohio, cost $1485 and was fitted with thirty-two tubes containing thirty-five pounds of oxygen each. Now, at seventy-six, M. Lussier still enjoys recalling the big event of his life.

When did you last see a tree or flagpole sitter? Through the twenties and into the Depression, we were a nation of stunt-lovers, and what better way could be devised to pass the idle, weary days than to perform or watch those foolhardy enough to be the performers? People did anything, no matter how ridiculous or risky, for unbelievably small rewards. It was easy to say, "What have I got to lose?"

Human flies were generally professionals who traveled from city-to-city to use any building high enough to present a breathtaking view of the feat. They scaled the

306

sides of structures by hanging to cornices and bric-a-brac, all of which has been eliminated from modern skyscrapers. There's little future left for the profession.

A barnstorming plane of the twenties; note the girls on the ladder and on the wing.

You won't see many barnstorming little planes with girls hanging by their teeth from ropes suspended under the plane. They used to dance on the flimsy linen wings of rickety aircraft with nothing to grasp but the quivering struts. Except for air shows, stunt-flying is mostly a memory. With the crash and death of the greatest stuntman, Paul Mantz, there aren't likely to be hordes of successors other than those who work for motion pictures. Many times in my childhood, I'd look to the sky to see a plane barrel-rolling, nosediving or looping-the-loop. Popular attention is now directed to sky diving.

The old-time horse-drawn milk wagon.

During the Depression we had marathon dances that were more revolting than entertaining as the wretched contestants staggered and dragged their disheveled bodies, barely moving when exhaustion set in. Sometimes they collapsed altogether. They chose to do this with the hope of winning the pitifully small amount of prize money. The owner of the hall was the one who made money from the agony.

Can you remember the horse-drawn milk wagon? Old Dobbin was gradually replaced by trucks and in our town the thirties saw them disappear entirely. The "hay-motor" was convenient as he sleepily plodded the route, knowing where to stop, how long to wait and when to start without commands. No truck can automatically do as much.

A sight seldom seen today: coal being rolled down a chute.

There was a distinctive sound like no other as coal rolled down a chute from the truck into the basement coal bin. Every house had a sizeable area reserved for the coal pile but when my folks converted the furnace to an oil-burner, they didn't find an effective use for the empty, dark basement corner. As a child I was always leery of the coalman with his smudged face and only the glaring whites of his eyes seeming to be free of black dust.

Nowadays a machine moves along a road, digging a uniform ditch with amazing speed. Do you remember when big crews used the muscles of backs and arms to lift out the dirt, one shovelful at a time?

Other sights on the street have vanished. Where is the organ grinder with his wheezy music and red-coated monkey that scrambled around to the squeals of delighted children? Now he'd land in the pokey for not having a license or disturbing the peace.

It would be nice to come upon a popcorn wagon some summer evening—to see the flickering gas jets as fluffy kernels in paper bags got their shots of butter and salt. It always tasted better than corn popped at home.

Have you had a telegram delivered lately by a boy in the uniform of Postal Telegraph? Of course not, because this company has long been gone along with postal savings accounts. The Western Union delivery is scarce too since it's easier to phone the message—or call long distance in the first place. How long is the line of jobs that have disappeared for young fellows!

Where are the grocery delivery boys? They're prob-

The organ grinder and his monkey have largely vanished from the scene.

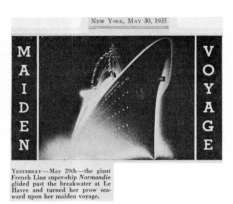

YESTERDAY—May 29th—the giant French Line super-ship *Normandie* glided past the breakwater at Le Havre and turned her prow seaward upon her maiden voyage.

The maiden voyage of the *Normandie*. (A house advertisement for N. W. Ayer & Son, Inc., Philadelphia, 1935)

ably box boys at the supermarket, and you'd need strong binoculars to find the grocer who now delivers.

When did you last walk around a game of mibs or hopscotch? These were like spring tonic along with roller skates and kites, robins and crocuses.

people for a day's outing. Crowds thronged to see her demise, but to me it was like watching the painful death of a dear friend.

Vital Link in Great Lakes Region Transportation

DETROIT & CLEVELAND NAVIGATION CO.

An advertisement for the now-defunct overnight boat line between Detroit and Cleveland. (A D&C Lake Lines advertisement, illustrated by the author)

Horses brought the circus to town.

Were you a water boy when the "big top" came to town? As a young fellow without enough coins in your knickers, you might have strained and puffed to lug enough buckets of water to the elephants for a free ducat to the inside magic of the big circus tent. Did you wiggle through the crowd to get a choice curb position when the circus parade went down Main Street? How wonderful was the sound of the steam calliope!

We've lost in the travel realm too. If you ever walked up the gangplank of the *Normandie* or *Queen Mary*, you knew the thrill of luxury travel afloat. As more and more trips converted to air, most of the small excursion boats gave up the ghost. Their leisurely diversion isn't appreciated now. Call it sentimentality, but tears flowed the day they burned the old Tashmoo that plied the Detroit River and Lake Erie for many years, taking carefree

The restful overnight boats to Cleveland and Buffalo from Detroit had to go as they got less and less fares and maintenance costs climbed. These are localized conditions, but you can match them with similarities in your community.

Since the revolution for agrarian reforms, you've seen no advertisements like the one pictured—and it's questionable whether in our lifetimes we'll see them again. We can only pray that Cuba is liberated soon from its "savior," so she may be visited. It's a delightful island just ninety miles from our shores and they're missing millions of dollars our tourists used to pour into their country.

Lately, seams in women's stockings are becoming a thing of the past. At least, it's eliminated the problem of twisted, crooked lines up the backs of legs—a sight deplored by men as they "watched the girls go by."

Have men's hard straw hats, derbys and top hats gone forever? How long has it been since you snuggled under a heavy, plaid lap blanket? Loss of the horse and buggy

Advertisements, like this one, are not likely to be seen again in the near future. (Cuban National Tourist Commission, courtesy of Fidel Castro)

Seams in stockings are becoming a thing of the past. (Courtesy *Harper's Bazaar*)

did not erase the need for these because it was a long time before the effective car heater. In the twenties heavy soapstones were still heated, especially in rural districts, to warm icy sheets on beds in unheated rooms.

Somewhere on the trail of years, Mr. Bones and Mr. Interlocutor got lost in the shuffle of more sophisticated entertainment. One day we realized that the Minstrel Show was gone along with a tent show that "praised the Lord" with entertainment—the Chatauqua.

Perhaps you should scurry around with a camera to photograph the many things you now take for granted as objects that will be with us eternally. One day you may turn your back and when you look again—they've gone!

37

Futuristic Dreamland

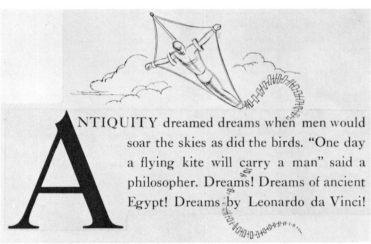

ANTIQUITY dreamed dreams when men would soar the skies as did the birds. "One day a flying kite will carry a man" said a philosopher. Dreams! Dreams of ancient Egypt! Dreams by Leonardo da Vinci!

This tribute to Leonardo da Vinci was designed by the author.

The United States will have a woman President by 1992. Does this sound like an irresponsible statement? No more than a prediction made in 1926 by Mrs. Helena Normanton, a Britisher, when she said we'd have a woman President before 1950. We see now that time and history have proved her wrong, but this doesn't discourage predictors. Thomas Jefferson expressed it accurately when he said he "liked the dreams of the future better than the history of the past."

We can indulge in no safer pastime than predictions because dead people can't argue that we were wrong, and if our ideas are far enough into the future, it won't be necessary to say, "I told you so" if they come true. What degree of insanity would you have suspected of a person who in 1920 would have said that by 1966 we'd have hundreds of pictures of the far side of the moon?

Every generation is blessed with dreamers, those who can strip through veils of time and clearly see "Things to Come," as did H. G. Wells. In 1935 his futurist story

A vision of the city of the future, as seen by H. G. Wells in 1935.

was filmed as science fiction. No one at that time had seen television sets, yet he not only saw them clearly but the model in the film was set in a wall flush. It looked very modern. At that time World War II hadn't crashed upon us, but Mr. Wells's movie showed a replica of the London blitzkreig with great fidelity.

All geniuses have earned an idiot's rating by being ahead of their times. Isn't it ironic that the inventions to benefit mankind the most have had a furious fight from those they'd most benefit? The early song lyrics could be parodied, 'They all laughed at Alexander Raymond when he said we'd fly in space . . . they all laughed when they said the atom could be smashed" (except the Japanese).

This traffic plan was considered a dream in the thirties. Today's experts would scoff at the two-way streets.

If you scoff at the idea of having picnics on the moon, remember that twenty-five years ago you'd have been laughed out of town if you'd have predicted man could walk in space. Prophets always run into trouble, but luckily our artists, scientists, designers and science writers aren't stoned for their far-out ideas. Instead, we read entertaining articles in Sunday paper supplements about their works.

It's exciting to stand here today and look in both directions, since we've lived to see some amazing concepts produce flesh and bones. Scarcely a sizeable city today lacks at least rudiments of super road systems with cloverleaf intersections, but artists and engineers had details of them worked out clearly in the 1930's and before. Some illustrators showed roads that traffic experts would shake a finger at because they had two-way traffic on super-streets, but the idea was germinating.

By 1938 the idea of the city of tomorrow was lucid enough to be photographed from a model.

Norman Bel Geddes, in 1929, foresaw the aerial restaurant and the diesel locomotive. (Courtesy Detroit News)

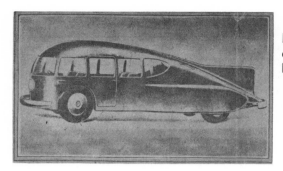

Bel Geddes's 1931 dream car incorporated many of the design features seen on today's automobiles. (Courtesy *Detroit News*)

Artist's rendering of a spaceship for a Flash Gordon movie.

Bel Geddes was less successful in his vision of the aircraft of the future. He failed to foresee the jet engine. (Courtesy *Detroit News*)

A giant of predictive ideas in our time was Norman Bel Geddes. As early as 1929 he designed an aerial restaurant built around a central shaft. A good existing example is in the Los Angeles International Airport. In 1931 Bel Geddes designed a locomotive similar to our diesel streamliners at a time when the huge iron steam locomotives were still firmly entrenched on our scene.

The Norman Bel Geddes motor car concept had a fin in 1931, before we were bristling with fin-happy cars. Otherwise, it had the rear shape of the presently popular fastback, plus the utility and general appearance of the Volkswagen Bus. Overall, it followed the "teardrop" design.

The only article that missed the mark was the Bel Geddes super airliner. In 1929 he didn't foresee the jet motor, which appeared in 1944. It was this new form of explosive propulsion that revolutionized all earlier theories about immense flying contraptions holding hundreds of passengers. His twenty-motored plane had an enormous weight with a pygmy speed. But he didn't miss the swept wing design.

A civilization has never raced wildly through so many "ages" in a few decades. Historians are overworked to record it and ordinary citizens crack up with incomprehensibility of the mechanized vortex. In the thirties fanciful artists depicted windowless shafts that defied the skies while jet-like planes streaked past. It wasn't far from future truth because although we have windows, many are unopenable and air is blown, washed and filtered.

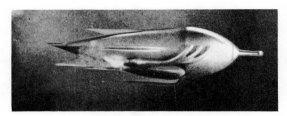

A spaceship model.

The possibility of probing space was talked about when I was young. It was fascinating to contemplate it, even before man had a means of speed that would break from our atmosphere. Artists and designers drew spacecraft for science fiction magazine stories and motion pictures. These illustrations are more artistic than realistic, but show what imagination could do for those who dreamed of the future.

We may have been born in the "horse and buggy" age, but we've survived the "machine age" with its growing pains, the "atomic age" that quickly fused into the "space age" as soon as the Russian, Yuri Gagarin, lifted away from the earth and whirled around it once. The dream of the man-in-the-moon has edged closer and closer to the man-on-the-moon. We're now so blasé about space shots that many would rather sleep than see the blast-off on television. Man will continue to dream and predict. What age next, prophet?

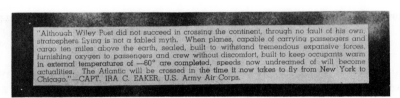

"Although Wiley Post did not succeed in crossing the continent, through no fault of his own, stratosphere flying is not a fabled myth. When planes, capable of carrying passengers and cargo ten miles above the earth, sealed, built to withstand tremendous expansive forces, furnishing oxygen to passengers and crew without discomfort, built to keep occupants warm in external temperatures of —60° are completed, speeds now undreamed of will become actualities. The Atlantic will be crossed in the time it now takes to fly from New York to Chicago."—CAPT. IRA C. EAKER, U.S. Army Air Corps.

As this clipping attests to, Captain Ira C. Eaker had an accurate vision of today's aircraft.

38

Tomorrow Will Be Yesterday

We've hedge-hopped in a Stinson Biplane over a unique period in American experience. Whether you grow nostalgic about it or wonder what the shouting was about, take a tip from today's teenagers and "don't knock it!" We can scarcely assess an era as good or bad when it happened only yesterday.

A Stinson Biplane.

We may say that the Depression and World War II were so bad we don't wish to think of them. Like labor pains or a sore that's healed, they should be forgotten. We can't condemn a whole tapestry for a single thread. If we morbidly remember troubles, the space reserved for pleasant happenings will be crowded. There were good aspects in the bad—if you're philosophic. At no time did we learn more of resourcefulness than in the Depression. Instead of jumping from windows after losing paper fortunes, the bulk of Americans had the courage to patch thin trousers, put cardboard in worn shoes, and plod on in search of work.

During the War we were probably more closely knit as a people than at any time. We worked hard and accomplished much, as Americans are capable of doing when all muscles pull in the same direction. We showed what a free country can do when provoked by unwarranted attack.

It has been said that the "good old days" only seem that way in retrospect because we were younger, more energetic, hopeful and our taste buds were sensitive. But the day we're living this moment will tomorrow be a "good old day." If the young person remembers this, he'll not be disdainful of his elders and their memories. Nor will we-of-the-silvered-locks be embarrassed when caught with our memories.

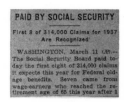

New York Times article describing the beginning of Social Security.

In the black ledger we have written many prideful accounts. Most people now enjoy the eight hour day, and there's a minimum wage that is higher than many maximums used to be. We had something to do with this struggle and the accompanying blessings of more leisure for recreation, paid vacations and other social benefits. As we approach later years, there's something to look forward to other than dependency on our children and interference in their lives—thanks to pensions and Social Security.

Today's manufacturers would never take the attitude depicted in this clipping. (Courtesy *The New York Times*)

Perhaps we've become unmindful of other improvements such as the pure food and drug legislation, sanitary regulations and requirements that manufacturers state the true contents of their merchandise on labels.

It once took us all day to go a distance we now travel in an hour or two. It's possible to do this without tire or engine failure and yet, the trouble-free drive used to be cause for boasting. We now jet across the nation in five hours.

We no longer huddle around a stove that crisped us on one side while the other was chilled. If it's oppres-

There are now better ways of cooling off than with this old-fashioned palmleaf fan.

sively hot, we cool ourselves more efficiently than by waving a palmleaf fan, or waiting for a breeze through open doors. Many of the advances that are taken for granted were the outgrowth or direct result of ideas spawned in our time. It's a boast to old and young, not a defense with apologies.

We're not downgrading our yesterdays by eulogizing today's life. It's only the review of a prelude and appraisal of qualities we had that are gone—maybe forever. Our regard for life and the pursuance thereof was somewhat different. We admired the good guys and their halos lasted a long time. Now the market for heroes is at low ebb, but the healthy need of them persists.

In the earlier decades we hadn't secured the final rivet that would forever enclose us in the tension machine of today. Everything wasn't computed and we didn't know the meaning of the word "automation." We weren't a long series of numbers on cards—we dared to be individuals, even if this meant being a hermit lost to civilization. Instead of being cogs in the gears of a grey, massive machine, we were brightened by colorful individuals.

This "strike sheet" from a color photography service is
a fine summation of the era described in our book.

We were more spiritual about many things. It wasn't against the law or high court decisions to mention God, for fear of offending an atheist. Crowds didn't watch someone in trouble and refuse to be involved. Someone would risk his life to save a stranger, simply because it was the human, humane thing to do. We were outspoken against indignities that we've now been conditioned to meekly accept.

There have been gradual changes of attitude and morale since the time when we were fiercely independent, self-sufficient and proud of our patriotism. If we made mistakes, (and certainly we did), we had to pay for them ourselves instead of blaming our parents and society in general. We wanted to belong to the "establishment."

America had the resilient tissue of youth instead of the deteriorating ailments of age.

Our era was both good and bad, as characters must be in a credible play. One wish for future Americans is that they cherish our heritage enough to never be satisfied with anything less than the ideals our forefathers laid as principles by which mankind could function freely and happily. We may yet have to fight and strain as never before, against powerful forces loose in today's world. They'll try to undermine not only what we've known, but the lifetimes of our young and those unborn. Let's hope that future generations can still look back fondly to their "good old days" and wistfully smile.

Index